CORPORATE PLASTICITY

HOW TO CHANGE, ADAPT, AND EXCEL

Laurent Chevreux
Wim Plaizier
Christian Schuh
Wayne Brown
Alenka Triplat

Illustrations by Tomaž Nečemar

Apress·

Corporate Plasticity: How to Change, Adapt, and Excel

ISBN-13 (pbk): 978-1-4302- 6749-2

ISBN-13 (electronic): 978-1-4302-6748-5

Publisher: Heinz Weinheimer
Acquisitions Editor: Jeff Olson
Editorial Board: Steve Anglin, Mark Beckner, Ewan Buckingham, Gary Cornell, Louise Corrigan, James DeWolf, Jonathan Gennick, Jonathan Hassell, Robert Hutchinson, Michelle Lowman, James Markham, Matthew Moodie, Jeff Olson, Jeffrey Pepper, Douglas Pundick, Ben Renow-Clarke, Dominic Shakeshaft, Gwenan Spearing, Matt Wade, Steve Weiss
Coordinating Editor: Rita Fernando
Copy Editor: Deanna Hegle
Compositor: SPi Global
Indexer: SPi Global
Cover Designer: Tomaž Nečemar

Distributed to the book trade worldwide by Springer Science+Business Media New York, 233 Spring Street, 6th Floor, New York, NY 10013. Phone 1-800-SPRINGER, fax (201) 348-4505, e-mail orders-ny@springer-sbm.com, or visit www.springeronline.com. Apress Media, LLC is a California LLC and the sole member (owner) is Springer Science + Business Media Finance Inc (SSBM Finance Inc). SSBM Finance Inc is a Delaware corporation.

For information on translations, please e-mail rights@apress.com, or visit www.apress.com.

Apress and friends of ED books may be purchased in bulk for academic, corporate, or promotional use. eBook versions and licenses are also available for most titles. For more information,referenceourSpecialBulkSales–eBookLicensingwebpageatwww.apress.com/bulk-sales.

Any source code or other supplementary materials referenced by the author in this text is available to readers at www.apress.com. For detailed information about how to locate your book's source code, go to www.apress.com/source-code/.

Apress Business: The Unbiased Source of Business Information

Apress business books provide essential information and practical advice, each written for practitioners by recognized experts. Busy managers and professionals in all areas of the business world—and at all levels of technical sophistication—look to our books for the actionable ideas and tools they need to solve problems, update and enhance their professional skills, make their work lives easier, and capitalize on opportunity.

Whatever the topic on the business spectrum—entrepreneurship, finance, sales, marketing, management, regulation, information technology, among others—Apress has been praised for providing the objective information and unbiased advice you need to excel in your daily work life. Our authors have no axes to grind; they understand they have one job only—to deliver up-to-date, accurate information simply, concisely, and with deep insight that addresses the real needs of our readers.

It is increasingly hard to find information—whether in the news media, on the Internet, and now all too often in books—that is even-handed and has your best interests at heart. We therefore hope that you enjoy this book, which has been carefully crafted to meet our standards of quality and unbiased coverage.

We are always interested in your feedback or ideas for new titles. Perhaps you'd even like to write a book yourself. Whatever the case, reach out to us at editorial@apress.com and an editor will respond swiftly. Incidentally, at the back of this book, you will find a list of useful related titles. Please visit us at www.apress.com to sign up for newsletters and discounts on future purchases.

The Apress Business Team

Contents

About the Authors

We have worked for many years with global companies and organizations to define strategies and improve performance and believe that classical management science is focusing too much on aspects that can easily be measured and thereby misses an important point.

The results of Plasticity are easily recognizable—they manifest themselves as true excellence. Understanding the mechanisms behind Plasticity—the magic in it—is much harder. We would highly value your views and can be reached at www.linkedin.com/groups/Corporate-Plasticity-8130818.

Laurent Chevreux is a partner in A.T. Kearney's Strategic Operations Practice. Laurent has more than 25 years of industry and consulting experience. His key areas of expertise encompass supply chain, value chain reconfiguration, and retail. As a former supply chain executive for a manufacturer and a distributor, and as a consultant, he has overseen distribution and operational turnarounds in various sectors and has become passionate about the topic of product availability in both brick-and-mortar and online retail. He holds a degree in manufacturing engineering from the venerable Ecole Nationale Supérieure de Techniques Avancées in Paris and a master's degree from the University of California Santa Barbara. Laurent is based in A.T. Kearney's Paris, France, office.

Wim Plaizier is a partner in A.T. Kearney's Energy & Process Industries Practice and the Operations Practice. Wim has close to 30 years of experience in consulting and industry. His key areas of expertise encompass operational excellence in asset-intensive industries, end-to-end value chain management, and postmerger integration. He has been A.T. Kearney's lead partner for the Benelux and global lead for the operations practice. He also served as a member of A.T. Kearney's global leadership team. Currently he heads A.T. Kearney's operations in Africa. Before joining A.T. Kearney, Wim worked with Shell in various roles in procurement and engineering. He earned an MBA from Henley Management College in the United Kingdom. Wim works out of both A.T. Kearney's Amsterdam and Johannesburg offices

Christian Schuh is a trained engineer with a degree in aero-mechanics and a doctorate in business administration from Graz University of Technology. After three years at Unilever, he joined A.T. Kearney in 1995. His career in consulting has taken him to exciting places like NASA's Johnson Space Center and 300,000-worker mega-factories in China. He has devoted many years to advising car makers in Germany, France, the UK, Italy, Brazil, and the US. Most recently, his focus has shifted to high tech firms in the US and in Taiwan. He is most passionate about creating game-changing products in engineering-driven environments. Christian is best known for his books *The Purchasing Chessboard* and *The CPO*. He lives in the historic center of Vienna, Austria.

 **Wayne Brown** is a member of A.T. Kearney's Strategic Operations Practice. He has over 20 years' industry and consulting experience and is passionate about human behavior in the workplace and effecting real and lasting change in individuals and organizations. His key areas of expertise include improvement in complex service environments, business transformation, and enterprise optimization. Before joining A.T. Kearney, Wayne held roles at Royal Sun Alliance Insurance and HBOS Bank. He is a chartered marketer and has first class bachelor's and master's degrees in business. Wayne lives with his family in Yorkshire, UK, and is based in A.T. Kearney's London office.

Alenka Triplat is a member of A.T. Kearney's Strategic Operations Practice. She is passionate about driving change, be it transformation of client organizations or improving a product's design to beat the competition. Doing so often requires establishing close links between procurement, engineering, marketing, and operations. In over 10 years with the firm in Vienna, Austria, she has led multiple projects across various industries, such as high-tech, industrial equipment, process industries, and financial institutions. Her flexibility and pioneering spirit led her not only to choose multinational clients, but also to move abroad for longer periods in the USA, China, and Taiwan. She has co-authored several books on procurement (most notably *The Purchasing Chessboard*), and articles on related topics. Alenka studied economics at the University of Ljubljana (Slovenia) and business administration at Vienna University of Economics and Business Administration (Austria). She currently shuttles between Taipei, Vienna, and Ljubljana.

The age-old science of business is all about corporate strategy and functional excellence. We believe it overlooks a third element.

We call this element Plasticity.

Part 1:
The Corporate Plasticity Manifesto

Part I
The Corporate History Manifesto

The Starting Point

For decades, executives have driven improvement along two dimensions: corporate strategy and functional excellence. And despite the many well-intentioned attempts to make management a reliable science, the outcomes have been mixed.

Corporate history is full of counterintuitive case examples and mysteries that management science fails to comprehend or explain. Why, for example, does one leader in the photographic film and paper industry nearly cease to exist while the other transforms into an imaging company and thrives in the digital world? Why does one carmaker successfully introduce a platform strategy while another fails miserably? How was a maker of rubber boots capable of dominating the mobile phone industry for decades? How does a PC maker emerge from near bankruptcy only to enter and totally transform the mature mobile phone industry as well as six other industries?

Also, as a long-term view on the S&P 500 would suggest, does growth make companies ultimately so complex and inflexible that they are destined to fail in the end? Is it all about luck and coincidence?

We don't think so. In our view, management science so far has overlooked a third dimension that is complementary to corporate strategy and functional excellence. We call this dimension *Corporate Plasticity*. The definition of Corporate Plasticity is twofold. It is

1. The ability of individual agents to collaborate in the pursuit of a common objective.

2. The ability of individual agents to reconfigure themselves to face a so far unknown challenge or reach a new state.

Surprisingly enough, Plasticity is everywhere. In nature, it allows a pack of wolves to hunt and kill prey that is several times heavier than a single wolf. In space, it brought the *Apollo 13* astronauts back safely. In World War II, it let the Allied naval, land, and air forces overrun the highly fortified German defenses in Normandy. Plasticity is at the core of the human race and has allowed our species to conquer and reshape the entire planet.

Absence of Plasticity—even when possessing superior strategy and capabilities—is a certain recipe for failure. The Roman legion, after having conquered most of the then-known world, experienced it when they were defeated by Germanic tribes that were superior in neither strategy nor capability but played by different rules. At the 1980 Winter Olympics, the USSR had the best ice hockey team in the world. They had won the gold medal every year since 1964 and had the highest-scoring players, the strongest defense, and the most reliable goaltender. But they didn't win. They were defeated in a medal-round game by a US team made up of amateur and collegiate players, who then went on to win the gold medal. Although Plasticity seems to be a winning formula just about anywhere you look, it has largely been ignored in business—until now.

When Plasticity meets functional excellence, a collection of great individual performances can turn into a grand masterpiece. Think of a symphony. The orchestra is composed of highly talented musicians who, over time, with practice and experience, could perform without a conductor. Yet like a great CEO, the conductor does not control the orchestra; he or she, rather, influences and guides the orchestra toward a perfection they could not achieve on their own.

When Plasticity meets strategy, the results are highly creative and sometimes surprising. Think of a jam session. The jazz musicians start off on a theme, and then they improvise. They react to what their peers are doing, carrying the theme into another iteration.

In business, the combination of functional excellence and Plasticity will enable companies to achieve true operational excellence. Plasticity will tear down the organizational and cultural boundaries between silos and create more vibrant, more stimulating workplaces.

Plasticity also makes a company continually rethink what it stands for and enables it to adapt its strategy to turbulent environments and create a competitive advantage. With Plasticity, the makers of steam engines in the 19th century would not have ceased to exist but would have evolved into propulsion companies, mastering diesel and electricity just as well as steam.

In our view, we are about to enter the era of Plasticity in business. It will largely shape competition in the decades to come. Strategies have become wholesale commodities, and functional excellence ultimately will not make the difference. Leading companies are already finding it increasingly difficult to make incremental gains in functional excellence. Emerging market competitors are quickly replicating excellence in engineering, procurement, manufacturing, and sales and marketing. A couple of years from now, it will be normal for companies—at least those that embrace the challenge—to find a sound balance between strategy, functional excellence, and Plasticity.

A Postmortem on Classic Management Science

Classic management science has been central to the modern corporation. Functional excellence and corporate strategies have enabled massive increases in productivity. Such advancements have lowered costs, prices, and barriers to entry, and they have created organizations with efficient functions and clear direction.

But not everything that has emerged is marvelous. The modern organization has inherent problems. These include silo thinking as well as a fixation on detail rather than on the big picture. Worse, beautiful and supposedly flawless corporate strategies fail. This has led to a deluge of theories for rectifying the issues by developing even better processes and more immaculate strategies.

Of course, having superior processes and better strategies than competitors is important. But has anyone considered whether the ills of the modern organization or the regular failures of strategy have the same root causes? And as a consequence, have we become too transfixed on management theories that began before the modern firm was even envisioned? On its own, can classic management science help resolve the new complexities emerging in modern organizations?

The Birth and Nurturing of Functional Excellence and Strategy

To consider if classic management science answers today's corporate questions, we must understand what gave rise to its development in the first place. In other words, what problems and challenges was classic management science seeking to resolve? Only by understanding the original intent behind functional excellence and corporate strategy can we begin to consider whether they are still suitable for solving today's problems.

GENEROSITY PRUDENCE
PROFIT
HUMANITY TRUST
JUSTICE
ECONOMY
THE STATE

As Adam Smith wrote in 1776, in *The Wealth of Nations*, "The division of labor, by reducing every man's business to some one simple operation, and by making this operation the sole employment of his life, necessarily increases very much the dexterity of the workman."

Thus were sown the seeds of functional excellence. Smith, widely cited as the father of modern capitalism, laid down the markers that would enable massive changes in productivity. Primarily, he insisted that the efficient production of goods requires a division of labor, which is driven by a social dimension: each of us has a different talent to be exploited.

The notion was further codified 140 years later when Frederick Taylor published his monographs, particularly *The Principles of Scientific Management* in 1911, which advocated the analysis and synthesis of workflows to discover the "one best way." At the same time, Henry Ford was demonstrating functional excellence with breathtaking boldness, making breakthrough changes in mass production that enabled massive—life changing in many cases—increases in salary for his workers.

But not everyone agreed with these ideas. Some argued that Taylorism and Fordism didn't build up the talents of people and that the notion of talent, talent management, personal growth, and the aspirations of human beings in general were at odds with the highly fragmented environment that Taylorism and Fordism had created. This was the kernel for the field of organizational behavior.

The notion of *strategy* goes back thousands of years. It is a word of military origin, deriving from the Greek *strategia*, meaning "office of general, command, generalship." The term *strategic management* is very much a business-related term developed in the 1950s.

Pulitzer Prize-winning business historian and author Alfred Chandler recognized that, as organizations grow, their various strategies need to be combined under a bigger strategy. He said a strategy was necessary to give a company structure, direction, and focus. Many theories followed. Applied mathematician and business manager Igor Ansoff developed his well-known growth matrix, while management consultant Peter Drucker recognized the need to disseminate strategy in a codified manner through performance objectives.

In fact, for the rest of the 20th century, interest in corporate strategy grew so much that each passing decade seemed to have a new management theme. In the 1970s, managing a portfolio through growth-share matrices began to emerge; the 1980s were about identifying and exploiting competitive advantage; and the 1990s were about core competencies.

Flaws Begin to Emerge

Privately, CEOs have conceded their frustration about the influence they have on the course their companies are taking. One prominent CEO compared his situation to the captain of a supertanker: "I can turn the steering wheel any way I want, but the ship keeps on going straight." Corporate strategies disappear in a sea of information. Great concepts are hardly managing to take off, let alone become successfully implemented; and the lack of feedback in the system leaves the CEO half blind.

Further, classic management science has so far offered only an inconsistent response to what, to us, is a very simple notion: senior executives have their own agendas. Sometimes these agendas align with the firm's goals, and sometimes they do not.

However, the ultimate failure of classic management science is that it has nurtured divided organizations that fail to see the big picture.

Attempting to Fix the Problem

Classic management science has been trying more of the same for too long. Rather than rethinking its paradigm, it has piled up complexity by overengineering. The frustration resulting from the difference between expectation and reality has led to the development of highly sophisticated forecasting systems. But even the most sophisticated forecasting systems fail because the challenge is not predicting the future—something that is impossible—but developing the ability to respond to change. Similarly, the difficulty to deliver consistently against the promise has led to more stringent rules and processes.

It is not that these theories and approaches have no merit; they have invariably been intellectual, compelling, and practical—but they have failed to make a lasting impact. While classic management science has been creating solutions, it has been asking the wrong questions.

For example, business process reengineering correctly diagnosed that organizations needed to rethink how they did their work. And what's more, its overarching answer was paradigm destroying at the time in that only after an organization rethinks what it should be doing can it go on to decide how best to do it. It was right to proclaim that functional silos needed to be broken, but it merely replaced them with horizontal silos.

Of course, the theories cited previously span 250 years and have laid the foundation for modern business. Nevertheless, gaps and flaws have always been there. The speed of today's technological innovation made these flaws more apparent but did by no means cause them. In any case, what is becoming more and more apparent is that the power of these flaws to keep companies from reaching their potential is growing.

The Third Dimension

Over the past decades, companies have tried to develop a competitive advantage through a cleverly cooked strategy and/or a deep focus on functional excellence. However, this approach has shown weaknesses in two areas:

- *Wastefulness and lack of measure*: Too much effort/money/resources have been dedicated to pushing functional excellence in one topic further and in many instances possibly too far. Examples are

  - Companies running cost reduction wave after cost reduction wave do not recognize that the real issue is the lack of appeal of their products.

  - Engineering-driven companies perform miracles but fail to market them appropriately.

  - Consumer goods companies develop innovative new brands but keep all their merchandizing and promotion power on their cash cows.

  - Retailers that push category management to the extreme leave shoppers clueless in front of endless shelves of similar products.

- *Groupthink and myopia:* Most or even all relevant players in any industry are moving in the same direction like herd animals. Examples are

- Most companies display similar values and mission statements in their headquarter reception halls and on the first page of their annual reports: client and shareholder focus, improving the lives of customers, integrity, care for employees and society, transparency, etc.

- Most marketing executives aim for skimming the most affluent consumer group and ignore the "One Laptop per Child" type of opportunities.

- Most innovations—no matter if they concern a product such as a smartphone with a multitouch display, a service such as cloud computing, or a management principle such as the platform strategy—take many years to finally take off. But once they are introduced successfully, everybody copies them.

Of course, all those behaviors are not wrong by themselves. But by saying mainstream things that are not controversial, executives are playing it safe at the expense of communicating a clear and unequivocal message.

As a consequence, signals contrary to expectation are ignored, and the ability to respond once the new situation is understood is greatly diminished.

We trust that the third dimension—Plasticity—will allow the curing of these fundamental weaknesses. Before we discuss the interaction of Plasticity with strategy and functional excellence, let's remember how we defined this third dimension:

1. The ability of individual agents to collaborate in the pursuit of a common objective.

2. The ability of individual agents to reconfigure themselves to face a so far unknown challenge or reach a new state.

The building blocks (Figure 1) that enable those two abilities, and therefore Plasticity, we call the "Magic 7":

*   *Purpose*: Has the company discovered, selected, and expressed what it is meant for?

*   *Focus*: Does the company have the courage to deselect and ignore everything that is not in line with its purpose and see it through?

*   *Culture*: Does the company create the conditions that allow people to work and excel across boundaries and outside of predefined roles?

*   *Spirit*: Does the company inspire people to feel part of a cause that is bigger than themselves?

*   *Network*: Does the company provide the means, freedom, and encouragement for people to continually nurture and grow their internal and external networks?

*   *Knowledge*: Does the company encourage experts to provide their knowledge and others to use expert knowledge, and how readily available is it?

*   *Leadership*: Do the company's leaders personify each of these principles?

Figure 1. The Magic 7 of Plasticity

We are now ready to discuss the interaction of Plasticity with strategy and functional excellence as illustrated in Figure 2, which shows that

- The right combination of strategy and functional excellence can at best provide a competitive advantage.

- When augmented by Plasticity, functional excellence can lead to operational excellence, and strategy can lead to versatility.

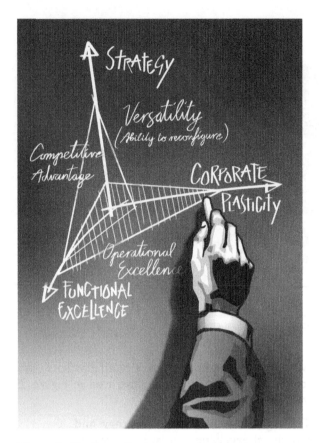

Figure 2. The "tripod"

Let's illustrate this with two examples: Company Red (with the horizontal orientation) and Company Blue (vertical orientation) in the tripod. Company Blue scores high across strategy and functional excellence. It has become very good at what it is doing and is the undisputed leader in its market. But despite its might, it is highly vulnerable to change.

Company Red is functionally as good as Blue. It does not pay a lot of attention to strategy but demonstrates a lot of Plasticity. It therefore has the ability to adapt quickly and can apply its skills in different markets seamlessly.

Let's put this into the context of the examples cited previously. Company Blue is the steam engine maker or the automaker or photographic film or mobile phone company. At some point, the company did something dramatically right. Its founders may have come up with a crucial invention or taken an invention made elsewhere and transformed it into a lasting market success.

Based on this success, its executives drew up elaborate plans on how to penetrate new product/market segments. Its operational people ventured out into the world to sell, produce, and service. Stock performance was great, and everybody involved felt very happy. Over the years and potentially decades, the original entrepreneurial spirit of the founding generation, however, ceased to exist. Hierarchical layer piled on hierarchical layer, and decision making became a highly complex process.

At a certain point in time, a weak signal appeared. Someone in the organization certainly picked that signal up. They connected the dots and came up with a breakthrough idea. In the photographic film company, it may have been the idea of digital imaging. Our hero immediately understood the potential of digital imaging and pitched it to her or his superiors. They probably were excited by it and reported it further up. Ultimately, the idea was presented to those who had a lot to lose. Concerns such as the following would gain the upper hand:

- We have invested billions in plants that produce photographic film and cameras—what is going to happen to those?

- Only high-tech geeks will get excited about digital cameras—the average consumer will shy away from it for decades to come.

- We should not divert funds and attention from our core business—we have the next annual report coming up and that one will determine our bonus.

- Who is that lady with the digital imaging idea anyway? She is not even one of our research staff and is clearly deserting her normal duties.

At best, our hero might have been given a budget to test the idea in a secure laboratory environment. But she was sidelined. Why disrupt things that have been running so smoothly for decades?

Company Blue hung on to its core business of photographic film in a declining market. Strategists came up with a "last man standing" concept. The hope behind it was that the market would not evaporate totally. So the one company that cut cost most rigorously would survive all its competitors and harvest healthy margins for eternity.

Unfortunately they were wrong. The market totally collapsed at breathtaking speed. Cheap and easy-to-use digital cameras, broadband Internet connections, and the advent of smartphones made just about everybody abandon analog photography.

Who is to blame here? Could Company Blue have been saved with more functional excellence? Certainly not. Producing photographic film at even higher productivity rates or squeezing suppliers even harder would not have made a difference. Could a better strategy have made a difference? Potentially it could have, but then Company Blue knew it all. Our hero clearly showed the trend that was developing to key decision makers. Still, they refused to recognize it because it came from an unauthorized source and it challenged the cozy status quo.

Let's look at Company Red for contrast. Let's say Company Red was the somewhat rogue competitor to Company Blue. Despite its operational people being at least as professional as those of Company Blue, it wasn't the darling of the stock market. Its mercurial leaders endorsed many different projects, and some of those inevitably failed. Also, its strategy looked messy, as it repeatedly cannibalized its own product lines.

Imagine our hero working at Company Red. She also got invited to pitch her idea to senior executives. But here, she met an audience ready to venture out into new, uncharted territories. Her pitch triggered thoughts that were very different from what we saw at Company Blue:

- Wow, this really could be something—with that technology we could finally bypass Company Blue.

- If this really is technically feasible, we should halt the investment program for additional photographic film manufacturing capacity.

- This will mean throwing our current strategy overboard—but in the end, who cares?

- How do we get our key stakeholders excited about this?

- Who could we partner with in other industries to make this a success?

At this crucial point in time, Company Red started to reconfigure. For many months, the process remained unnoticed by the outside world. Of course, that process was painful for many individuals involved. People saw their pet projects get canceled to focus on the new technology, teams got reshuffled, and hierarchies got turned upside down. But Company Red had the versatility to reinvent itself. At the same time, its leaders did not waste time pondering ideas but got into action. It soon reached operational excellence levels in the new technology that frightened competitors. By the time Company Blue started to appreciate the magnitude of change that was happening, it was far too late. Our hero became a star at Company Red.

The Company Blue and Company Red examples perfectly illustrate some of the benefits Plasticity offers to companies: it allows them to choose their destiny, become versatile, and dare more.

Choose Your Destiny

Plasticity guides companies to base critical decisions on inner strengths and convictions rather than on alleged external needs.

When an auto executive finally made it to the top of the carmaker he was deeply in love with, one of his first actions was to abolish car clinics. His rationale was that the purpose of car clinics is to show prototypes of new cars to customer groups repeatedly until a majority would agree to its design features. In his view, this was a sure recipe for failure: "The result of a car clinic is a model 80% of people like but nobody gets excited about. I only want us to build cars that I like. Those cars will be disliked by 80% of people but the remaining 20% will be excited about them and buy!"

Indeed, in the world of modern management, decisions—even the so-called strategic decisions—are based on an analysis of market needs through focus groups, benchmarks, and all sorts of techniques that supposedly reveal where to go no matter where the starting point is or what the equipment for the journey is. In reality, basing decisions on focus groups means asking people who have never seen a product whether they would want it when they actually cannot see themselves using it, and where founding a strategy by benchmarking against another company is deciding not to be number one.

The history of entrepreneurship is full of success stories about products no one believed in except their creator, but perhaps this is the difference between entrepreneurship and management. Here, among the Magic 7 of Plasticity, the crucial factor is *purpose*: the unbreakable conviction about what the company stands for, something that cannot be traded for something else. Having this vision is probably the most indispensable element. To develop and survive in a competing world, companies also must have a reason for being. If they are only followers mimicking the leaders, they are destined to die.

American entrepreneur Warren Buffet said, "It's far better to buy a wonderful company at a fair price than a fair company at a wonderful price." It is similarly better to decide on a robust strategy that perfectly fits the company's purpose than choosing a super sophisticated strategy and fail at executing it.

Become Versatile

Being at the forefront of human development, NASA has accumulated an incredible wealth of experience on what it takes to succeed in an ever-changing environment. Indeed, what NASA people will tell you is that their key competence is not to develop spaceships but to manage complex missions. The most visible manifestation of NASA's experience is the mission control room in the Johnson Space Center in Houston. Depending on the mission profile, 25 to 30 people staff mission control, each of them representing the tip of an iceberg of hundreds of experts working below them in real time. NASA's lessons learned are simple and effective:

- *Colocate key decision makers*: You cannot expect people to come up with useful decisions if you manage them in a series of meetings.

- *Constantly incorporate the latest insights*: The plan does not survive the first day of enemy contact, so continuous replanning is the name of the game.

- *Visualize key goals and information to create transparency and support conflict resolution*: Create situation awareness and give consistent information to everyone involved.

- *Agree on detailed decision-making rules up front:* In times of stress, the problem-solving capability of humans is greatly diminished, so it is much better to perform as much problem solving as possible without an immediate disaster looming.

- *Delegate decision-making authority to the operational level that is actually close to the crucial information:* Rather than escalating difficult decisions to top management as is often done in business, delegate to those who will have the most informed opinion.

Watching the movie *Apollo 13* gives a good flavor of how these principles work in practice. As soon as the first sensor reading suggested that something had gone wrong, the mission objective changed from landing on the moon to bringing the crew back home safely. All decision making was kept within the mission control team, and neither the chief administrator of NASA nor the US president interfered.

The difference between this fine and heroic example and business reality could not be more striking. In almost any given company, decision making is the result of an opaque series of meetings in which different sets of people base their opinions on different sets of data. The plan (e.g., a budget) is almost sacred and needs to be adhered to, no matter what. In the typical corporation, breaking the news that the plan will not be met does not make you popular. This means that a sales executive who sees that he or she will fall short of ambitious growth targets will remain silent about it as long as possible. The executive may never have to come clean because there is the hope that manufacturing cannot make the planned number of products anyway. Collectively, both the sales and the manufacturing executive add to the bullwhip effects that have plagued sales and operations planning over the past century.

We are not advocating throwing the baby out with the bathwater. In virtually no company would it be acceptable to have no clear budget or forecast at the beginning of the year, rich with details about geography, client segment, product type, and so forth. Of course, each month there must be confirmation of adherence to the initial statements. Our point is that there are many things on the road that cannot be anticipated. In business, there are many types of these incidents: an unanticipated move of a competitor, a product that becomes a top seller with no warning, a change in regulations, and so on. The desired reaction should be to pick up the weak signal the moment it appears and to reward rather than punish the person that brings it to our attention.

Among the Magic 7 of Plasticity, the crucial ones for versatility are *culture, network,* and *knowledge.* Among them, knowledge is first. The instant availability of information is a must, in a stressful situation—even more so than under normal conditions. Information must be easily searchable, structured, and meaningful, and not a long list of key performance indicators (KPIs) that are usually overlooked and contribute to the panic when everybody is scrambling for the exit. Next comes network. In a stress situation, the key players of the company must reach out to whoever they believe can help. Collaboration, which is encouraged in normal times, is a must in difficult times. And the final element, culture, should reflect the idea that it is everyone's common goal to succeed rather than trying to find one person or department to blame. This prevents the people who might believe—rightly or wrongly—that they are the cause of the problem, or who feel that they are not skilled enough to solve it, from hiding the problem or refusing to face it.

The famous statement, "Houston, we have a problem," is certainly one of the exemplars of a situation in which extremely skilled experts in their field (functional excellence), striving toward a clear and thoroughly vetted goal (strategy), would have failed miserably without Plasticity skills.

Dare More

Some years ago, in front of an audience composed of the top 100 executives of a multinational company, a guest speaker asked, "What is the difference between soccer and rugby?" Immediately, consultation started among the participants, each passing their ideas about the shape and weight of the ball, the number of players, playing with the feet or the hands, the role of referee and the respect the players have, the money involved, and so forth. The speaker was smiling, savoring the effect of his forthcoming revelation. He said, "The difference is in rugby, you can only pass the ball backwards." When the one who carries the ball is running to the defensive goal line, he must pass the ball to his teammates backward. In other words, when paying attention to adversaries who are determined to block him, the player must pass to someone he can scarcely see and often to someone he cannot see at all. This is very different from what happens in soccer, where passes are made between players who see 360 degrees.

In rugby, then, the whole team is engaged in the same goal and has only one immediate goal: Support the runner. Therefore, the runner does not need to check to see if his teammates are there. They are. And knowing that gives the runner strength and audacity.

In business, the same should apply—but generally does not. People typically do not expect others to be there and support whatever happens. Much too often, people believe that others would not help in a crucial situation but would rather capture the opportunity to score a cheap point, not because they are mean but because management procedures and incentive systems nurture competition rather than solidarity.

Take a look at the life cycle of a successful high-tech company. It is often founded by like-minded college students who share the same passion for the initial cause. As the company grows, they get seriously rich and bring in additional people who are motivated by the prospect of getting wealthy in a relatively short time frame. They know that anything that is

good for the company will increase the value of their stock and are therefore aligned behind bold ideas. This works well for a couple of years until growth eventually plateaus out. The third generation of people joining now will neither become billionaires nor millionaires; they just have regular jobs and work for their monthly salaries. Their well-being in the company is very much determined by their ability to impress their superiors. For them, coming up with an unconventional idea will first and foremost put them at odds with their boss. Having the very different cultures of these three generations under one roof is a tremendous challenge that is still waiting for the silver bullet.

Among the Magic 7 of Plasticity, the crucial ones for daring more are *leadership*, *focus,* and *spirit*. Among these, spirit is first. If there is passion, if there is belief that the community is bigger than the individuals—and that individuals will get satisfaction from the accomplishment of the community—then individuals offer themselves to solve problems, which in return allows the group to be daring and target ambitious goals. Focus is also important: the ability and the courage to deselect or ignore what is not aligned with the corporate vision and values is important for creating the unspoken discipline that none of the members will even consider overstepping. Obviously, leadership is crucial in many dimensions. The example top management sets in terms of behavior, courage, integrity, and ability to sanction improper actions reinforces feelings of community and solidarity, which are necessary before embarking toward ambitious goals.

Leadership is also crucial in allowing members of the community to fail. If failure is shameful, then fear wins and progress stops. Too often, incentive systems do not value failure, generally celebrating success and adherence to plan but at the same time systematically downgrading community members who fall short. In response, goals are set too low so that failure is avoided.

As Cynthia Copeland Lewis wrote in her book *Really Important Stuff My Kids Told Me,* "If you wait until you're really sure, you'll never take off the training wheels."

Does Plasticity Solve It All?

Exactly as functional excellence and fine strategy are necessary, Plasticity is a must for a company. And this is not because it helps you be most efficient and effective and therefore profitable in steady times, but more to be able to be truly competitive and survive disruption—and possibly to create disruption that will destabilize and anesthetize competition.

What will your journey to Plasticity look like? The purpose of this book is to get your thought process started. We are firmly convinced that Plasticity will mean very different things for different companies. Therefore we refrained from writing a classic "how-to" book.

Instead we want you to take inspiration from examples in which Plasticity is at play. This is what the next part of the book is about. You will notice that business examples in it are few and far between. The reason for that is that Plasticity is a concept that the corporate world has not yet had the time or interest to embrace. But now is the time. The times demand it.

Part 2:
Plasticity at Play

Come Together: Did The Beatles Deploy Plasticity?

Purpose, focus, culture, spirit, network, knowledge, leadership

"I Want to Tell You"

On Saturday, July 6, 1957, a band called The Quarrymen was playing at St. Peter's Church garden fête in Woolton, a suburb of Liverpool in England. They were a skiffle and rock 'n' roll group formed by friends from Quarry Bank High School. The band's leader was 16-year-old John Lennon. Another member of the band, bass player Ivan Vaughan, brought someone along who he thought could make the band better.

While the band set up in the church hall for their perfor-mance, introductions were made: "John Lennon, this is Paul McCartney." McCartney tuned their guitars and sang Eddie Cochran, Gene Vincent, and Little Richard songs. It didn't take long for Lennon to ask McCartney to join his band. Five years later, The Beatles hit the big time, and Beatlemania began.

Lennon and McCartney never forgot Ivan Vaughan's role in bringing them together. For a while, they made him an Apple Records employee. It was Vaughan's wife, Jan, who sat down with Lennon and McCartney to write the French lyrics in the song "Michelle." However, it is the Plasticity of Vaughan's act that is interesting: his recognizing that McCartney was a bet-ter musician than any of the current band members and being strong enough to seek his input had untold consequences. It set a precedent and became the first of many Plasticity acts displayed by this band.

The Beatles, four young men from Liverpool, strode the world like a colossus during the 1960s. Generation after generation has loved their music. Current bands, with members born decades after The Beatles broke up, credit them as a major influence. Was Plasticity crucial to this? We believe so.

"Listen, Do You Want to Know a Secret?"

There is no doubt that The Beatles comprised four terrific performers, but a fact often overlooked is just how much Plasticity they needed to be successful. The Beatles were more than the Fab Four. "The Fifth Beatle" is a name given to a whole range of people with strong connections to the band. Manager Brian Epstein decided on all business matters and public image; producer George Martin contributed to most songs and wrote their string arrangements; CEO of Apple Records and road manager Neil Aspinall supervised the marketing of music, videos, and merchandising; and press officer Derek Taylor was in charge of all media liaisons. These people were not just influences on the band: they were active participants. Responsibilities and contributions were shared in a highly flexible, responsive way to ensure that The Beatles' creativity was channeled and commercially successful. But it was not just this wider entourage that made them deploy Plasticity.

Musicianship? Plasticity.

The Beatles were four highly talented musicians; but individually, they might not be considered the best musicians of their era. The band members' post-Beatles careers suggest that the sum of the parts far exceeded the whole. Paul McCartney might point to Wings, but he would surely acknowledge that creatively and commercially, that band didn't come close to The Beatles.

In the seedy caldron of Hamburg clubs, The Beatles delivered more than 1,000 performances in an intense two-year period. They learned to play off each other, knowing instinctively what each would do next, ultimately providing the key to perfect Plasticity: Ringo Starr's drum fills bouncing off Paul

McCartney's assertive bass and George Harrison's melodic soloing style against John Lennon's junky, aggressive chords. Bring in the selective use of strings and other instruments, add groundbreaking experimentation in the studio, and you have a perfect sound.

Songwriting? Plasticity.

The Beatles were keen for others to contribute: often when writing at John's house, John's wife Cynthia offered advice. In the studio, producer George Martin offered crucial input, such as beginning "Strawberry Fields Forever" with the chorus. They were also happy to turn Ringo's oft-used phrases, such as "a hard day's night" and "tomorrow never knows," into songs.

The Beatles, particularly John Lennon, loved 1950s American rock 'n' roll; they were also influenced by the "rom-pom-pom" of the British Music Hall and, later, by the mysticism of the Indian sitar. They were happy to credit their peers. For example, they were pleased to say that the *Sgt. Pepper* album of 1967 could not have been created without The Beach Boys' 1966 *Pet Sounds* album. There is no doubt The Beatles were happy to be influenced.

They understood the need to share responsibility. The main songwriting was shared by Lennon and McCartney, but Harrison would also get at least one song per album, and Ringo Starr would always get a song to sing on each album. As we've noted, there were many others involved in the band with discrete responsibilities that ensured songwriting remained an inner strength and core to the band's modus operandi.

Ability to change? Plasticity.

The Beatles drove the sound of popular music during the 1960s. From their foundation as a skiffle group, through rock 'n' roll, into pop ballads, through psychedelia and out the other side, their music is a genre-busting assortment covering every conceivable style. Their ability to adapt and evolve sustained them and propelled them forward.

They sacked their first drummer, Pete Best, after the sound test for their first album, *Please Please Me*. In 1962, Ringo Starr was playing drums in a holiday camp when John Lennon and Paul McCartney arrived and asked him to join the band. Despite the band being formed many years earlier, the last piece of the jigsaw fell in very late after an extremely agile move.

With a desire to evolve, they pushed themselves to create new sounds: looping tapes backward, using feedback from their guitars, even having a dog whistle on the play-out loop. They acknowledged that the sounds they were making were hard to recreate on stage and consciously made a decision to move from a live band into a recording band.

"It's Getting Better All the Time"

The Beatles had an abundance of functional excellence and a clear strategy that drove them on; but with Plasticity, they progressed from being a good band to one of the greatest of all time. They never did the same thing twice; they didn't overuse instruments and gained precisely the right sound they needed; they didn't imitate others but surpassed them; they were not satisfied with mediocrity; and they gave credit where credit was due. Their Plasticity gave them a versatility and breadth that other leading acts of the era couldn't match; it gave them an eagerness to dare more and not just push but smash the boundaries of popular music. And it gave them the confidence, and the inner strength, to know that everything they wanted to achieve was within their capability. From *Please Please Me* to *Abbey Road*, Plasticity was at the heart of The Beatles' success.

The Miracle on Ice

Purpose, focus, culture, spirit, network, knowledge, leadership

At the 1980 Winter Olympics, the USSR had the best ice hockey team in the world. They had won the gold medal every year since 1964 and had the highest scorers, the strongest defense, and the most reliable goaltender. But they didn't win. They were defeated in a medal-round game by a US team made up of amateur and collegiate players who then went on to win the gold medal. Could Plasticity be behind "The Miracle on Ice," one of most renowned sporting upsets of all time?

The USSR was considered a vastly superior team to the US: it had beaten the US 27 times and lost only 7 games. In the previous year, they had crushed the NHL All Stars 6–0 in a challenge game; and just 13 days before the famous game, they had beaten the US 10–3 in an exhibition game. But behind the scenes, the US was working on the Magic 7 and creating the opportunity for a famous win:

- The US coach, Herb Brooks, provided a clear *purpose* and showed strong *leadership*. He knew his team would have to defeat the USSR to win the Olympics, so he spent 18 months identifying a team that could combine to specifically combat Soviet strengths.

- He held a multitude of camps to ensure he had a team comprising individual personalities that could develop the team *spirit* he wanted.

- A unique *culture* was developed during a grueling four-month schedule to enable players to learn each other's style and combine as a single unit. This also instilled in the team single-mindedness and a clear *focus* of what they needed to do to beat the Soviets.

- The players came from different colleges and cities, and the coaching staff transformed this into an opportunity to acquire knowledge from each other and build an effective *network*.

- Brooks accumulated a wealth of *knowledge* on his opponents and recognized he could not match their skills. In response, he accentuated speed, conditioning, and discipline. And he ruthlessly ensured the team combined correctly when responding to specific situations such as moving a main attacker to defense to create better mobility when the Soviets moved forward aggressively.

While the US was leaning on Plasticity, the USSR was moving in the opposite direction. In the early Olympic rounds, the USSR often had to come from behind, but that didn't appear to worry them. Did they lack purpose and focus? Were they sharing knowledge properly? They were resting most of their best players, choosing to let them study plays instead of playing; and all the evidence suggests a heavy reliance on the individual skills of their starting lineup rather than a combined, more team-like effort.

In the Miracle game itself, the Soviets were dominant from the beginning; and approaching the first break, they were leading 2-1. However, at the first period buzzer, the US scored an equalizing goal. In response, the Soviets, incredibly, chose to make a substitution for goaltender Vladislav Tretiak, widely considered to be the best goalie in the world at the time. This had a huge impact on the US team and lifted their spirits.

By the start of the final period, the USSR was defending a slender 3–2 lead. Now the US's preparation paid off. They began to rotate their lineup to ensure the freshest and most versatile five were always on the ice. Disastrously for the Soviets, they did not replicate this strategy and continued to rely on their star players. It did not take long for the results of the two strategies to reach a predictable conclusion. The Americans were playing as one team throughout their entire roster and were conditioned, fast, and disciplined. The Soviets, on the other hand, were effectively playing as a smaller unit and their veteran center and wingers were exhausted. The Americans began to find what they needed to win the game and midway through the final period, the US took a 4–3 lead, which they would keep until the final buzzer.

It is wonderfully romantic to think that a group of students beat the world's greatest team through courage and patriotism. But this quixotic and sentimental idea is somewhat facile: the US team had a stronger purpose, more focus, tougher leadership, fiercer spirit, greater knowledge, a more effective network, and a better culture. They won because they deployed Plasticity.

D-Day
Purpose, focus, spirit, network, leadership

Nazi-occupied Europe was ripe for an allied invasion, but the big question remained: when? Just doing the weather forecast was a daunting endeavor. The first requirement was to pick a day with a full or new moon to have low water levels that would make spotting submerged barricades easier. Second, the day should have two low tides because the invasion would be staged in two waves. Third, there should be a mild breeze from the sea that would prevent the Germans from using gas. And then, of course, there should be no rain, neither in England from where most of the heavy equipment would be shipped nor on the French coast.

General Dwight Eisenhower, Supreme Commander of the Allied Expeditionary Forces, had three teams of meteorologists that finally agreed on a date: June 5, 1944. Yet the invasion still had to be postponed to June 6 due to bad weather.

The landings started with an airborne assault landing 24,000 parachute and glider troops behind enemy lines shortly after midnight. At 6:30 a.m., the amphibious landing commenced along an 80-km stretch of the Normandy coast divided into five sectors: Utah, Omaha, Gold, Juno, and Sword. With over 160,000 soldiers landing the first day, supported by nearly 200,000 navy personnel in 5,000 ships, it was the largest amphibious invasion in world history.

Guiding the land, sea, and air forces from the United Kingdom, the United States, Belgium, Canada, Free France, the French

Resistance, Poland, Norway, Australia, New Zealand, and the Netherlands to a coordinated push toward the heavily fortified German Atlantic Wall required an outstanding amount of networking.

Despite the magnitude of the endeavor, Eisenhower and his staff managed to write very simple orders for D-Day and the ensuing Operation Overlord:

> Land on the Normandy coast. Build the resources needed for a decisive battle in the Normandy-Brittany region and break out of the enemy's encircling positions. Land operations in the first two phases under the tactical direction of Montgomery.
>
> Pursue on a broad front with two army groups, emphasizing the left to gain necessary ports and reach the boundaries of Germany and threaten the Ruhr. On our right we link up with forces that are to invade France from the South. Build up our new base along the western border of Germany, by security ports in Belgium and in Brittany as well as in the Mediterranean.
>
> While building up our forces for the final battles, keep up an unrelenting offensive to the extent of our means, both to wear down the enemy and to gain advantages for the final fighting. Complete the destruction of enemy forces west of the Rhine, in the meantime constantly seeking bridgeheads across the river.

> Launch the final attack as a double envelopment of the Ruhr, again emphasizing the left, and follow this up by an immediate thrust through Germany, with the specific direction to be determined at the time. Clean out the remainder of Germany.

This clear purpose and the overall Plasticity of the plan was shared and understood by all the allied forces that were engaged in the hundreds of battles that followed.

Steam Locomotives

(A lack of) vision, purpose, network, knowledge, leadership

The year 1689 saw the first commercial application to the millennia-old idea to use boiling water to produce mechanical motion. What started in Thomas Savery's water pump evolved into the main power source of the industrial revolution over the subsequent 150 years or so.

The use of high-pressure steam reduced the weight of the engine so much that eventually it could be put on wheels. That gave birth to the steam locomotive. In 1825, George Stephenson built the Locomotion No. 1 (originally called Active) for the Stockton and Darlington Railway, the first public steam railway in the world. With the success of his 1829 Rocket, Stephenson's company was established as the preeminent builder of steam locomotives in the United Kingdom, the United States, and much of Europe.

Following Stephenson's example, steam locomotives were built by companies in virtually every industrializing country in the world. In a fierce competitive race, they made locomotives ever faster and more powerful. Over decades, the market leaders in the United States were Baldwin Locomotive Works, American Locomotive Company (ALCO), and Lima Locomotive Works.

Baldwin built its first steam locomotive in 1831. The Pennsylvania-based company was very successful; its sales peaked in 1906 with 2,666 steam locomotives delivered to customers. The emergence of first the diesel and later the electric locomotive were challenges that Baldwin failed to master. It stopped producing locomotives altogether in 1956 and went out of business in 1972.

Baldwin, and other steam locomotive manufacturers, defined themselves poorly. They created a myopic view based on the product they could see (the steam engine) rather than have the vision to see themselves as industrial manufacturers that could create trains powered in a range of ways.

Had Baldwin known about Plasticity and leveraged it for choosing the company's destiny, we might be able to click on Baldwin's web site and read, "Baldwin stands for speed and power. Whenever you want to harness the power of steam in boilers and turbines or start thinking about a new high-speed railway either with diesel or with electricity, we are the people to talk to."

Teleonomy
Purpose

With science advancing, the very definition of life has become a hot topic for biologists and philosophers. When high-powered microscopes confirmed that viruses are essentially just proteins storing genetic information but lack all other elements of living cells, there was substantial debate. Are viruses alive at all, or are they just nonliving matter? In his essay, *Chance and Necessity: Essay on the Natural Philosophy of Modern Biology*, Nobel Prize winner and French biologist Jacques Monod discussed teleonomy, or goal directedness, and stated that the common denominator of life is that it follows a clearly identifiable purpose. In viruses, this purpose is reproduction. They enter the cells of a host organism and force them to produce copies of themselves—more viruses. In more complex life forms, the underlying purpose of reproduction is covered with other layers that can still be traced back to reproduction. Take the playful behavior of young animals as an example. In playing, they mimic the actions of adults and thereby practice skills that will be essential for their survival. Teleonomy is closely related to concepts of complexity theory and self-organizing systems. Some philosophers of biology resist the term, whereas others endorse it.

Because purpose is so essential to the very fabric of living beings, it would appear natural for leaders of companies to have it their top priority to make the purpose of the company very clear to each and every employee. With the purpose understood and embraced by everybody, the right structures to fulfill this purpose will emerge on their own—if not hindered by the leaders.

Arcimboldo

Plasticity

Giuseppe Arcimboldo, a 16th-century painter, started as a fairly traditional and well-respected painter of dignitaries and sceneries. At some point in his career, he abandoned tradition and started to represent the people he was painting with a collection of other objects. These objects were mostly the ones you would expect to find in a still life, such as fruits, vegetables, and other agricultural products.

Similar to Salvador Dali's famous painting of Abraham Lincoln, close up to the painting you see the individual objects. At a certain distance, your brain connects these objects to the overall representation of the person portrayed. Interestingly, of the many paintings Arcimboldo produced throughout his life, only these portraits gained fame.

In these iconic representations, none of the fruits or vegetables has a perfect shape or color, but the association of them is powerful and harmonious.

The lesson for Corporate Plasticity is that it does not take perfect elements to create something great and unexpected. What really matters is how you get the elements to work together.

Golden Ratio

Plasticity

The *golden ratio* was first defined by Euclid in ancient Greece. Two quantities are in the golden ratio if their ratio is the same as the ratio of their sum to the larger of the two quantities, meaning that the larger quantity is 1.618 times the smaller quantity.

The golden ratio is a measure that can be found all over in nature and our lives. We can find it when looking at the arrangement of branches along stems of plants, and of veins in leaves. The mathematician Jacob Bernoulli investigated an appearance of a logarithmic spiral that, when it is in golden ratio, he called Spira mirabilis, "the marvelous spiral." It can be found in shells and other plants, such as in the arrangement of artichoke leaves.

The golden ratio proves to be one of the most optimal ways to use space. For example, the growth of seeds in the sunflower follows the golden ratio. As new seeds grow, the older ones move to the outskirts, and the distance between new and old seeds equals the golden ratio.

The ratio has been applied in architecture since the ancient Greeks or perhaps even Egyptian times, and it governs the proportions of many classical buildings such as the Parthenon.

We can find traces of the golden ratio in art, be it in Leonardo da Vinci's works or in paintings by artists such as Salvador Dalí or Piet Mondrian.

It seems that the human eye perceives things made in the golden ratio as beautiful, complete by themselves. Is there a golden ratio for the design of organizations that will enable Corporate Plasticity?

Communication of Ants

Purpose, network

How often have you come across a large ant nest during a casual walk in the woods? You can usually spot a trail of working ants delivering some kind of material into the nest. These ants can travel miles and still find their way back to the nest and then navigate the maze of the nest itself. How come they don't get lost? They don't, after all, have a global positioning system built into their brains, and there is no central control mechanism. The truth is that each ant only follows the movements of its most proximate ants, and in addition it follows the smell markings that previous ants have left on the ground.

This method of ant communication is a system in which each node communicates only with adjacent nodes to enable the quickest and most efficient communication. It is so efficient that it inspired analogies that have been applied in computer science to identify the shortest-route optimization algorithms.

This is an example of a well-organized system of interconnected parts communicating only with related adjacent parts being more efficient than one central system.

It appears that in organizations with Plasticity, central control is not always required.

Public Spaces
Culture, network

Public spaces have been created since ancient times to provide an area for people to gather to trade goods, exchange
ideas, or just stop by to see and be seen. The medieval public
space was in the form of a central marketplace in a city or a
village, usually in an irregular and closed format so that people
could access it from many sides. Great examples for vivid
medieval public spaces are the shell-shaped Piazza del Campo
in Siena, Italy, or the many narrow alleys in London.

In more modern times, architects have planned public spaces
that have perfect geometric shapes. They exist in open spaces,
which enable a lot more fresh air to flow through them, and
they often have one or two main axes leading to them. The
trees and obstacles of any type are usually small or omitted
completely to allow openness of the space and to emphasize
clear geometric forms.

If they are so good, though, why are they so often empty,
without people lingering there?

Arguably it's because people prefer more closed public
spaces, because they like to observe and interact with other
people, and it is more comfortable to sit in the shade of a
tree or be protected from wind by the adjacent walls. The
random obstacles make it more interesting, even after return-
ing for the hundredth time to the same place. Architects have
learned their lessons, and Times Square in New York City is a
shining example of a successful contemporary public space.

Encouraging random interaction between people is one of the core elements of a livable community. If we want to encourage networking within a company, we need to foster random interaction between its members.

Not surprisingly, we can find elements of good public spaces in great companies that nourish networking and collaboration. Let's take Apple's current HQ in Cupertino, California. In addition to multiple informal gathering places on campus, such as cafeterias and break rooms, there is a large atrium that many Apple workers have to cross several times a day that makes chance encounters almost inevitable.

The new Apple HQ, Apple Campus 2, nicknamed "the Mothership" or "flying saucer," will be a 2.8-million-square-foot facility located on a 175-acre lot. It will house 12,000 employees and feature a 1,000-seat auditorium, 300,000 square feet of research space, and its own power plant.

To bring Plasticity to corporate life, leaders should bring life to office buildings. Let's tear down cubicles and walls. Establish a coffee shop wherever possible and tear down cubicles and walls!

The Human Brain
Plasticity

The human brain as a biological processing system can be described by a few core properties:

- *It consists of modular parts*: That is, different network parts have relatively well-defined functions.

- *The parts are plastically connected*: Modularity is not absolute; rather, it is plastic, meaning a brain can rewire itself on slow timescales, and previously disconnected regions/neurons can become connected. Plasticity enables the system to constantly rewire and makes learning possible. The brain tries to predict the future, compares the predictions to the real outcomes, and rewires itself to make predictions even better. This is a constant process; the brain does not go through "periods" of restructuring.

- The system is adaptive. The building blocks are able to compensate, within themselves and without top-down instructions, for certain variations in their environments. This would be as if, for example, electronic components could operate with alternating current or direct current without any special adaptors or converters.

An interesting experiment illustrating the amazing ability of the human brain to adapt was conducted by psychologist George M. Stratton in the 1890s. Stratton designed reversing glasses that made him see things upside down. When he put these glasses on for just a couple of hours, he had great difficulties orienting himself in his house and he repeatedly bumped into furniture.

Stratton wondered if his brain would adapt if he wore the reversing glasses for longer periods of time. And there it was—after four days of permanently wearing the glasses during his waking hours, the image suddenly flipped. Despite his wearing the reversing glasses, he saw things the normal way. Somehow his brain had rewired the information received from his eyes to make sense for him.

He continued another four days and then took the reversing glasses off for good. As expected, he then saw things upside down. To Stratton's relief, this rewiring was not permanent; a couple of days after ending the experiment, his normal eyesight returned.

The ability of the human brain to constantly adjust itself is the ultimate example of Plasticity.

The Roman Military

Purpose, focus, culture

The Roman military existed for 2,000 years and was arguably the greatest military machine in history. Its ability to learn, reconfigure, and reach a new state was critical to the longevity and superiority of Rome's Republic and Empire.

Its army and navy underwent numerous transformations in configuration, structure, equipment, and tactics. In the end, the Roman military was more versatile than its enemies, dared more than its enemies, and helped Rome choose a destiny that echoes to this day. Let us consider two examples from the mid-Republic era.

The Manipular Army—Daring More

Up until the mid-Republic era, the Romans had used a battle formation they had inherited from the Etruscans—the phalanx formation. This was essentially a rectangular mass of soldiers lined up in close order. During the Second Samnite War, the terrain of Samnium drew attention to the lack of maneuverability in this formation, and the result was a series of defeats and a calamitous surrender of a legion at the Caudine Forks without even a fight. The defeat humiliated Rome, which was subjected to a five-year peace treaty and embarrassing terms.

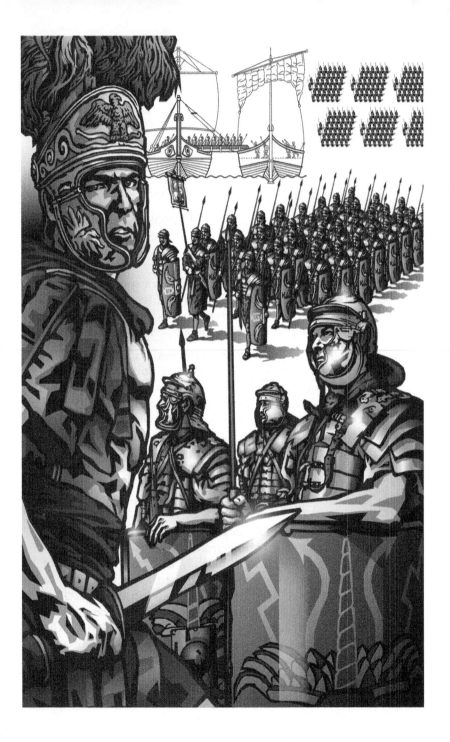

As Rome waited for the treaty to expire, it mused on its defeat and, with a renewed focus, strengthened its military. It increased recruitment, constructed its first military roads, increased the size of its military levy and—perhaps most importantly—abandoned the phalanx formation that it had deployed for 200 years.

The new formation was called the maniple. In this formation, the army was organized into three lines, positioned in a checkerboard pattern, and divided by experience: youngest soldiers at the front, experienced soldiers in the middle, and hardened fighters at the rear. This allowed true Plasticity when engaging: each line would draw back to the next when it reached the peak of its capability, thus immediately supplementing the frontline with increased capability when it was required; its best fighters were kept fresh for the hardest fights; and the youngest and rawest fighters were exposed to action early, being coached by the more experienced people immediately behind them.

Over the next decade, Rome perfected the maniple, won a series of battles against the Samnites, and gained control of most of central Italy. The maniple became the Roman army's mainstay formation for the next 200 years.

The Corvus—Versatility

The Punic Wars were bloody and vicious wars between two great powers separated by the Mediterranean Sea: Rome and Carthage. At the time of the first Punic War, Carthage had a navy and a great deal of maritime experience with its sea-based trade. Rome, on the other hand, had almost no experience in naval warfare. Indeed, at this stage, its military had never campaigned outside the Italian Peninsula. To defeat Carthage, Rome would have to win a naval war. But Romans were not sailors, and the strength of the Roman military was the discipline and courage of its soldiers. Rome's path to victory, despite this clear disadvantage, is a display of Plasticity at its finest.

The first step to triumph was a victory that used its traditional functional excellence at the Battle of Agrigentum. This was a land battle in Sicily and the first large-scale confrontation of the war. The Carthaginians were trapped in the city. The Romans first laid siege and then won a fierce, pitched battle. The Romans then displayed strategic excellence to capture Carthaginian ships and, with the assistance of their new Sicilian allies, quickly built a sizable navy. The next step was to bring their superior knowledge of land military tactics to the sea.

No one knows who invented the corvus. Polybius describes it as a bridge 1.2 m (4 ft) wide and 10.9 m (36 ft) long. It was fixed in the bow of the ship, and could be raised or lowered like a drawbridge. The key was the heavy spike on the bottom that penetrated the enemy ship's deck when it was lowered. The corvus allowed Rome to evade Carthage's naval strength and promote its own military strength by using marines to board Carthaginian ships via the corvus and fight in hand-to-hand combat. The corvus had immediate impact, as Rome was victorious in the first naval battle of the war, the Battle of Mylae.

The corvus was used for no more than a decade. Indeed, by the time of Rome's ultimate victory at the Battle of the Aegates Islands, there is no mention of its use. But its creation and deployment demonstrates the Roman military's Plasticity and its ability to overcome groupthink and myopia and reconfigure itself to reach a new state.

Rugby

Purpose, culture, spirit

As the story goes, rugby was invented by a rule breaker, William Webb Ellis, in 1823 at Rugby School. He allegedly caught the ball while playing football and ran toward the opposition goal line and put the ball down.

In critical elements of the game, players must combine to win the ball. Interestingly for some elements, such as the scrum, players from both sides have to come together to make it work. In other words, it requires both teams to cooperate to actually compete.

After certain stoppages in play, a scrum is formed by eight players from each team binding together in three rows. The two sets of players engage so that the players' heads on the front row are interlocked with those of the other side. If players don't use a certain technique, then the whole thing ends up in a collapsed heap!

There is a role for everybody in rugby, regardless of size. Everyone has a clear position and a task to fulfill. Invariably, if everyone completes the tasks for their role and supports others in doing theirs, the team will play cohesively and put themselves in a position to win.

The blind pass can be an important element in winning a game.

A player's entire body shape will be used to mislead defenders. He will look, run, and aim for contact in a totally different place than where he passes the ball. The aim is to deceive defenders and make them commit to tackling the player, which will free up space for the receiver of the ball.

A blind pass is high-risk, though: a dropped pass may mean that the opposition gains possession. To accomplish successful blind passing, all players in a team need to be highly skilled and confident in each other's ability. The player receiving the ball needs high concentration—the receiver may also be fooled by the blind pass if it is not anticipated—while the player passing the ball must have a heightened sense of awareness about where teammates are on the field.

Rugby is a brutal sport, but it has strong Plasticity credentials. It was created by a visionary breaking convention. And its game elements, particularly those that require both sides to participate, require an implicitly agreed-upon culture that creates the conditions for the game to work.

Wikipedia

Knowledge, culture, spirit, network

Encyclopedias are anthologies of reference material. The name is Greek in origin and means "general education." Encyclopedias have existed for at least two millennia, but they have undergone an unprecedented and radical transformation in the last 20 years.

In 1993, Microsoft launched Encarta on CD-ROM with entries supplemented with video and audio. It changed forever the way encyclopedic information was conveyed. Despite being lauded as a massive breakthrough in the way that encyclopedias worked, within a mere 16 years Encarta had been discontinued and was relegated to history. In that astonishingly short period, people had changed the way they sought information and the traditional reference material market died. The trigger was Wikipedia.

Wikipedia is the largest and most popular reference site on the Internet and has 365 million readers worldwide. It has transformed the way that reference material is created and shared. Its articles are written collaboratively by volunteers around the world and can be edited by anyone with access to the site.

Users' acceptability of material from a mass of amateur content providers rather than a small set of experts has been crucial to Wikipedia's success. The network of contributors, colloquially known as *Wikipedians*, has its own online and

offline community, and a culture driven by the same ideology and based on shared values has emerged. The combination of having this community and Wikipedia's readers crowdsourcing the content enables the web site to match the intellectual depth that just a few years ago was only possible with a small number of experts and a lot of time.

Wikipedia has disrupted a millennia-old approach to the curation of knowledge. It is down to a strong network and the spirit of its contributors that Wikipedia is now an established reference work.

Oakland Athletics

Purpose, focus, knowledge, leadership

The Oakland Athletics, an American professional baseball team, plays in Major League Baseball's American League. In 2002, they had the third-lowest team salary in the league ($40 million), a staggering $80 million behind the highest-salaried team, the New York Yankees. With no sign of a change in available funds, the general manager, Billy Beane, sought a new way to get an advantage over the richer clubs. Beane, along with a mostly reluctant scouting team, chose a different approach to building a team: the goal was not to buy players, the goal was to buy wins; and to buy wins, the club needed to buy runs. The whole ethos of the team building was switched to focus on obtaining and nurturing players that, when combined, would best facilitate runs. Deploying this approach meant making some seemingly astonishing purchases.

Baseball has been the national pastime in the United States since the mid-19th century. Since that time, coaches and scouts have used virtually the same analysis to assess the quality of a player. Basic statistics such as runs batted in, stolen bases, and batting average were combined with subjective physical and mental assessments such as a "strong arm" or "good under pressure." The Oakland Athletics decided to challenge this approach to build a championship team they could afford.

Oakland systematically deployed an approach called saber-metrics. This is a statistical approach that questions the traditional values of baseball skill and places emphasis on a player's ability to help his team score more runs than the opposing team. Measures were created (rather than just sterile statistics) to determine the probability of players' success. For example, sabermetricians contended that the ability to control the strike zone was the biggest indicator of a hitter's future success. Oakland recognized that by assessing players this way, they could identify players that the rest of the league consistently undervalued.

Oakland built a team with significant Plasticity. As individuals, the players they recruited were mostly so-called misfits; but when combined, they created a powerful unit. The approach had an immediate impact, and even though their salary level remained steady, the team went to the playoffs in 2002 and 2003. The club did not just deploy Plasticity on the field though—many of the Magic 7 can be seen off the field:

1. *Leadership*: Authority and so-called experts were challenged. Oakland had reached a point where tradition was killing them and they had to "change the game" if they wanted to progress.

2. *Focus/purpose*: They developed a philosophy and stuck with it under pressure to change.

3. *Knowledge*: Oakland understood and knew every element of their business. From this they were able to set the goal of wins and the runs needed to get those wins. From there they were able to recruit the players that would combine and fit into this plan.

Oakland recognized that there is always a weakness in a market and that when it can't be seen, you simply need to look at the market differently. Billy Beane had a strong vision that was countercultural. He was ostracized by his own scouts for disowning what scouts have done for 150 years. He demonstrated a relentless focus on the critical problem (i.e., building a winning team for $40 million) and utilized techniques that turned otherwise seemingly meaningless data into knowledge of considerable value. The rest of baseball had no choice but to follow or be left behind, and now most Major League Baseball clubs use sabermetrics in one way or another. With the help of Plasticity, Oakland changed the world of baseball.

NATO Forces

Plasticity

The North Atlantic Treaty Organization (NATO) is an inter-governmental military alliance that began in 1949 as an orga-nization of collective defense. After the fall of the Berlin Wall in 1989, it began to intervene militarily in locations such as Yugoslavia, Bosnia, and Kosovo. By 1999, a new Alliance Strategic Concept had been enshrined that emphasized con-flict prevention and crisis management.

NATO comprises 26 nations and Plasticity—which it recog-nizes as a useful concept that it calls "interoperability"—is essential for the militaries to work together successfully in out-of-area expeditionary operations. This has meant forces from different nations working together have a combined mil-itary structure, but it must of course also include a degree of technical capability and the ability to contribute to coalition military goals. This is no mean feat: bureaucracy kills Plasticity, and too many stakeholders with too many requests in the pipeline is a recipe for slow decision making.

Plasticity in NATO works on four levels: strategic (balancing national views and building agreed policy), operational (inter-change of forces and units), tactical (using best combinations available; e.g., a maritime task group may combine minesweepers clearing the way, submarines then following to ensure that below surface is clear, battleships next, and then finally aircraft carriers), and technological (sharing communications and systems). The best Plasticity is dependent on data sharing. For example, even within NATO, there is not a full share—only the United States, Britain, and Australia have truly open books with each other. It is no coincidence that they exemplify good Plasticity.

Kodak

(A lack of) purpose, culture, spirit, network, leadership

George Eastman formed Eastman Kodak in 1888 in Rochester, New York. Kodak transformed photography from something done in a studio by a professional to something that was integral to modern family life. It established the practice of popular photography, and throughout the 20th century was one of the world's most recognized brands. Yet by 2012, this industrial icon filed for Chapter 11 bankruptcy protection. What went wrong?

Kodak's early history illustrates that it once had substantial Corporate Plasticity. George Eastman was an innovator and entrepreneur, and he boldly transformed the business twice: dry-plate photography was abandoned to move to film, and when Kodak dominated the black-and-white film market, that was abandoned to invest in color film (even though it was poorer quality than black and white at that time). Eastman wrote that he wanted his business to create "a rapid succession of changes and improvements.... If we can get out improved goods every year nobody will be able to follow us and compete with us. The only way to compete with us will be to get out original goods the same as we do."[1]

---

[1]Alfred D. Chandler, Jr. (1977). *The Visible Hand.* Cambridge, MA: Belknap Press, p. 572.

In the 1970s and 1980s, this ethos had run aground. Kodak's laboratories were groundbreaking, and the skill and capability to take a lead in new technologies was within their grasp. However, the reaction of the corporate suite was not exactly encouraging. Kodak engineers invented the first digital camera in 1975, but they were told to keep quiet about it so it would not impact the film business. By 1981, photo finishers were asking about digital photography and Kodak conducted research on the technology and adoption curves. The results indicated that digital photography would eventually replace film and that Kodak had about 10 years to prepare. Nothing was done with this research.

By the 1990s and into the 21st century, Kodak tried to ignore what was happening and then tried to explain it away. Thus they hung on to obsolete assumptions that reaffirmed their existing business model and they failed to spot market movements for what they were:

- They believed digital products were merely a substitute for analog products rather than a catalyst that would drop the high barriers to entry in the film market and transform the industry.

- They failed to recognize the move from cameras being photography equipment to being gadgets that were sold through new channels in new ways.

- They believed that people would still want to print photos; they could not bring themselves to admit that hard prints would die out.

- They failed to track the changes in their market segments. Women had always been Kodak's key customers; but with the move away from hard print archiving toward sharing through social media, this segment had fundamentally changed its behaviors.

Kodak had an incredibly prescient market assessment and the skills and capability to deliver digital technology, so how could these mistakes be possible in an industrial icon? It collapsed because it failed to address some important fundamentals of Corporate Plasticity:

- Kodak's spirit had become diminished, and it was complacent. It was already beginning to lose ground to Fuji in the roll-film business before the digital revolution. There was no leader willing to take on the corporate behemoth and instill much-needed urgency.

- People saw the problem coming, but the network that would have gotten the message through was not functioning. There were people that didn't agree with the obsolete assumptions and had the solutions, but these people were buried in the firm and had no voice.

- Kodak lacked the vision to recognize the world around them was changing and that what the organization did would need to change. It could easily have invested in a few start-ups to explore digital photography alongside its traditional business, but it failed to do so.

In December 2012, Kodak announced that in a bid to end its bankruptcy it was selling its patents in digital photography for $500 million. Deploying Corporate Plasticity would have cost a lot less and kept an icon going and growing.

The European Union

(The lack of) purpose, focus, leadership

The European Union (EU), having brought an unprecedented period of peace, stability, and prosperity to at least the western half of the European continent, is a success story. Or is it?

Let's take a closer look at how the EU operates. There are three main institutions: the European Commission, the European Parliament, and the European Council (made up of the national governments).

The European Commission traditionally has its strengths in functional excellence and strategy. Specifically, functional excellence has always been high on the agenda and had been inspired by the proven model of British administration. The European Commission employs nearly 30,000 people representing an impressive pool of expertise, knowledge, and experience. Emphasis is put on people development, which starts from very high levels. The sheer need to operate in a multilanguage environment forces people to take broader perspectives. The European Commission also has a pretty clear strategy.

Since the start of the financial crisis in 2008, across all ups and downs, it has become clear that functional excellence and strategy are not sufficient. Established rules and procedures were replaced by informal agreements between heads of states to fix issues through aligning national legislation. All players interpret any agreement based on their individual

background. That interpretation heavily impacts the way and the stamina with which the agreements are put in place. This is compounded by the way people collaborate. Leadership capabilities, teamwork, and the ability to constructively digest feedback remain key challenges. In that respect, Plasticity is a highly relevant topic for the European Commission.

Purpose, focus, and leadership—key aspects of Plasticity—are serious shortcomings in the EU. This is aggravated by the fact that the overall philosophy behind the EU is based on the French model that requires a visionary leader at the center. Without that, the model tends to stagnate.

Imagine what the European Union could be with true Plasticity.

The Conservation Biologist Facing Synthetic Biology

Purpose, focus, culture, spirit, network, knowledge

Conservation biologist Kent Redford is about to bring together two camps that so far have not talked to each other at all—conservation biologists and synthetic biologists. To kick start what he deems to be a long overdue exchange of ideas and perspectives, he organized a conference in Cambridge, U.K. in April 2013 titled "How Will Synthetic Biology and Conservation Shape the Future of Nature?"

Redford makes the case that conservationists have so far sat at the rear of the bus, looking out the back window, cataloging and bemoaning the extinction of species. In his words, every new event "hit conservationists at the back of their heads." With his efforts to open up to synthetic biology, he wants conservationists to look out the front window of the bus, very much the way synthetic biologists are doing.

One of many examples he gives is the white nose syndrome that is believed to have killed some seven million North American bats since it was first recorded in 2006. The disease is caused by a fungus called Geomyces Destructans and has mortality rates of up to 95% in some bat populations. Conservation biologist approaches have been limited to recording losses in the bat population and identifying that European bats appear to be immune to the fungus. Redford now argues that it might be possible for synthetic biologists to identify the portion in the genome of European bats responsible for the immunity and

introduce it to American bats. Because both camps of biologists historically have not really talked to each other, conservation biologists don't really understand what synthetic biology could do for them, while synthetic biologists are widely ignorant of the problems keeping conservation biologists awake at night.

Plasticity might enable the two camps of biologists to put their differences aside and cooperate in a cause to save the North American bat. It may be a North American bat with a tiny portion of European genome, but it would play its crucial role in its natural habitat.

Guns, Germs, and Steel

Plasticity

In his book *Guns, Germs, and Steel*, Jared Diamond makes a compelling case for why world history turned out to be what it is. Many of us may have speculated about the question of why the native Americans did not board big ships to invade Europe. Why did it instead happen the other way around?

Diamond's answer to this question goes like this. Eurasia had many big animals that could be domesticated, and because the continent stretches from East to West, the same plants and animals could be used over vast stretches of territory. In contrast, the Americas had only one large animal that can be domesticated, the llama. Other large American animals, such as the bison, turned out to be too aggressive for domestication. In addition, the North–South orientation of the continent, with many different climate zones, created a huge obstacle to sharing plants and animals.

Based on this, Eurasian farmers were far more productive and provided the basis for population growth, urbanization, and division of labor. In addition, living close to animals led to diseases such as smallpox and measles jumping from the animals to the humans. Initially, these diseases killed many humans. Gradually, however, Eurasians developed resistance.

The lesson for business leaders is that Plasticity should also encompass building entire ecosystems. Great people, great ideas, and great products are not created and developed in isolation. Their surroundings play a vital, but often imperceptible part, in their gestation. A continuously growing ecosystem that is guided by the principles of Plasticity will be almost impossible to beat.

Pack of Wolves

Culture, spirit, leadership

Many teams of behavioral scientists around the world have studied wolf packs. Wolves live in complex social structures that can be likened to human societies to a certain extent.

The interesting aspect about wolf packs in the context of Plasticity is how fluid their structure is. Wolf packs are dominated by a male and female couple called the *alpha wolves*. The alpha wolves lead the pack on hunts for prey and when there is a need to defend the territory. Being an alpha wolf comes with significant perks. They are the first to feed on prey and maybe even more importantly, they are the ones to breed.

But alpha wolves are never allowed to rest on their laurels. Periodically, they will be challenged by others for leadership. If alpha wolves lose the challenge, they move down the social ladder and follow the new leader. And they know that there will be a chance in the future to reclaim their cherished position as alphas.

Entrenched hierarchies can stifle Plasticity. Leaders should consider shaking up their structures regularly, just like in a wolf pack. The challenged alpha may not like it, but it will be better for the competitiveness of the entire group.

Orcas

Purpose, culture, network, knowledge

Orcas, the largest dolphins, are the top predators in the ocean. They live in highly structured populations that are determined by matrilineal relations. Orcas are very chatty animals and communicate with each other using complex sound patterns. These patterns vary by populations, and some scientists name these variations as dialects or even different languages. Orcas are very sophisticated and effective predators. They adapt to any type of prey with a great level of Plasticity. When hunting small fish such as herring, orcas deploy a tactic known as carousel feeding. A group of orcas will swim circles around a school of herrings and continuously blow bubbles. This disorients the herring and forces them to form a tight knot. One of the orcas will then shoot upward with his mouth open and swallow a couple of fish. The orcas take turns to ensure that none of their group leaves the carousel hungry.

When hunting sharks—orcas are the only predator going after great white sharks—they induce tonic immobility by holding them upside down, which renders them helpless. A great white shark would be a fearsome opponent to a single orca, but with their tightly coordinated attacks, they can overwhelm the shark that lacks any Plasticity and always hunts alone.

When hunting for large whales, the orcas first try to separate a young or weak individual from its family by chasing them until they are worn out. They then collectively prevent the whale from surfacing to breathe and drown it.

Maybe the most stunning hunting tactic of orcas can be observed in the Antarctic. There, orcas spy-hop to locate seals that rest on ice floes. Once they have identified a suitable target, they deploy a tactic called *wave hunting*. A group of 5–10 orcas swims in sync in the direction of the ice floe. These orcas will dive right in front of the floe, which will have two effects. First, the floe will sway, and second, a wave will gush over the floe. Combined, these effects will push the seal over the opposite side of the flow. There another orca will already lie waiting with his jaws wide open.

Orcas never go it alone. Despite being the top predator in the ocean, they cooperate and learn from each other to increase the rate of success and minimize risk. Leaders should learn from the Plasticity of orcas to focus more on how to collaborate, reduce political infighting, and adapt their strengths for each challenge.

Symphony Orchestra

Purpose, leadership

One musician cannot make a symphony, but neither can an orchestra without a conductor. The best musicians in the world cannot create the best symphony without a conductor. And the most musically gifted conductor cannot be effective without the skill of leadership. They are directive and do not fear anyone, even star performers.

If someone is out of tune, it is their job to say so. Likewise, they don't simply lead through discipline; they know that to be effective, they must encourage, often publicly, to achieve the best performance from thin-skinned superstars. The conductor is always leading with a view on succession. An orchestra is a large group of people, and at any time an individual may choose to leave. Knowing this, the conductor is also a scout, constantly looking for the best up-and-coming talent. The conductor is also best placed to help current orchestra members develop their music and fulfill their potential. The role of a conductor is often lightheartedly questioned by those not familiar with classical music. However, the role is at the heart of the orchestra, and the conductor embodies all the virtues of a great leader.

Actor and Director

Culture, spirit

Austrian actor Christoph Waltz was looking back at three largely frustrating decades of German TV when he was contacted by Quentin Tarantino for a role in *Inglourious Basterds*. That role brought him the Oscar for best supporting actor. Waltz and Tarantino repeated that feat with *Django Unchained*.

What had happened? Had Waltz in his mid-50s suddenly become a better actor? Hardly. Tarantino had been looking for an actor who could give what Waltz was longing to give.

Waltz's role in *Inglourious Basterds* was Hans Landa, the primary antagonist. The role required an actor with the highest capability in language. Tarantino had searched in vain for an actor to fill the role and became convinced that he had written a role that was un-playable. He became so frustrated that he was just days away from calling off the movie when Waltz auditioned for the role.

The lesson for leaders is that if you have a clear view of what really matters, the superstar you need is often in your midst. Deploy Plasticity to unlock their potential.

Humans

Purpose, focus, culture, spirit, network, knowledge, leadership

Plasticity is at the very core of human nature. As we come to the end of this book, let us review the Magic 7 of Plasticity, what they have meant in the development of the human race, and how they distinguish us from the other animals.

Purpose: Many animals collaborate, but none at the size of humans. Humans can collaborate in groups much larger than a family or a clan. The underlying logic of that collaboration can manifest itself in many forms. We may call it philosophy or religion, but they invariably make the individual perceive itself as just one element in a much bigger cause.

Focus: The human ability for long-term planning made activities such as farming possible. The farmer needs to set aside a portion of the harvest to have seeds for the next season. So the hungry farmer had to overcome his immediate hunger for the benefit of a much bigger reward later in time. Only that human quality led to the development of towns, the division of labor, and everything that is associated with civilization.

Culture: The division of labor ultimately leads to a group of people that neither produce nor hunt nor fight enemies. That group is dedicated to honing the purpose of society. Job descriptions range from priests, kings, and judges to philosophers.

Spirit: Closely related to the aforementioned cultural group is the cast of artists. Song, music, and dance made feasts and celebrations memorable events.

Network: Humans have very distinct facial features. For humans it is not difficult to recognize an acquaintance amid a sea of faces immediately. This ability is the basis for networking. With it, exchanging favors or paying back debt is something that works over long periods of time.

Knowledge: Language made it possible to transmit vast amounts of information in short periods of time. It made humans far more effective hunters than, say, wolves, and it allowed us to accumulate knowledge from generation to generation.

Leadership: Organizing and rallying large groups of people is a skill that turned out to be more valuable and decisive than other factors.

In summary, Plasticity has always been there and it is the finest quality of the human race. When will large corporations acknowledge this fact and start using it to their benefit?

Let's look at some examples of each of these areas.

Purpose

Apple's Steve Jobs gave the finest example for defining the purpose of a company. At the unveiling of the first generation iPad on January 27, 2010, Jobs said, "We've always tried to be at the intersection of technology and liberal arts, to be able to get the best of both, to make extremely advanced products from a technology point of view, but also have them be intuitive, easy to use, fun to use, so that they really fit the users—the users don't have to come to them, they come to the user."

This message not only works internally for Apple's employees. It also works externally with Apple's customers and makes them queue up in front of Apple stores every time the firm launches a new product. These customers are so convinced by Apple living to its purpose that they are willing to spend money on products they have never had a chance to lay a hand on.

Focus

The famous Dutch yachtsman Conny van Rietschoten, who won the Whitbread Round the World Race in 1978 and 1982, is an example of focus. Before participating in this race, he was entirely unknown in international long-range sailing; he had instead built his family business.

What set him apart from all the sailors of his time was his professional approach to the sport and his focus. He put great emphasis on rehearsing and training, and he invested in research to improve the crew's clothing and the ability to forecast weather.

What makes van Rietschoten relevant for this book is his feat in the 1982 race. His yacht, *The Flyer II*, was in heavy seas in the Southern Ocean when van Rietschoten had a heart attack. Unimpressed by this serious and immediate threat to his life, he had his crew press ahead:

> The nearest port was 10 days away and the critical period is always the first 24–36 hours," he recalled later. "*Ceramco* was already breathing down our necks. If they had known that I had a health problem, they would have pushed their boat even harder.

When you die at sea, you are buried over the side. Perhaps those Ceramco boys might then have spotted me drifting by. And that I was determined would be the only thing they would see or hear from Flyer on the matter![1]

Van Rietschoten's gamble with his own life paid off, and he was the only skipper to win the Whitbread Round the World Race twice. He continued sailing, enjoyed his fame, and lived on until 2013.

---

[1] http://blog.boats.com/2013/12/eight-bells-cornelis-van-rietschoten/#.U2pcCIFdWzs

Culture

Many companies demand that their employees do all kinds of things. As priorities shift, people can lose sight of what really matters. With priority piled on priority, one can be busy just ticking boxes. This is not exactly the climate that will foster innovation.

Google is going down a very different route. Trying to preserve its start-up culture despite being a huge multinational corporation, Google is following 3M's example of allowing and encouraging all employees to dedicate 20% of their time to projects they deem important.

With this freedom and independence, a lot of projects will not lead to anything. But a critical few projects feed the pipeline of breakthrough ideas with which Google does not cease to surprise us.

Some examples of projects (in total, 50% of all products) at Google that are results of "20% time":

- Gmail
- AdSense
- Google Latitude
- Orkut
- Google Suggest
- Transit directions on Google Maps
- Google Talk
- Google News
- RechargeIT

Spirit

There are companies run by accountants and companies run by people who are passionate about the products they make. Volkswagen falls into the latter category and is making a credible push to becoming the world's number one carmaker soon.

Let's take a look at how a board-level executive at Volkswagen spends his day. Many decision-making meetings don't happen in the board room but in a laboratory looking at prototypes. Final decisions are made by gut feeling; rather than looking at spreadsheets, the executive asks the question, "Is this a product I like?"

Getting to a board-level position at all requires a skill that may come as a surprise. Throughout their careers, Volkswagen executives spend a lot of time test-driving the cars they make. Board members are routinely taken to places with extreme weather conditions, be it the North of Norway in winter or Death Valley in summer. There they challenge each other in race-like conditions. Passionately knowing how their vehicles feel under extreme driving conditions sets Volkswagen executives apart from their competitors.

Intimacy with the group's products leads to ambition at all levels, creates a strong team spirit, and positively feeds back on end customer experience. That, in turn, fosters Plasticity.

Network

The Human Brain Project is one of several similar ambitious endeavors to simulate a human brain sometime in the 2020s. The first challenge of the project is to collect, categorize, and link the millions of research papers published on the mammalian and human brains.

The next challenge will be bringing together all the different disciplines that are required to understand what it takes to build an artificial brain. The team will encompass computer scientists, operating system developers, biologists, neurolinguists, psychologists, and a host of other experts.

If all goes well and the network of thousands of experts can work together effectively, we are supposed to see an artificial cat brain around 2019.

NEUROINFORMATICS
BRAIN SIMULATION
HIGH PERFORMANCE COMPUTING
MEDICAL INFORMATICS
NEUROMORPHIC COMPUTING

NEUROROBOTICS

Knowledge

The age-old challenges of knowledge have consistently been the following:

- How to encourage experts (those who possess knowledge) to provide their knowledge

- How to store knowledge so that it can be accessed easily

- How to encourage nonexperts to accept knowledge

At least the second of these three challenges seems to edge toward a solution. Google is increasingly talking about a Star Trek–type of search engine. Rather than keying in search words and receiving links to other web sites, we will interact with the search engine like Captain Kirk on starship Enterprise.

Captain Kirk never used a keyboard to interact with the ship's computer, and the computer talked to him like a human being.

Imagine the long-standing promise of computer systems to have all information readily available. With rapidly advancing technology, we may finally get there. The race is on.

Leadership

As a global leader in complete life cycle power solutions for the marine and energy markets, the Finnish company Wärtsilä can look back at an impressive growth trajectory that includes several large acquisitions.

In 2005, Wärtsilä was organized by country and functional silos. These have gradually been replaced by cross-functional collaboration that in itself could merit a long chapter in this book. What we would like to highlight though, because it is more unusual than anything else we have observed, is Wärtsilä's approach to leadership.

Historically, Wärtsilä did what any other company in the world did: they promoted experts into leadership positions. Sometimes this worked, but often it did not. When it did, the company had lost an expert but won a leader. When it did not, the company had lost an expert and in return had a poor leader in place.

In Wärtsilä's new model, experts are rewarded for what they are without necessarily promoting them into leadership positions. All people are now measured against hard performance and behavior standards. Managers are required to give feedback on performance and behavior to all employees, including

white collar and blue collar. What Wärtsilä is doing now is bringing in people specifically for leadership positions. Often, these people are recruited from the military in the countries Wärtsilä is operating in. Wärtsilä is growing faster than the competition in a market that is increasingly challenged by low-cost competitors. It's clear they are getting leadership right.

Part 3:
The Way Forward

Case Studies

You will have noticed that the previous section was called Plasticity at Play and not Corporate Plasticity at Play. Also, the examples given in that part cited all kinds of fields ranging from art to biology with only a few references to the corporate world.

We believe that the message of this book can help save struggling companies and make the most innovative even stronger. At the same time, this is not a cookbook. We do not provide a recipe to introduce Corporate Plasticity because there is no one recipe. Even less do we want to award Corporate Plasticity certificates. Every organization will need to figure out what exactly Corporate Plasticity means for them, and this will not be done by benchmarking or copying what others have done.

Having said this, we still want to highlight three notable case studies about companies and their leaders who chose their destiny, became versatile, and dared more. In our view, these selected few have come very close to what we call Corporate Plasticity. May their stories serve as inspirations for all of us.

Case Study 1: Changi Airport

Every business traveler has war stories to tell of horrible airports that are notorious for delays, long walks through maze-like corridors, and unfriendly staff. Yet one airport sticks out for the right reasons—Singapore's Changi Airport. With more than 370 awards in the past 30 years, it is the world's most awarded airport. Changi Airport even receives high marks when it cannot permit you to fly. When passengers were stranded in the airport in April 2010 due to the Iceland volcano flight disruption, passengers were well taken care of. Close coordination with airlines to source hotel accommodation, and the provision of blankets, food/drinks, and resting space at the airport when no more hotels were available were highly appreciated by many.

At a closer look, it is striking that Changi Airport operations continue to be top-notch and score the highest in benchmarks despite many ground services outsourced to third parties (such as ground baggage handling, security, cleaning, etc.). So how do they do it?

The airport has a deeply ingrained culture. Yes, there are many parties involved and many different missions, but there is only one Changi. First and foremost, there is a widely shared element of pride to work at Changi and most regard it as a national icon.

To keep it that way, contractors are selected very carefully. Changi Airport engages directly with the employees of third

parties and tries to make them feel part of Changi Airport and proud of their work. On a regular basis, feedback sessions with those third-party employees are conducted to identify areas where their work environment can be improved. Little measures such as multilanguage signs and the provision of hot drinking water for cleaners during their shift had a big impact.

How many companies ever wonder what they could do for the employees of subcontractors? This is Plasticity in action.

Case Study 2: SpaceX

Elon Musk is a serial entrepreneur who, after founding PayPal, set out to change the world. Tesla Motors, a maker of electric vehicles, would warrant a case study of its own, but here we would like to focus on SpaceX, one of his lesser-known ventures.

Disappointed by the slow progress of humans into space over the past decades, Musk seriously considered donating a large share of his wealth to fund a manned mission to Mars. After analyzing his options, he came to the sobering realization that this at best would fund a one-off stunt similar to the Apollo missions to the Moon but would not lead to a lasting presence of humans on the red planet.

Musk then concluded that the big hurdle to sending humans into space was the cost of transport to orbit. Access was controlled by large government-sponsored aerospace and defense companies living in a cost-plus mindset with little incentive to change the rules of the game.

These companies are focused on preserving the status quo and making incremental improvements against it. Their inherent conservatism is best expressed in the infamous quote: "You can only fly a material and a technology that has already flown." This cautious approach is attributed to mission assurance, pedigree reviews of suppliers, and a long list of risk-mitigation activities required for winning government contracts. After all, when launching a defense satellite that costs more than $1 billion and takes six years to manufacture, losing this satellite due to a mission failure is a key concern.

In contrast, SpaceX was founded with the overriding objective of bringing a step change to the cost of launching into orbit. Musk concluded that when that hurdle is removed, everything else that it takes to travel to Mars and beyond would fall into place. He focused SpaceX on disrupting the status quo with breakthrough technology. One of the key milestones SpaceX is working toward is to have fully reusable launch vehicles. One comparison drawn by Musk is a commercial airliner. Like in an airliner, the cost of the fuel in the rocket is almost negligible compared to the cost of the hardware. The big difference is that the rocket is thrown away after each flight. If the same was true for airliners, intercontinental travel would be as rare as going to space is today.

To achieve Musk's vision, SpaceX has a highly entrepreneurial culture with strong individual employee empowerment and accountability akin to a high-tech start-up. Unlike anybody else in the launch business, SpaceX has a predominantly vertical supply chain. It has a strict rule that it will not be held captive by any supplier, and has notable examples where it has taken components production in-house rather than having to rely on an external supplier.

Day after day, Elon Musk is demonstrating purpose and leadership. With SpaceX he is challenging just about every paradigm of the international aerospace industry, and he is doing the same with Tesla in the automotive industry.

Case Study 3: Din Tai Fung

Din Tai Fung is the only Taiwanese restaurant to have earned a Michelin star so far. Launched originally as a cooking oil retailer on Taipei's Xinyi Road, the founding family moved into selling steamed dumplings as a side business in 1980. Quickly, the dumpling business overtook the cooking oil business in importance. As a consequence, the entire place was converted into a restaurant.

Today, Din Tai Fung operates branches in Australia, China, Hong Kong, Indonesia, Japan, Malaysia, Singapore, South Korea, the United States, and Thailand. Most of Din Tai Fung's restaurants are not more than a couple of steps from other restaurants specializing in dumplings that are often offering their products at a fifth of Din Tai Fung's prices. Yet, customers are willing to stand in line up to 100 minutes to get a seat, and tables at Din Tai Fung turn up to 19 times a day, a record in the restaurant business.

Over the years, many competitors have tried to copy Din Tai Fung. They even went as far as enrolling their children as apprentices there, sometimes under false names. Despite all of these attempts, no serious competitor to Din Tai Fung has emerged, and the company is marching on and opening restaurant after restaurant.

What is Din Tai Fung's secret sauce? In our view, it is total dedication to giving the customer a great experience. This experience starts with queuing up. On registration in front of the restaurant, you are given a fairly accurate estimate of the

waiting time and you are handed a full menu plus an ordering card. With this, at least some of the waiting time is not lost, and the prospective patrons have ample time to pick the delicacies they are going to enjoy.

When your time is up, a hostess takes you to a preassigned table with cups of steaming green tea ready to be enjoyed. Jackets that are flung over seat rests are covered with custom-made bags to prevent them from getting spoiled by any parts of food that might fall on them in the process of serving. Likewise, lady's handbags get stored in cradle-like contraptions with protective covers on top.

Once seated, the time for the first course to arrive is less than two minutes, and the waiters who serve the food wear face masks and hair nets to prevent any contamination. In many of Din Tai Fung's newer branches, patrons can observe the process of making the dumplings through large bay windows. Like the waiters, the people making the dumplings look more like operators in a high-tech clean room than traditional cooks. To observers literate in industrial engineering, the kitchen processes are remarkably efficient, echoing many of the lean principles employed by the automotive industry.

When your dumplings are served, you receive an instructive leaflet written in several languages that explains to you how to best enjoy the dumplings and what to do to avoid burning your tongue with the hot soup inside.

If you have to go to the bathroom, you will be greeted by a caretaker who checks every stall before you enter it, sprays alcohol on the toilet seat and wipes it. After washing your hands, you are handed fresh towels.

On leaving your table, someone will make sure that you don't forget smartphones or other valuable items.

Ensuring this unique customer experience does not stop with the expected as described here, the attentive staff will keep an eye on you to spot any needs you might have. If you fiddle with a box of pills, expect to receive a glass of water within a few moments.

On average, Din Tai Fung trains its employees for half a year before they are allowed to operate in their restaurants. By then, every employee fully understands that Din Tai Fung is all about creating a unique customer experience.

Din Tai Fung evolved from a modest retailer of cooking oil to a cult-like chain of dumpling restaurants by defining a crystal-clear purpose that is shared by all of its employees.

. . .

We hope that we have inspired you to deploy Corporate Plasticity for helping your company to choose its destiny, become versatile, and dare more.

I

Index

Get the eBook for only $10!

> Now you can take the weightless companion with you anywhere, anytime. Your purchase of this book entitles you to 3 electronic versions for only $10.

This Apress title will prove so indispensible that you'll want to carry it with you everywhere, which is why we are offering the eBook in 3 formats for only $10 if you have already purchased the print book.

Convenient and fully searchable, the PDF version enables you to easily find and copy code—or perform examples by quickly toggling between instructions and applications. The MOBI format is ideal for your Kindle, while the ePUB can be utilized on a variety of mobile devices.

Go to www.apress.com/promo/tendollars to purchase your companion eBook.

Apress®
THE EXPERT'S VOICE™

Other Apress Business Titles You Will Find Useful

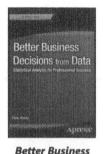
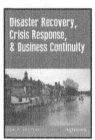

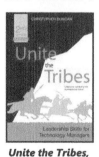

CROW LAKE

Mary Lawson was born and brought up in a farming community in Ontario. She came to England in 1968, is married to an Englishman, has two grown-up sons and lives in Surrey.

Mary Lawson

CROW LAKE

VINTAGE

Published by Vintage 2003

6 8 10 9 7 5

First published in Great Britain in 2002 by
Chatto & Windus

Vintage
Random House, 20 Vauxhall Bridge Road,
London SW1V 2SA

Random House Australia (Pty) Limited
20 Alfred Street, Milsons Point, Sydney
New South Wales 2061, Australia

Random House New Zealand Limited
18 Poland Road, Glenfield,
Auckland 10, New Zealand

Random House (Pty) Limited
Endulini, 5A Jubilee Road, Parktown 2193,
South Africa

The Random House Group Limited Reg. No. 954009
www.randomhouse.co.uk

A CIP catalogue record for this book
is available from the British Library

ISBN 0 09 942932 2

Papers used by Random House are natural, recyclable
products made from wood grown in sustainable forests.
The manufacturing processes conform to the environ-
mental regulations of the country of origin

Printed and bound in Great Britain by
Bookmarque Ltd, Croydon, Surrey

FOR ELEANOR,
FOR NICK AND NATHANIEL,
AND MOST OF ALL
FOR RICHARD

Author's Note

CROW LAKE is a work of fiction. There are so many lakes in Northern Ontario that there are bound to be half a dozen named after a crow, but none of them is the Crow Lake in this novel. Likewise, with two exceptions, all the characters in the novel are figments of my imagination. The first exception is my great grandmother, who did indeed fasten a book-rest to her spinning wheel. She had four children rather than fourteen, but she lived on a farm on the Gaspé Peninsula and time for reading was hard to come by. The second exception is my younger sister, Eleanor, whose infant self was the model for Bo. My thanks to her for permitting me to use her infancy, and also for her unceasing support, advice and encouragement in the writing of the book.

I would like to thank my brothers, George and Bill, not only for their humour, faith, and encouragement over the years, but also for advising on the 'natural history' of Crow Lake. They both know the North a thousand times better than I ever will, and their love for it played a part in the inspiration for the book.

There are others to whom I owe a great debt:

– Amanda Milner-Brown, Norah Adams, and Hilary Clark for their insight and their support, and for being honest when it would have been easier and more polite to lie.

– Stephen Smith, poet and teacher, for his encouragement and inspiration.

– Penny Battes, who helped me to get started all those years ago and who never seemed to doubt that I would get there in the end.

– Professor Deborah McLennan and Professor Hélène Cyr of the Zoology Department of the University of Toronto, for giving me a glimpse into the world of academic research. (It's a safe bet that I've still got it all wrong, but that's my fault and not theirs.)

– Felicity Rubinstein, Sarah Lutyens and Susannah Godman, all of Lutyens and Rubinstein, for their skill, tact, energy and enthusiasm.

– Alison Samuel of Chatto & Windus in London, Susan Kamil of the Dial Press in New York, and Louise Dennys of Knopf Canada in Toronto, for the perceptiveness, sensitivity and skill with which they steered *Crow Lake* through the editing process.

I would also like to acknowledge the publication, *Animals of the Surface Film* by Marjorie Guthrie (Richmond Publishing Company Ltd, Slough), which was an invaluable source of technical information.

Finally, and above all, my thanks to my husband, Richard, and to my sons, Nick and Nathaniel, for years and years of unfaltering faith, comfort and support.

PART ONE

PART ONE

Prologue

My GREAT Grandmother Morrison fixed a book-rest to her spinning wheel so that she could read while she was spinning, or so the story goes. And one Saturday evening she became so absorbed in her book that when she looked up she found that it was half-past midnight and she had spun for half an hour on the Sabbath day. Back then, that counted as a major sin.

I'm not recounting that little bit of family lore just for the sake of it. I've come to the conclusion recently that Great Grandmother and her book-rest have a lot to answer for. She'd been dead for decades by the time the events occurred that devastated our family and put an end to our dreams, but that doesn't mean she had no influence over the final outcome. What took place between Matt and me can't be explained without reference to Great Grandmother. It's only fair that some of the blame should be laid at her door.

There was a picture of her in my parents' room while I was growing up. I used to stand in front of it, as a very small child, daring myself to meet her eye. She was small, tight-lipped and straight, dressed in black with a white lace collar (scrubbed ruthlessly, no doubt, every single evening and ironed before dawn each day). She looked severe, disapproving, and entirely without humour. And well she might; she had fourteen children in thirteen years and five hundred acres of barren farmland on the Gaspé Peninsula. How she found time to spin, let alone read, I'll never know.

Of the four of us, Luke, Matt, Bo and I, Matt was the only one who resembled her at all. He was far from grim, but he had the same straight mouth and steady grey eyes. If I fidgeted in church and got a sharp glance from my mother I would peer sideways up at Matt to see if he had noticed. And he always had, and looked severe, and then at the last possible moment, just as I was beginning to despair, he would wink.

Matt was ten years older than I, tall and serious and clever. His great passion was the ponds, a mile or two away across the railroad tracks. They were old gravel pits, abandoned years ago after the road was built, and filled by nature with all manner of marvellous wriggling creatures. When Matt first started taking me back to the ponds I was so small he had to carry me on his shoulders – through the woods with their luxuriant growth of poison ivy, along the tracks, past the dusty box-cars lined up to receive their loads of sugar beets, down the steep sandy path to the ponds themselves. There we would lie on our bellies while the sun beat down on our backs, gazing into the dark water, waiting to see what we would see.

There is no image of my childhood that I carry with me more clearly than that; a boy of perhaps fifteen or sixteen, fair haired and lanky; beside him a little girl, fairer still, her hair drawn back in braids, her thin legs burning brown in the sun. They are both lying perfectly still, chins resting on the backs of their hands. He is showing her things. Or rather, things are drifting out from under rocks and shadows and showing themselves, and he is telling her about them.

'Just move your finger, Kate. Waggle it in the water. He'll come over. He can't resist . . .'

Cautiously the little girl waggles her finger; cautiously a small snapping turtle slides over to investigate.

'See? They're very curious when they're young. When he gets older though, he'll be suspicious and bad-tempered.'

'Why?'

The old snapper they had trapped out on land once had looked sleepy rather than suspicious. He'd had a wrinkled, rubbery head and she had wanted to pat it. Matt held out a branch as thick as his thumb and the snapper chopped it in two.

'Their shells are small for the size of their bodies – smaller than most turtles – so a lot of their skin is exposed. It makes them nervous.'

The little girl nods and the ends of her braids bob up and down in the water, making tiny ripples which tremble out across the surface of the pond. She is completely absorbed.

Hundreds of hours, we must have spent that way over the years. I came to know the tadpoles of the leopard frogs, the fat grey tadpoles of the bullfrogs, the tiny black wriggling ones of toads. I knew the turtles and the catfish, the waterstriders and the newts, the whirlygigs spinning hysterically over the surface of the water. Hundreds of hours, while the seasons changed and the pond life died and renewed itself many times, and I grew too big to ride on Matt's shoulders and instead picked my way through the woods behind him. I was unaware of these changes of course – they happened so gradually, and children have very little concept of time. Tomorrow is for ever, and years pass in no time at all.

One

WHEN THE end came, it seemed to do so completely out of the blue, and it wasn't until long afterwards that I was able to see that there was a chain of events leading up to it. Some of those events had nothing to do with us, the Morrisons, but were solely the concern of the Pyes, who lived on a farm about a mile away and were our nearest neighbours. The Pyes were what you'd call a problem family, always had been, always would be, but that year, within the privacy of their big old grey-painted farmhouse — offstage as far as the rest of community was concerned — their problems were developing into a full-scale nightmare. The other thing we didn't know was that the Pye nightmare was destined to become entangled with the Morrison dream. Nobody could have predicted that.

There's no end to how far back you can go, of course, when you're trying to figure out where something started. The search can take you back to Adam and beyond. But for our family there was an event that summer catastrophic enough to be the start of practically anything. It took place on a hot still Saturday in July when I was seven years old, and brought normal family life to an end; even now, almost twenty years later, I find it hard to get any sort of perspective on it.

The only positive thing you can say about it is that at least everything ended on a high note, because the previous day – our last day together as a family – my parents had learned that Luke, my 'other' brother – other than Matt – had passed his senior matriculation and won a place at teachers' college. Luke's success was something of a surprise because, to put it mildly, he was not a scholar. I remember reading somewhere a theory to the effect that each member of a family has a role – 'the clever one', 'the pretty one', 'the selfish one'. Once you've been established in the role for a while you're stuck with it – no matter what you do people will still see you as whatever-it-was – but in the early stages, according to the theory, you have some choice as to what your role will be. If that's the case, then early on in life Luke must have decided that what he really wanted to be was 'the problem one'. I don't know what influenced his choice but it's possible that he'd heard the story of Great Grandmother and her famous book-rest once too often. That story must have been the bane of Luke's life. Or one of the banes – the other would have been having Matt as a brother. Matt was so obviously Great Grandmother's intellectual heir that there was no point in Luke even trying. Better, then, to find what he was naturally good at – raising our parents' blood pressure, say – and practise, practise, practise.

But somehow, in spite of himself, here he was at the age of nineteen having passed his exams. After three generations of striving, a member of the Morrison family was about to go on to higher education.

It was not only a first for the family but also, I think, for Crow Lake, the small farming community in northern

Ontario where all four of us were born and brought up. At that time Crow Lake was linked to the outside world by one dusty road and the railroad tracks. The trains didn't stop unless you flagged them down and the road led only south, there being no reason for anyone to want to go further north. Apart from a dozen or so farms, a general store and a few modest houses out by the lake, there was nothing there but the church and the school. Historically, as I say, Crow Lake hadn't produced much in the way of scholars, and Luke's achievement would have made banner headlines in the church newsletter the following Sunday if our family catastrophe hadn't got in the way.

Luke must have received the letter confirming his place at teachers' college on Friday morning and told my mother, who phoned my father at the bank where he worked, in Struan, twenty miles away. That in itself was almost unheard of; never, ever, would a wife disturb her husband at his work if that work was at a desk. But she phoned him, and the two of them must have decided to announce it to the rest of us at supper that evening.

I've gone over that mealtime many times in my mind, less because of Luke's astounding news than because it turned out to be our last family supper. I know that memory plays tricks on you and that events and incidents your brain has invented can seem as real as those which actually took place, but I do believe that I remember every detail of that meal. And looking back, what seems most poignant to me is how low-key it was. Understatement was the rule in our house. Emotions, even positive ones, were kept firmly under control. It was the Eleventh Commandment, carved on its very own tablet of stone and presented specifically to those of Presbyterian persuasion: Thou Shalt Not Emote.

So, supper that evening was exactly as it always was, rather formal, rather dull, with occasional diversions from Bo. There are several photographs of Bo at that time. She was small and round and had a fine, fair fluff of hair that stood straight out from her head as if she'd been struck by lightning. In the photographs she looks placid and sweet, which only goes to show the extent to which the camera can lie.

We all sat in our proper places, Luke and Matt, aged nineteen and seventeen, on one side of the table; myself, aged seven, and Bo, aged one and a half, on the other. I remember my father starting to say grace and being interrupted by Bo, asking for juice, and my mother saying, 'In a minute, Bo. Shut your eyes.' My father started again and Bo interrupted again and my mother said, 'If you interrupt once more you'll go straight to bed,' whereupon Bo stuck her thumb in her mouth and started sucking it, balefully, with a regular clicking noise, like a time bomb biding its time.

'We'll try again, Lord,' my father said. 'Thank you for the meal you have set before us tonight, and thank you particularly for the news we received today. Help us always to be aware of our great good fortune. Help us to make the most of our opportunities and to use such small gifts as we have in Thy service. Amen.'

Luke and Matt and I stretched. My mother passed Bo her juice.

'What news?' Matt said. He sat directly across from me. If I slid down in my chair and stretched out my legs I could touch his knee with my toe.

'Your brother,' my father inclined his head in Luke's direction, 'has been accepted at teachers' college. The school confirmed it today.'

'No kidding?' Matt said, looking at Luke.

I looked at him too. I'm not sure that I'd ever really looked at Luke before – really considered him. For one reason or another we'd had very little to do with each other. The difference in our ages was even greater than that between myself and Matt, of course, but I don't think it was that. We just didn't have much in common.

But I noticed him now, sitting beside Matt as he presumably had for the last seventeen years. In some ways they were very similar – you wouldn't have had any difficulty guessing that they were brothers. They were of similar height and both were fair, with long Morrison noses and grey eyes. The main difference was in build. Luke was broad-shouldered and heavy-boned and must have weighed a good thirty pounds more than Matt. In his actions he was slow-moving and powerful, where Matt was agile and quick.

'No kidding!' Matt said again, overdoing the astonishment a little. Luke gave him a slant-eyed look. Matt grinned and dropped the astonishment and said, 'That's great! Congratulations!'

Luke shrugged.

I said, 'Are you going to be a teacher?' I couldn't imagine it. Teachers were people of great authority. Luke was merely Luke.

'Yeah,' Luke said.

He was slouching, but for once our father didn't tell him to sit up. Matt slouched too, but he didn't work at it like Luke did, he didn't *sprawl*, so compared to Luke he always looked relatively upright.

'He's a very fortunate young man,' my mother said. In her effort to hide her unseemly pride and pleasure she sounded almost cross. She was serving the meal – pork from the Tadworths' pigs, potatoes, carrots and runner beans from Calvin Pye's farm, apple sauce from Mr Janie's ancient battered apple trees. 'Not everybody gets an opportunity like that. Not everybody, by any means. Here you are, Bo, here's your dinner. And eat properly. Don't play with it.'

'When do you go?' Matt said. 'And where? Toronto?'

'Yeah. End of September.'

Bo picked up a fistful of runner beans and clasped them to her chest, crooning.

'We may have to get you a suit,' my mother said to Luke. She looked at my father. 'Will he need a suit?'

'I don't know,' my father said.

'You have to get him a suit,' Matt said. 'He'd look so lovely.'

Luke only snorted. In spite of their differences and the fact that Luke was always in trouble and Matt never was, there was seldom real friction between them. Both of them were what you would call slow to anger. And most of the time they inhabited separate worlds, I suppose, so they didn't often rub up against each other. Having said that, occasionally they did fight, and when they did, all of the emotions which weren't supposed to come out at all came out all at once, shattering the Eleventh Commandment. For some reason the fighting itself didn't seem to be against the rules – maybe my parents put it down to normal adolescent-male behaviour, reasoning that if the Lord hadn't wanted them to fight he wouldn't have given them fists. Once though, in the heat of the moment, having swung at Matt's head and missed and smashed his fist into the door-frame, Luke said, 'Shit! You bastard!' and was banned from the dining room for a week and made to eat standing in the kitchen.

But I was the one who was really upset by their fights. Matt was the quicker but Luke was by far the stronger, and I was terrified that one day one of his massive swings would connect and Matt would be killed. I would scream at them to stop, and my screaming annoyed my parents so much that frequently I was the one who was sent to my room.

'What he will need,' my father said, still pondering the question of a suit, 'is a suitcase.'

'Oh,' my mother said. The serving spoon paused above the bowl of potatoes. 'A suitcase,' she said. 'Yes.'

Just for an instant I saw her face stricken. I stopped fiddling with my knife and watched her anxiously. I suppose until that moment she hadn't quite grasped the fact that Luke would be going away.

Bo was singing to her runner beans, rocking them gently to and fro against her shoulder. 'Baby, baby,' she sang. 'Baby baby baby bean.'

'Put them down, Bo,' my mother said absently, the serving spoon still hovering. 'They're to eat. Put them down and I'll cut them up for you.'

Bo looked horrified. She shrieked and clutched the beans passionately to her chest.

'Oh for heaven's sake!' my mother said. 'Stop it. I'm tired of you.'

And whatever it was that had been in her face was gone, and all was normal again. 'We'll have to go to town,' she said to my father. 'To the Bay. They have suitcases. We can go tomorrow.'

So on the Saturday they drove into Struan together. There was no real need for both of them to go. Each of them was capable of choosing a suitcase on his own. And there was no need for them to rush off and do it that weekend – it was more than six weeks before Luke's term would start. But I guess they just wanted to. Odd though the word seems when applied to such calm, practical people, it's possible that they were excited. This was their son, after all. A Morrison was going to be a teacher.

They didn't want to take Bo and me with them, and of course we were too young to leave alone, so they waited until Luke and Matt got back from Calvin Pye's farm. Both of them worked on the farm at weekends and during holidays. Mr and Mrs Pye had three children of their own but two of them were girls and Laurie, the boy, was only fourteen and too small for heavy work, so Mr Pye was obliged to hire muscle.

Matt and Luke got home about four. My parents asked Luke if he would like to come and choose his own suitcase but he said no, he was too hot and needed a swim.

I believe I was the only one to wave goodbye. It's possible that I have invented that wave – that I dreamed it up later because I couldn't bear not to have said goodbye – but I think it's a genuine memory. The other three didn't because Bo was in a rage at being left behind and Matt and Luke were staring gloomily at her, wondering who was going to be lumbered with her for the rest of the afternoon.

The car turned out onto the road and disappeared from sight. Bo sat down on the gravel of the driveway and bellowed.

'Well I'm going for a swim,' Luke said, loudly, to be heard over Bo. 'I'm hot. I've been working the whole damned day.'

'So've I,' Matt said.

'So've I,' I said.

13

Matt prodded Bo's bottom with his toe. 'How about you, Bo? Have you been working the whole damned day?'

Bo roared.

Luke said, 'Why does she have to make that God-awful noise all the time?'

'She knows how much you love it,' Matt said. He reached down, prised Bo's thumb out from her fist and plugged her mouth with it. 'How about a swim, Bo. Do you want a swim?'

She nodded, moaning around her thumb.

It must have been the first time we'd been for a swim together, all four of us. The lake was less than twenty yards from the house so you just went in when you felt like it and I suppose we'd never all felt like it at the same time before. In any case, my mother would always have taken Bo. But we passed her around between us, using her as a beach ball, and it was good fun. I remember that.

I also remember that Sally McLean came along not long after we'd got out of the water. Mr and Mrs McLean owned the one and only store in Crow Lake and Sally was their daughter. In the last few weeks she'd taken to dropping by quite often, and each time she looked as if she were on her way somewhere and just happened to come across us. This was odd because there was nowhere for her to be on her way to. Our house was the last in Crow Lake and a fair way out; beyond it there was about three thousand miles of nothing and then the North Pole.

Luke and Matt had been skipping stones but when Sally appeared Matt stopped and came and sat down and watched me bury Bo. Bo hadn't been buried before and she was delighted. I'd scooped out a little hollow for her in the warm sand and she sat in it, round and brown and naked as an egg, and watched wide-eyed and beaming while I piled the sand up around her.

Sally McLean had slowed down when she got close to Luke and came to a halt a few feet away and stood there, her weight on one hip, drawing lines in the sand with her toe. She and Luke talked in low tones without looking at each other. I didn't pay much attention. I'd buried Bo right up to her armpits and now I was making patterns on the mound with pebbles and Bo was picking the pebbles out and poking them in again in the wrong places.

'Don't, Bo,' I said. 'I'm making a pattern.'

'Peas,' Bo said.

'No they're not. They're pebbles. They're not to eat.'

She put one in her mouth.

'Don't!' I said. 'Spit it out!'

'Idiot,' Matt said. He leaned over and squeezed Bo's cheeks until her mouth popped open and then fished out the pebble. She snickered at him and stuck her thumb in her mouth and then took it out and looked at it. It was gooey with saliva and sand. 'Beans,' she said, and stuck it in again.

'Now she's got sand in her mouth,' I said.

'It won't hurt her.'

He was watching Luke and Sally. Luke was still skipping stones but more carefully now, taking a long time to choose the flattest ones. Sally kept reaching up and smoothing back her hair. It was long and thick and a bright copper-red, and the breeze off the lake kept lifting little strands of it and blowing them across her face. I thought the two of them were pretty boring, but Matt was watching them with the same thoughtful interest with which he studied the inhabitants of the ponds.

15

His interest interested me. I said, 'Why's she here? Where's she going?'

He didn't answer for a minute and then he said, 'Well, I suspect it has something to do with Luke.'

'What? What to do with Luke?'

He looked at me and narrowed his eyes. 'I don't actually *know*. Do you want me to guess?'

'Yes.'

'OK. It's only a guess, but everywhere Luke goes, there's Sally. So I'm guessing she's in love with him.'

'In *love* with *Luke*?'

'Hard to believe, isn't it? But females are very strange, Katie.'

'Is *Luke* in love with *her*?'

'Dunno. I guess it's possible.

After a while Sally left and Luke wandered up from the shore, frowning deeply at the sand, and Matt raised his eyebrows at me in a warning way which meant I would be wise to keep quiet on the subject of Sally McLean.

We unearthed Bo from her burial mound and brushed the sand off her and took her back to the house to get dressed. Then I took my bathing suit outside to hang it on the line, so I was the one to see the police car come down the drive.

You didn't often see police cars in Crow Lake and I was curious. I ran down to the driveway to look at it, and the policeman got out and to my surprise so did Reverend Mitchell and Dr Christopherson. Rev. Mitchell was our minister and his daughter Janie was my best friend. Dr Christopherson lived in Struan, but he was our doctor – in fact the only doctor for about a hundred miles. I liked both of them. Dr Christopherson had an Irish Setter called Molly who could pick blueberries with her teeth and who came with him on his rounds. I skipped up to them and said, 'Mum and Dad aren't here right now. They went shopping. They went to get a suitcase for Luke, because he's going to be a teacher.'

The policeman was standing by his car, looking intently at a small scratch on the fender. Rev. Mitchell looked at Dr Christopherson and then back at me and said, 'Is Luke here, Katherine? Or Matt?'

'They're both here,' I said. 'They're getting changed. We've been for a swim.'

'We'd like a word with them. Could you tell them we're here?'

'OK,' I said. And then remembering my manners, 'Do you want to come in? Mum and Dad will be back about half-past six.' I had a happy thought. 'I could make you a cup of tea.'

'Thank you,' Rev. Mitchell said. 'We'll come in, but I don't think . . . tea, thank you. Not right at the moment.'

I led them into the house and excused the noise Bo was making – she'd got all the pots and pans out of the bottom cupboard and was bashing about with them on the kitchen floor. They said it didn't matter so I left them in the dining room while I went to get Luke and Matt. I brought them both back and they looked curiously at the two men – the policeman had stayed by his car – and said hi. And then I saw Matt's face change. He'd been looking at Rev. Mitchell and suddenly he didn't look polite and curious any more. He looked afraid.

He said, 'What?'

Dr Christopherson said, 'Kate, I wonder if you could go and see to Bo? Could you just . . . um . . . ?'

I went out to the kitchen. Bo wasn't doing anything wrong but I picked her up and carried her outside. She was getting big but I could still just carry her. I took her back down to the beach. The mosquitoes were starting to come out but I stayed there anyway, even when Bo began to rage at me, because I was afraid of the expression on Matt's face and I didn't want to know what had caused it.

After a long time, half an hour at least, Matt and Luke came down to the beach. I didn't look at them. Luke picked Bo up and carried her down to the water's edge and began to walk along the shore with her. Matt sat down beside me, and when Luke and Bo were a long way down the curve of the shore he told me that our parents had been killed when their car was hit by a fully loaded logging truck whose brakes failed as it was coming down Honister Hill.

I REMEMBER being terrified that he would cry. His voice was shaking and he was struggling very hard with himself, and I remember being rigid with fear, not daring to look at him, scarcely daring to breathe. As if that would be the worst thing; much worse than this incomprehensible thing he was telling me. As if for Matt to cry was the one unthinkable thing.

Two

MEMORIES. I'm not in favour of them, by and large. Not that there aren't some good ones, but on the whole I'd like to put them in an airtight cupboard and close the door. And in fact, until a couple of months ago I'd managed to do that quite successfully for some years. I had a life to live, after all. I had my work and I had Daniel, and between them they took up a lot of time and energy. It's true that things hadn't been going too well in either department for a while, but I didn't think to connect that with 'the past'. I did genuinely feel, up until a couple of months ago, that I'd put all that behind me. I felt that I was doing fine.

And then, back in February, I found a letter from Matt waiting for me when I got home from work one Friday evening. I saw the writing and instantly I saw Matt – you know how handwriting conjures up the person. And also instantly, I got the same old ache, centred more or less mid-chest, a heavy, dull pain, like mourning. In all those years it hadn't lessened a bit.

I opened the envelope as I climbed the stairs, clutching my bag full of lab reports under my arm. It turned out not to be a proper letter after all. It was a card from Simon, Matt's son, inviting me to his eighteenth birthday party at the end of April. Attached to it was a scribbled note from Matt saying, 'You have to come, Kate!! No excuses!!!' A total of five exclamation marks. And then a tactful PS: 'Bring someone if you want to.'

Behind the note was a photograph. It was of Simon, but at first I thought it was Matt. Matt at eighteen. They're absurdly alike. And naturally that triggered a whole raft of memories of that disastrous year and its slow-moving chain of events. And that in turn took me back to the tale of Great Grandmother Morrison and her book-rest. Poor old Great Grandmother. The photograph of her hangs in my bedroom now. I took it with me when I left home. No one seemed to miss it.

I put my bag down on the table in my living-cum-dining room and sat down to read the invitation again. I would go, of course. Simon is a very nice boy and I am his aunt, after all. Luke and Bo would be there – it would be a family reunion and I am in favour of family reunions. Of course I would go. There was a conference in Montreal that weekend which I had already arranged to attend but I wasn't giving a paper so I could cancel that. And I had no classes on Friday afternoons so I could leave straight after lunch. Get on Highway 400 and head north. It's a 400-mile trip, still a long haul, though the roads are paved most of the way now. It's only for the last hour or so, when you fork off the main road, heading west, that the paving runs out and the forest closes in and you really feel you're going back in time.

As for 'bringing someone' – no. Daniel would love to go, Daniel is consumed by curiosity about my family and would be simply *delighted* to go, and his fascination and enthusiasm would be altogether more than I could cope with. No, I would not invite Daniel.

I looked at the photograph, seeing Simon, seeing Matt, knowing how it would be. Fine, really. Everything would be fine. The party itself would be loud and cheerful, the food would be terrific, we'd all laugh a lot and crack jokes at one another's expense. Luke and Matt and Bo and I would talk about old times, though only specific old times. Certain things would be left out, and certain names wouldn't come up. Calvin Pye, for instance. His name wouldn't be mentioned. Or Laurie Pye's, come to that.

I would give Simon a very expensive present to demonstrate both my affection for him, which is genuine, and my continued commitment to the family.

On Sunday afternoon, when the time came for me to leave, Matt would come out with me to my car. He'd say, 'Somehow we never got time to talk,' and I'd say, 'I know. It's ridiculous, isn't it?'

I'd look at him, and he'd look back out of Great Grandmother Morrison's steady grey eyes, and I'd have to look away. And part way home I would discover that I was crying, and I'd spend the next month trying to figure out why.

*

IT KEEPS coming back to Great Grandmother.

With no trouble at all I can call up an image of her and Matt, deep in conversation. Great Grandmother is sitting very straight in a high-backed chair and Matt is sitting opposite her. He is listening attentively to what she says, nodding when he agrees with her, politely waiting to put his own case when he does not. He is respectful but he

21

isn't cowed by her, and she knows it and is pleased. I can see it in her eyes.

Strange, isn't it? Because of course they never actually met. Great Grandmother lived to a ripe old age, but even so, by the time Matt appeared on the scene she was long gone. She never visited us – never left the shores of the Gaspé – but nonetheless, when I was a child I had the impression that she was 'with us' in some mysterious way. She was a powerful enough influence, heaven knows; she might as well have been in the next room. As for her and Matt – I think I sensed from early on that there was a link of some kind between them, though I couldn't have told you what it was.

My father used to tell stories about her – far more than about his own mother – most of them illustrating some high moral principle. Unfortunately he wasn't much of a story teller and the tales were longer on message than they were on suspense. There was the one about the Protestants and the Catholics, for instance, about the friction between them within the community, which led to battles between rival gangs of boys. But the sides weren't evenly matched – there were more Protestants than Catholics – so Great Grandmother decreed that her sons must fight 'on the other side' in order to even things up. Fair play was what we were meant to glean from that one. No battle scenes, no blood and glory, just the lesson: fair play.

And then there was Great Grandmother's famous devotion to education – the subject that made Luke's eyes glaze over. All fourteen of her children finished elementary school, which was almost unheard-of in those days. Homework came before farm work – never mind that every mouthful of food had to be wrung from the land. Education was her dream of dreams, a passion so strong it

22

was almost a disease, and she infected not only her own children with it but generations of little Morrisons yet unborn.

In his references to her our father made her sound like a paragon; fair-minded, kindly and wise as Solomon – a description I had some difficulty reconciling with her photograph. In the photograph she looks like a battle-axe, pure and simple. You can see at a glance why there are no stories about her children misbehaving.

And where was her husband, our great-grandfather, in all this? Out in the fields, I supposed. Someone had to be.

But we all knew she was a remarkable woman; not even our father's lack of story-telling skills could disguise that. I remember Matt asking once what books she had propped on that book-rest of hers, apart from the Bible, of course. He wanted to know if they were novels – Charles Dickens maybe, or Jane Austen. But our father said no. Fiction didn't interest her, not even great fiction. She didn't want to 'escape' from the real world, she wanted to know about it. She had books on geology, on plant life, on the solar system; there was one called *The Vestiges of Creation*, over which he remembered her tutting and shaking her head, which discussed the geological formation of the world. It pre-dated Darwin, but like him was not in complete accord with the teachings of the Bible. It was a sign of how greatly she revered knowledge, our father said, that although it troubled her, she did not forbid the children or grandchildren to read it.

Much of what was in the books must have been completely beyond her – she had never had a day's schooling in her life – but still she read them, and struggled to understand. I was impressed by that, even as a child. Now I find it touching as well. That hunger for knowledge, that determination in the face of so much grinding labour – I do find it both admirable and sad. Great Grandmother was a born scholar, in a time and place where the term was unknown.

But she had her successes. I've no doubt our father was the apple of her eye, because it was through him that she finally saw her dream of getting her family educated and off the land begin to come true. He was the youngest son of her youngest son; his brothers did his share of the farm work so that he could finish high school – the first member of the family to do so. When the celebrations were over (he came top of the class in every subject; I can imagine Great Grandmother, her face grim with suppressed pride, presiding over the feast) they packed a hacksack for him – clean socks, a handkerchief, a bar of soap and his high-school certificate – and sent him out into the world to better himself.

He headed west and south, travelling from town to town, taking work where he could find it, always following the wide blue path of the St Lawrence. When he reached Toronto he stopped for a bit, but he didn't stay long. Maybe the city alarmed him – all the people, all the noise – though my memory of him is not of someone easily alarmed. More likely he found city life frivolous and lacking in purpose. That fits in better with what I know about him.

When he set off again, he headed north and a bit west, away from so-called civilization, and by the time he was twenty-three he was settled in Crow Lake, which was much the same sort of community as the one he'd left a thousand miles behind.

When I was old enough to think about such things, it seemed to me that my father's family must have been disappointed that he had settled in such a place when they had sacrificed so much to launch him out into the world. It was a while before I realized that they would have approved of his choice. They would have known that in spite of the location there were huge differences in his new life. He had a job in a bank in Struan, and wore a suit to work and owned a car and built a low, cool, tree-shaded house out by the lake, away from the dust and the flies of the farmyards. In the living room of his house he had a bookcase full of books, and rarer still, he had the leisure time to read them. If he had settled in a farming community it was because he felt at home with the values he found there. The point was, he had a choice. That was what they had won for him.

The bank gave my father two weeks annual leave (the first holiday anyone in his family had ever had) and a year after settling in Crow Lake he used that leave to go back to the Gaspé and propose to his childhood sweetheart. She was a girl from a neighbouring farm and had a good solid Scottish background like his own. She must have had a sense of adventure as well, because she said yes and came back to Crow Lake as his bride. There is one photograph of them, taken on their wedding day. They are standing at the entrance to a little church on the shores of the Gaspé; two tall, strong, big-boned, fair-haired, serious-minded people, who could as easily have passed for brother and sister as husband and wife. You can tell they're serious-minded by their smiles: honest, direct, but essentially serious. They don't think their life will be easy – neither of them has been brought up to expect that – but they think they are capable of taking it on. They will give it their best shot.

The two of them travelled back to Crow Lake together

and set up their home, and in due course produced four children: two boys, Luke and Matt, and then, after a ten-year gap and presumably much deliberation, two girls: myself (Katherine, known as Kate) and Elizabeth, known as Bo.

Did they love us? Of course. Did they say so? Of course not. Actually, that's not quite true – my mother did say she loved me once. I had done something wrong – it was a spell when I was always doing something wrong – and she was cross with me and wouldn't speak to me for what felt like days, though it was probably only hours. And finally, in fear, I said to her, 'Mummy, do you love me?' And she looked at me in surprise, and then said simply, 'To distraction.' I didn't know what 'to distraction' meant, on one level, but on another level I did know, and was reassured. I am still reassured.

At some stage, probably quite early on, our father banged a nail into the wall of the bedroom he shared with our mother and hung upon it the picture of Great Grandmother Morrison, and we all grew up knowing about her dreams and being aware of her gaze. As far as I was concerned it wasn't an entirely comfortable experience. I was always convinced that she disapproved of us all, with just one exception. I could tell by her expression that she thought Luke was lazy and I was a dreamer and Bo was so strong-willed she'd be nothing but trouble the whole of her life. It seemed to me that the only time those fierce old eyes showed any sign of softening was when Matt walked into the room. Then her expression would change, and you could see what she was thinking. She was thinking, That one. He's the one.

*

I FIND it hard to remember much of what happened in the days immediately following the accident. Most of my memories seem to be merely images, caught in time like a photograph. The living room, for example – I remember what a mess it was. We all slept in there the first night; probably Bo wouldn't settle or I couldn't get to sleep, and in the end Luke and Matt brought Bo's cot and three mattresses into the living room.

I have an image of myself lying awake, staring at the darkness. I kept trying to sleep and sleep would not come and time would not pass. I knew that Luke and Matt were awake too but for some reason I was afraid to talk to them, so the night went on for ever.

Other things seemed to happen over and over but I'm not sure, looking back, if that was only in my mind. I can still see Luke standing at the front door, holding Bo in one arm and with his free hand accepting a large covered dish from someone. I know that happened, but in my memory he spent practically the whole of the first few days in that pose. Though that could have been true – every wife, every mother, every maiden aunt in the community must have set her lips and started cooking as soon as she heard the news. Potato salad figured largely. And cooked hams. Also nourishing stews, though it was far too hot to eat them. Every time you went out the front door you tripped over a quart basket of peas or a vat of stewed rhubarb.

And Luke holding Bo. Did he really carry her for every waking moment of those first days? Because that's how I remember it. I suppose she was affected by the atmosphere in the house and was missing our mother and cried if he put her down.

And myself clinging to Matt. I held on to his hand or his sleeve or the pocket of his jeans, anything that I could get hold of. I was seven, I should have been beyond such behaviour, but I couldn't help myself. I remember him gently disengaging my fingers when he needed to go to the toilet, saying, 'Just wait, Katie. Just give me a minute.' And myself standing at the closed bathroom door, asking, 'Have you finished yet?' with a shaking voice.

I cannot imagine what those first days must have been like for Luke and Matt; the funeral arrangements and the phone calls, the visits of neighbours and the kindly meant offers of help, the practicalities of looking after Bo and me. The confusion and anxiety, to say nothing of the grief. And of course, nothing was said of the grief. We were our parents' children, after all.

A number of phone calls were from the Gaspé or Labrador, from various branches of the family. Those with no phone of their own called from call-boxes in the nearest town, and you could hear the coins clanging into the box and then heavy breathing while whoever it was, unused to phones and certainly unused to long-distance calls in times of crisis, tried to work out what to say.

'It's Uncle Jamie.' A windy bellow from the wastes of Labrador.

'Oh. Yes. Hello.' From Luke.

'I'm calling about your father and mother.' He had great lungs, Uncle Jamie. Luke was forced to hold the phone out from his ear and Matt and I could hear him from the other side of the room.

'Yes. Thank you.'

Painful whistling silence.

'Is that Luke I'm speaking to? The oldest one?'

'Yes. It's Luke.'

More silence.

28

Luke, sounding more tired than embarrassed. 'It's nice of you to call, Uncle Jamie.'

'Aye. Well. Terrible thing, lad. Terrible thing.'

The main message seemed to be that we were not to worry about the future. The family was sorting things out and everything would be looked after. We weren't to worry. Aunt Annie, one of my father's three sisters, was coming and would be there as soon as she could, though it was unlikely to be in time for the funeral. Would we be all right on our own for a few days?

I was fortunate in being too young to understand the implications of those calls. All I knew was that they worried Luke and Matt; whichever one of them had taken the call would stand staring at the phone afterwards. Luke had the habit of running his hands through his hair when he was anxious and in the days and weeks following the accident his hair looked like a well-ploughed field.

I remember being struck, suddenly, while watching him search through the chest of drawers in the room Bo and I shared, looking for something clean for Bo to wear, by the notion that I didn't know Luke any more. He wasn't the same person he had been a few days ago – the half-defiant, half-embarrassed boy who had scraped into teachers' college – and I wasn't sure who he was. I hadn't been aware that people could change. But then, I hadn't been aware that people could die. At least not people you loved and needed. Death in principle I had known about; death in practice – no. I hadn't known that could happen.

THE FUNERAL service was held in the churchyard. Chairs had been brought out from the Sunday School and placed in neat rows beside the two open graves. We four children sat in the front row and tried to keep the chair legs from wobbling on the hard-baked earth. Or rather, three of us sat in a row; Bo sat on Luke's lap with her thumb in her mouth.

I remember being very uncomfortable. It was extremely hot, and Luke and Matt had been consumed by the need to do everything properly so we were all in our darkest clothes — in my case a winter skirt and jersey, in Bo's a flannel dress from the previous year, much too small. The boys were in dark shirts and trousers. All four of us were shiny with sweat long before the service began.

All I can remember about the service itself is that I could hear several people snuffling and I couldn't turn around to see who they were. I think I was protected from the reality of what was happening by disbelief. I could not believe that my mother and father were in those two boxes by the gravesides and certainly I could not believe that if they were, people would lower them into the ground and heap earth onto them so that they could never again get out. I sat quietly beside Luke and Matt, and then stood beside them, holding Matt's hand, as the coffins were lowered into the ground. Matt held my hand very tight; I remember that.

Then it was over, except that it wasn't, because everyone in the village had to pay their respects to us. Most of them didn't actually say anything, they just filed past and nodded at us or patted Bo's head, but still it took a long time. I stood beside Matt. A couple of times he looked down at me and smiled, though his smile was just a white line. Bo was very well behaved, even though she was beet-red with the heat. Luke held her and she leaned her head against his shoulder and watched everybody around her thumb.

Sally McLean was one of the first to come up. She was

one of the ones who'd been crying – you could see by her face. She didn't look at Matt or me but she turned her tear-stained face to Luke and said, 'I'm so sorry, Luke,' in a broken whisper.

Luke said, 'Thanks.'

She looked at him, her mouth quivering with sympathy, but then her parents stepped up so she didn't say anything else. Mr and Mrs McLean were small, shy, quiet people, nothing at all like their daughter. Mr McLean cleared his throat but didn't actually say anything. Mrs McLean smiled unhappily at all of us. Then Mr McLean cleared his throat again and said to Sally, 'We'd better be getting along now, Sal,' but she just gave him a reproachful look and stayed where she was.

Calvin Pye came up next, herding his wife and kids before him. Calvin Pye was the farmer Matt and Luke worked for in the summers and he was a bitter-looking man. He had a scared-looking wife called Alice whom my mother had felt sorry for. I'd never been quite sure why. She'd just said, 'That poor woman,' from time to time.

She'd been sorry for the children too. The eldest child was Marie, who'd been in Matt's class at high school until the year before, when she'd left to help at home, and the youngest was Rosie, who was seven and in my class. The boy, Laurie, was fourteen, and should have been in high school, but he'd missed so much school due to having to work on the farm that he was never going to make it out of grade eight. Both the girls were pale and nervous-looking like their mother but Laurie was the spitting image of Mr Pye. He had the same lean, bony face and the same dark, furious eyes.

Mr Pye said, 'We're sorry for your loss,' and Mrs Pye said, 'Yes.' Rosie and I looked at each other. Rosie looked as if she'd been crying, but she always looked like that. Laurie stared at the ground. I think Marie wanted to say something to Matt but Mr Pye herded them all away.

Miss Carrington came up. She was my teacher and had taught both Luke and Matt. The public school had only one room, so she taught everybody until they went to the high school in town or left to work on their fathers' farms. She was young and quite nice, but very strict, and I was a bit afraid of her. She said, 'Well, Luke. Matt. Kate.' Her voice was unsteady and she didn't say anything else, just gave us a rather shaky smile and patted Bo's foot.

Dr Christopherson and his wife were next, and then four men I didn't know who turned out to be from my father's bank, and then, in ones and twos and whole families, all the people I had known since the day I was born, all looking upset and saying, 'Anything we can do . . .' to Luke and Matt.

Sally McLean was still standing as near to Luke as she could. She looked at the ground as people paid their respects and every now and then stepped closer to Luke and whispered something. Once I heard her say, 'Would you like me to hold your little sister?' and Luke said, 'No,' and tightened his grip on Bo. After a minute he said, 'Thank you, but she's fine.'

Mrs Stanovich was one of the last to come up, and I remember what she said very clearly. She'd been crying too, and still was. She was a large soft lady who looked as if she didn't have any bones and who talked to the Lord all day, not just during grace and prayers like the rest of us. Matt had said once that she was as mad as a hatter like all the Evangelicals and my parents had banished him from the dining room for a whole month. If he'd just said she was mad as a hatter he might have got away with it. It was

32

disparaging her religion that got him into trouble. Religious tolerance was a family creed and you defied it at your peril.

Anyway, she came up to us and looked from one to the other, tears rolling down her cheeks. We didn't know where to look. Mr Stanovich, who was known as Gabby because he never said a word, nodded at Luke and Matt and headed speedily back to his truck. To my alarm, Mrs Stanovich suddenly pulled me into her huge bosom and said, 'Katherine, sweetie, great will be the joy in Heaven this day. Your parents, bless their dear souls, have gone to join our Lord, and the Heavenly Host will *rejoice* to welcome them. It's hard, my lamb, but think how happy our Lord will be!'

She smiled at me through her tears and squeezed me again. Her bosom smelled of talcum powder and sweat. I'll never forget it. Talcum powder and sweat, and the idea that up in heaven they were rejoicing that my parents were dead.

POOR LILY Stanovich. I know she was genuinely grief-stricken by our parents' death. But that memory of her is the clearest one I have of their funeral, and to be honest I still resent that, even after all this time. I'd have liked a pleasanter memory, that's all. I'd have liked a clear strong picture of the four of us, standing very close together, supporting each other. But every time I get it fixed in my mind, in wallows Lily Stanovich, bosom to the fore, and smothers it in tears.

Three

IT WAS a long time before I told Daniel much about my family. When we first started going out we exchanged bits of personal information, like you do, but it was all very general. I think I told him that my parents had died when I was young but that I had other family up north and I went to visit them sometimes. It was hardly more detailed than that.

I knew quite a bit about Daniel's background because a lot of his background was in the foreground, so to speak, right there at the university. Daniel is Professor Crane of the Zoology Department. His father is Professor Crane of the History Department. His mother is Professor Crane of the Fine Art Department. It's a little Crane dynasty. Or as I learned later, it's a small sub-section of a large Crane dynasty. Daniel's forebears roamed the cultural capitals of Europe before emigrating to Canada. They were doctors or astronomers or historians or musicians, each of them without doubt eminent in his field. Against all that, Great Grandmother Morrison's little hand-made book-rest seemed a bit pathetic and I kept it under wraps.

But Daniel is a curious man. He shares with Matt – and it is the only thing they share, don't get the idea that in Daniel I have chosen a replacement for Matt – a curiosity which extends to almost everything. One evening when we'd been going out for a couple of weeks he said, 'So tell me the story of your life, Kate Morrison.'

As I say, this was at the beginning of our relationship. I didn't know it at the time but that little request from Daniel was the beginning of what was going to be a problem between us, a problem which I described to myself as Daniel asking more of me than I could give, and which Daniel described to me as my shutting him out of my life.

I am not from a background where people talk about problems in their relationships. If someone does or says something that upsets you, you don't say so. Maybe it's another Presbyterian thing; if the Eleventh Commandment is Thou Shalt Not Emote, the Twelfth is Thou Shalt Not Admit to Being Upset, and when it becomes evident to the whole world that you are upset, Thou Shalt on No Account Explain Why. No, you swallow your feelings, force them down inside yourself, where they can feed and grow and swell and expand until you explode, unforgivably, to the utter bewilderment of whoever it was who upset you. In Daniel's family there is vastly more shouting and accusing and slamming of doors but far less bewilderment, because people say why.

So I did not, in the months to come, say to Daniel that sometimes he made me feel that he would like to put my life and everything in it on one of his little glass slides and slide me, like some poor hapless microbe, under his microscope, where he could study my very soul. But he did say to me, quietly but very seriously, that he felt that I was not willing to give him very much of myself. That there was a barrier somewhere, which he could feel but not identify, and that he was finding it a real problem.

All that was in the future, however, on this particular night; our relationship was still very young and very exciting. We were in a deli at the time. Neon strip lights and yellow plastic tables on spindly metal legs, a constant clatter from the kitchen. Reuben sandwiches and cole-slaw and excellent coffee, and this little request: Tell me the story of your life.

I couldn't figure out at the time why I felt such a resistance to the idea. Partly I guess I'm just not given to soul-baring. I never was the sort of teenager who sat on friends' beds, whispering and giggling and exchanging secrets behind cupped hands. And I've always thought there was something a bit distasteful about laying your family out in front of a relative stranger, sacrificing their privacy on the altar of the getting-to-know-you ritual of dating. But I now think that most of my reluctance was due to the fact that the story of my life is all bound up with the story of Matt's life, and there was no way I was going to dissect that over a cup of coffee with anyone, far less someone as successful as Daniel Crane.

So I hedged. I said, 'I think I've already told you most of it.'

'You've hardly told me anything. I know your name and I know you come from somewhere up north. I think that's about it.'

'What else do you want to know?'

'Everything,' Daniel said. 'Tell me everything.'

'All at once?'

'Start at the beginning. No, start before the beginning. Start with that place you come from.'

36

'Crow Lake?'

'Yes. What was it like growing up in Crow Lake?'

'Fine,' I said. 'It was fine.'

Daniel waited. After a minute he said, 'You're a born story teller, Kate. You really are.'

'Well I don't know what would interest you!'

'Everything. How big was it? How many people? How big was the downtown? Was there a library? A Dairy Queen? A laundromat?'

'Oh no,' I said. 'No no. There was a store. There wasn't a downtown. There was a store and a church. And a school. And the farms. Mostly just farms.'

He was hunched over his coffee, trying to visualize it. Daniel is tall and thin and has a slight stoop from spending his life peering into microscopes. In the circumstances the name Crane is a bit unfortunate and you'd think his students would give him a hard time, but apparently not. He is reputed to be the best lecturer in the department. I have considered sneaking in to one of his lectures to see how he does it, but I've never had the nerve. When it comes to lecturing, I believe I am considered a bit dry.

'Real old-world stuff,' he said.

'It's not old-world,' I said. 'It's still like that now, more or less. There are lots of places like that. They're not so isolated, because the roads are better and the cars are better. Struan is only twenty miles away. Twenty miles used to be a long way. Now it's nothing. Except in the winter.'

He was nodding, still trying to visualize. I said, 'Haven't you ever been up north?'

He pondered. 'Barrie. I've been to Barrie.'

'Barrie! Good God, Daniel! Barrie's not north!'

I was quite shocked, to tell you the truth. He's such an

intelligent man, and he's been everywhere. His childhood was spent packing and unpacking as one or other of his parents took up a year's posting as Visiting Professor somewhere or other. He's lived for a year in Boston and a year in Rome and a year in London and a year in Washington and a year in Edinburgh. And to find this enormous gap in his knowledge of his own country! It's not as if he's an Egyptologist and has spent his life crawling into tombs – he's a microbiologist. A life-scientist! A life-scientist who's never been out in his own backyard.

I was shocked out of my normal reticence, I guess, because I started telling him all about Crow Lake, about how it was nothing at all, true wilderness, until the logging companies started to push their way north, and how they built a road all the way up to a little blue patch of water that they called Crow Lake, and how up that road in due course came three young men. Three stony-broke young men who were fed up with working on other men's farms and wanted farms of their own. Between them they had three horses, an ox, a cross-cut saw and assorted other tools and they pooled their resources and began to clear themselves some land. It was Crown Land – they claimed fifty acres apiece – and because it was located smack in the middle of nowhere and the Government wanted it settled, they got it free. They cleared an acre each to begin with, and built rough log cabins, one for each of them. And then they went back, one at a time, down the road to New Liskeard, and found themselves wives, one for each of them. They brought their wives back to those cabins.

'Four walls and a roof,' I said to Daniel. 'A dirt floor. That's all it would have been. Water, by bucket, from Crow River. That really was old-world stuff.'

'What did they do about food? Before they could grow any?'

'Brought it in by horse and wagon. Along with wood-stoves and sinks and beds and everything else. A bit at a time. And they kept clearing the land, a bit at a time. Clearing the land took years. Generations. It's still going on.'

'And did they all make it? Did their farms take off?'

'Oh yes. The soil's not too bad up there. Not wonderful, but good enough. There's a short growing season, of course.'

'How long ago was all this?' Daniel said.

I thought about it. 'Three or four generations.' It hadn't occurred to me before, but they would have been Great Grandmother's contemporaries, those three.

'Are their families still there?'

'Bits of them,' I said. 'Frank Janie – he was one of the three – he had a big family and they eventually got into dairy farming. They're still going strong. Stanley Vernon was the second man. His farm was taken over somewhere along the way but one of his daughters still lives there. Old Miss Vernon. She must be about a hundred.'

'Do they still live in log cabins?'

I looked at him to see if he was joking. It can be hard to tell with Daniel and I wasn't sure.

'No, Daniel. No. They do not live in log cabins. They live in houses, like real people.'

'That's a shame. What happened to the cabins?'

'They were probably used as sheds or barns once the houses were built. And then they probably rotted and fell down. This tends to happen with untreated wood, as you may know, being a biologist. All except Frank Janie's, which was bought and taken away on the back of a truck to be part of a heritage site for the tourists, in New Liskeard.'

'A heritage site,' Daniel said. He pondered some more, then shook his head. 'How do you know all this? It's incredible! Think of knowing the history of your whole community!'

'There's not that much to know,' I said. 'You just kind of soak it up, I guess. Osmosis.'

'How about the third guy. Is his family still there?'

'Jackson Pye,' I said. I saw the farm as I said the name. The big, grey-painted house, the large, shambling barn, bits of farm machinery scattered about, the fields lying flat and yellow under the sun. The ponds, still and quiet, reflecting the hard blue sky.

Daniel was waiting expectantly. I said, 'The third man was Jackson Pye. The Pyes were our nearest neighbours, actually. But things didn't work out too well for them, in the end.'

AFTERWARDS I found myself thinking about old Miss Vernon. About something she had told me, which I would much rather have left un-remembered. Miss Vernon of the teeth and the long whiskery jaw, whose father had been one of those first three men. This was in my teens, when during the summers I helped Miss Vernon with her vegetable garden. She seemed about a hundred even then. She had arthritis and couldn't do anything much, only sit on a kitchen chair which she had me bring outside so she could keep an eye on me. That was what she said, but really she just wanted company. She talked while I weeded. Despite what I said to Daniel there's a limit to what you can learn by osmosis, and Miss Vernon is the source for most of what I know about Crow Lake.

This day she was telling me about her childhood, about the games they played and the trouble they got into. She said that one day in early winter she and her brother and two of the Pye boys – Jackson Pye's sons – were playing by the shore of the lake. The lake hadn't been frozen long and all of them had been expressly forbidden to go out on it, but Norman Pye, who was older than the rest of them, said that it would be safe if they slid out on their bellies. So they did.

'We thought it was exciting as all get out,' Miss Vernon said. 'We could hear the ice cracking but it didn't give and we slid across it like seals. Oh it was tremendous fun. The ice was clear as glass and you could see right to the bottom. All the stones lying there, brighter and more colourful than they ever are when you look through water. You could even see fish swimming about. And then all at once there was this louder crack and the whole sheet gave way and there we were in the water. It was awful cold. But we were right near the shore so we just climbed out. But Norman wouldn't go home. He said he'd be better off not.'

She stopped there and started rattling her teeth about as she does, as if that were the end of the story. After a minute I said, 'You mean he didn't go home till he dried out?' I thought of him, teeth chattering, skin blue, trying to figure out how to keep from freezing while his clothes dried, afraid of the beating he'd get if his father found out. Being the eldest, he'd be in the most trouble.

Miss Vernon said, 'No no. He didn't go home at all.'

'You mean ever?'

'He reckoned he'd just head off down the road and maybe a logging truck would pick him up. We didn't see him again.'

It haunted me afterwards. It kept coming back to me, throughout my teenage years. The image of that boy walking down the road. Flailing himself with his arms, his feet numb, boots stumbling on the frozen road. Darkness coming on. Snow drifting down.

What haunted me most of all was the thought that three generations back, there was a Pye son who was prepared to risk freezing to death rather than face his father.

Four

A UNT Annie arrived two days after the funeral. You
need to know about Aunt Annie; she played a part in
what happened. She was my father's eldest sister, a worthy
descendant of Great Grandmother Morrison, and equal to
most tasks. It was the first time she had left the Gaspé, and
although Luke and Matt had met her – our parents had
taken them 'home' for a visit once, when they were small
– Bo and I never had.

She was many years older than my father, short where
he had been tall, fat where he had been thin and with a
behind I'm glad I didn't inherit, but she had something of
him about her and she seemed familiar to me straight
away. She was unmarried. My father's mother had died
some years previously, not long after Great Grandmother
in fact, and since then Aunt Annie had kept house for her
father and brothers. I suppose the family might have
chosen to send her simply because it was seen as women's
work and having no children she could most easily be
spared, but I suspect there was a better reason than that.
The message she had to deliver – the arrangements the

43

family had made for us – was a painful one, and I imagine there weren't many volunteers.

'I'm sorry to be so long in coming,' she said when Rev. Mitchell had presented her to us – since the accident we had no car and he had picked her up at the railway crossing for us – 'but this country is just too big. Do you have a lavatory? I assume you have a lavatory. Kate, you look just like your mother, aren't you the lucky one. And this is Bo. Hello, Bo.'

Bo regarded her stonily from Luke's arms. Aunt Annie seemed unperturbed. She removed her hat, which was small and round and brown and did her no favours, and looked around for somewhere to put it. Everything was a mess but she didn't seem to notice. She put her hat down on the sideboard beside a plate with a dull white crescent of ham fat on it. Then she reached up and patted her hair.

'Do I look a fright? I feel a fright. Never mind. Show me the lavatory and then I can get started. I expect there's lots to do.'

Her tone was cheerful and matter-of-fact, as if this were a regular visit and our parents just happened to be out of the room for the moment. But it seemed right that she should be like that. That was how they would have been. I decided that I liked her. I couldn't think why Luke and Matt were looking so anxious.

'There we are,' she said a few minutes later, emerging from the bathroom. 'Now then. What's the time? Four o'clock. That's fine. We all need to get to know each other but I expect that will look after itself. What I think we should do now is sort out what needs doing most – cooking, cleaning, washing, that sort of thing. Reverend Mitchell says you've managed marvellously, but there must be things . . .'

She paused. Something in Luke's and Matt's expressions must have distracted her, because she didn't finish her sentence. Instead, her tone a little less brisk and a little more gentle, she said, 'I know we have matters to discuss, but I think we should leave all that for a day or two, don't you? We'll need to go through your father's papers and we'll need to talk to his lawyer and the bank. Then we'll know where we stand. There's not much point in discussing things until then. Is that all right with you?'

They nodded, and both of them suddenly looked looser, as if they'd been holding their breath and now they had let it out.

So WE had a couple of days of what I suppose you could call a honeymoon period, during which Aunt Annie restored order and gave Luke and Matt a chance to get their breath back. Laundry had been the biggest problem, so she started there, and then cleaned the house and discreetly disposed of our parents' clothes and dealt with unanswered mail and unpaid bills. She was efficient and tactful and made no demands on our affections. I'm sure that under different circumstances we would have grown to love her.

On a Thursday, almost two weeks after the accident, she and Luke went up to town to see my father's lawyer and the bank. Rev. Mitchell drove them up while Matt stayed with Bo and me.

We went down to the lake after they'd left. I wondered if Matt would suggest a swim, but instead, after standing for quite a few minutes watching Bo stomp around at the water's edge, he said abruptly, 'Why don't we go back to the ponds?'

'What about Bo?' I said.

'She'll come too. It's time we educated her.'

'She'll fall in,' I said anxiously. Unlike the lake, the ponds were steep-sided. I felt tragedy lurked around every corner now; I was afraid all the time. I went to bed with fear at night and woke up with it in the morning.

But Matt said, 'Sure she'll fall in, won't you, Bo? That's what ponds are for.'

He carried Bo through the woods on his shoulders, the same way he had carried me all those years ago. We did not talk. We never said much on these excursions but there was a difference in the silence this time. Back then, it had been because there was no need to talk; now it was because our minds were full of things we couldn't say.

It was the first time we had been back to the ponds since our parents' death and when I saw them again, when we slid down the bank to the first of them, I felt my spirits rise in spite of everything. The first one was 'our' pond, not just because it was the closest but because on one side there was a shelf four or five feet wide where the water was less than three feet deep. The water was clear and warm and many of the pond dwellers congregated there, and of course you could see right to the bottom.

Bo gazed around from her perch on Matt's shoulders. 'Dat!' she said, pointing at the water.

'You should see what's in it, Bo,' I said. 'We'll tell you the names of everything.'

I lay down on my stomach, as I always did, and peered in. Tadpoles which had been hugging the edges of the pond swarmed away as my shadow fell over them and then gradually wriggled back. They were well developed, their hind legs fully formed, their tails short and stubby. We had watched them grow, Matt and I, as we did every year, from the very first day they began to move inside the tiny clear globes of their eggs.

Sticklebacks were drifting aimlessly about. The breeding season was over so it was hard to tell the males and the females apart. When they were breeding the males were very beautiful, with red underparts and silvery scales on their backs and brilliant blue eyes. Matt had told me – it had been in the spring, just a few months ago, though it seemed to be in another lifetime – that the male sticklebacks did all the work. They made the nests and courted the females and fanned the nests to keep the eggs supplied with oxygen. Once the eggs had hatched it was the males who guarded them. If a baby strayed from the group, the father sucked it into his mouth and spat it back into the pack.

'What do the females do?' I'd asked him.

'Oh, laze around. Go to tea parties. Gossip with their friends. You know what females are like.'

'No, but *really* Matt. What do they do?'

'I don't know. Eat a lot, probably. Probably they need to recover their strength after producing all those eggs.'

He'd been lying beside me then, his chin on the back of his hands, gazing into the water, and all that had been on our minds was this small world lying so still before us.

I looked around at him now. He was standing a few feet back from the pond, staring at it in the way you stare at something you're not really seeing. Bo was craning forward on his shoulders. 'Down!' she said.

I said, 'Aren't you coming to look?'

'Sure.'

He set Bo down and she staggered to the water's edge. Matt said, 'Lie down, Bo. Lie down like Kate and watch the fish.'

Bo looked at me. She squatted down beside me. She was wearing a little blue dress and her diaper hung down beneath it, so when she squatted it bunched up on the ground and made her look as if she had an enormous behind.

'Luke's not very good at diapers,' I said. Aunt Annie had offered to take over the task of changing Bo, but Bo would have none of it, so that was one job Luke and Matt still shared.

Matt said, 'I did that diaper, thank you, and I'm proud of it.'

He smiled at me, but when I looked at his eyes there was no laughter there. I saw suddenly that there was no happiness in him now. No *real* happiness; just a show, for my sake. I turned my head quickly away from him and stared hard into the water. The fear and dread lying inside of me rose up like a river, like a flood. I stared into the pond and pressed everything down hard.

After a minute Matt lay down beside Bo, so that she was between us. He said, 'Look at the fish, Bo.' He pointed at the water and Bo looked at his finger. 'No, look in the water. See the fish?'

Bo said, 'Ooooh!' She stood up and jumped up and down, yelling with excitement and the fish vanished as if they had never been. She stopped jumping and stared into the water. She looked at Matt in disbelief.

'You scared them all away,' Matt said.

'No fish!' she said. She was incredulous and grief-stricken, and her face caved in and the tears started to roll.

'Cut it out, Bo. Just stay still and they'll come back.'

She looked at him doubtfully and stuck her thumb in, but then squatted down again. After a minute, while Matt talked to her to keep her still, a small stickleback drifted towards us.

'There he is,' Matt whispered.

And Bo leapt up in excitement, stepped on the dangling tail of her diaper, and fell in.

ON THE way back along the railway tracks we met Marie Pye, carrying a bag of groceries in each arm. The Pyes' farm was back beyond the gravel pits – in fact the land the pits were on belonged to them – and the tracks were a shorter route to the McLeans' store than the road. Matt slowed down as she came towards us and Marie did likewise, and then she stopped and let us come up.

'Hi, Marie,' Matt said, shifting Bo a little on his shoulders.

'Hi,' Marie said nervously. She glanced past us in the direction of the farm as if she expected her father to come raging up the path from the gravel pits to tell her off. My mother had said once that Marie was the only normal member of that whole sorry family, but she looked just as twitchy as the rest of them to me. She was big-boned and strong-looking, but pale, with a halo of fine pale hair and wide anxious eyes. She and Matt must have known each other quite well – or at least for quite a long time. Marie was a year older but Matt had skipped a grade, so they'd been in the same class at school. And they'd have seen each other, if only from a distance, when he was working for her father.

This was the first time they'd met since the funeral though, and neither of them seemed to know what to say. I couldn't see why they needed to say anything. I was tired and wanted to go home.

'Bo's been fishing,' Matt said at last, jerking his head back against Bo's belly.

Marie looked at Bo, who was soaking wet and covered in pond weed, and smiled uncertainly. Then she looked back at Matt, and flushed, and said all in a hurry, 'I . . . I was really sorry about your parents.'

'Yeah,' Matt said. 'Thanks.'

'Do you . . . do you know what you're going to do? What's going to happen?'

'Not yet. We should find out . . .' He stopped, and though I wasn't looking at him I knew that he had nodded at me.

'Oh,' Marie said. 'Anyway, I'm really sorry.'

We stood for a minute more, and then Marie looked at Bo and me and smiled vaguely.

'Well, bye,' she said.

We walked on. I thought, What's going to happen? Is something else going to happen? What didn't he know yet? What's going to happen? Something so bad that he wouldn't talk about it in front of me.

We came to the path which led from the tracks down into the woods. Once we were there, protected by the dark privacy of the trees, I tried to ask him. I opened my mouth, but the need not to know was greater than the need to know, and I couldn't say anything. Then the paralysis of my brain affected my feet and I came to a halt. Matt turned and looked at me.

'Got something in your shoe?'

I said, 'What did she mean?' and my breath came out in little jerks.

'Who?'

'Marie. When she asked you what was going to happen? What did she mean?'

He didn't reply for a minute. Bo was examining his hair, lifting long strands of it straight out from his head and crooning over it. His shirt was as wet and pond-weedy as she was.

I said, 'What did she . . .' and then all at once I was crying, standing there, straight and still with my arms at my sides. Matt put Bo down and knelt and took my shoulders.

'Katie! Katie, what is it?'

'What did she mean? What's going to happen? What did she mean?'

'Katie, it's going to be all right. We'll be looked after. Aunt Annie is arranging it.'

'Then what did she *mean*? You said you didn't know yet. What don't you know?'

He took a deep breath, then let it out. 'The thing is, Katie, we won't be able to stay here. We'll have to go and live with the family.'

'Isn't Aunt Annie coming to live with us?'

'No. She can't. She has her parents to look after, and she works on the farm. She's too busy.'

'Who then? Who are we going to?'

'I don't know yet. That's what I don't know. But whoever it is, it will be all right. They'll be nice. The whole family is nice.'

'I want to live here. I don't want to leave here. I want Luke and you to look after us. Why can't Luke and you look after us?'

'It costs money to look after people, Kate. We wouldn't have any money to live on. Look, you mustn't worry. It'll be all right. That's why Aunt Annie is here. To arrange things. It'll be all right. You'll see.'

LUKE AND Aunt Annie got back from town just after five. Aunt Annie asked us to come and sit down in the living room, which we did, all but Luke who stood looking out of the window at the lake. Aunt Annie sat very straight in her chair and told us the following:

That our father had left some money, but not much.

That from the lawyer's office she had made a number of phone calls to the rest of the family and it had been agreed that Luke should go to teachers' college as planned. It would use up most of the money, but everyone felt that it was what our parents would have wished.

That when it came to the rest of us . . . here Aunt Annie, for all her straight back, had some difficulty. She looked away, then looked back, her eyes skating over Matt and me and finally coming to rest on Bo . . . when it came to the rest of us, unfortunately none of the various branches of the family was in a position to take on three extra children. Indeed, financial circumstances were such that none of them could afford to take on even two. Therefore, in order to keep at least Bo and me together, it had been decided that if Matt were willing, he would go back with her to the farm. He would be an asset there, and the money he earned would go towards supporting his sisters. Luke, it was hoped, would be able to contribute as soon as he had qualified and found a job. In the meantime, Matt's earnings, plus contributions from the rest of the family, would enable Aunt Emily and Uncle Ian, who lived in Rivière-du-Loup and who had four children of their own, to take in Bo and me.

Five

YOU SEE the suffering of children all the time nowadays. Wars and famines are played out before us in our living rooms and almost every week there are pictures of children who have been through unimaginable loss and horror. Mostly they look very calm. You see them looking into the camera, directly at the lens, and knowing what they have been through you expect to see terror or grief in their eyes, yet often there's no visible emotion at all. They look so blank it would be easy to imagine that they weren't feeling much.

And though I do not for a moment equate what I went through with the suffering of those children, I do remember feeling as they look. I remember Matt talking to me – others as well, but mostly Matt – and I remember the enormous effort required even to hear what he said. I was so swamped by unmanageable emotions that I couldn't feel a thing. It was like being at the bottom of the sea.

*

'KATE?'

I was looking at his knees. My knees were thin and

brown and knobbled. Matt's, extending from his shorts, were at least twice as big around.

'Kate?'

'What?'

'Are you listening?'

'Yes.'

'Look at the map. It isn't far, see? I'll be able to come and visit you. It isn't all that far. D'you see?'

There were fewer hairs on his knees than on his thighs or calves, and the skin was different. Creased, from bending. I had no hairs on my knees at all, and the creases were smaller.

'Look at this, Kate.'

We spent a lot of time here, sitting on the sofa. He and Luke were working for Mr Pye again, but in the evenings he took me back to the ponds, or if it was raining or too late to go to the ponds, he sat with me and talked about what our new lives would be like and how we would get together. I listened. Or I tried to listen. But there was a whirlwind howling through me and it made it difficult to hear.

'We can work it out,' Matt said. 'There's a scale here, see? It tells you how many miles to an inch.'

It wasn't a very good map. New Richmond, which was the nearest town to Aunt Annie's farm, wasn't marked on it, but Matt had asked Aunt Annie to show us where it was and then he took a pen and although you weren't ever supposed to write in books he had put a dot in the right place and then printed the name, New Richmond, very neatly beside it.

We were all to stay on in Crow Lake until Luke went to college and then the four of us, Aunt Annie, Matt, Bo and myself, would travel east together. Matt and Aunt

Annie would come to Rivière-du-Loup with Bo and me and stay there with us for three days while Bo and I got used to our new home. Then they would leave us, and travel on to Aunt Annie's farm.

In the meantime, Calvin Pye was desperate for help and Aunt Annie said there was no reason why the boys shouldn't earn a bit of money. She did not intend me to hear her tell them that it would also help Bo and me get used to not having them around.

'Put your thumb against the scale, Kate. That's right. Now look. That first joint of your thumb, from there to there, is about a hundred miles. See? Now lay it against the map. Look at that. It's not much more than a hundred miles, is it? A hundred and fifty at the most. I'll be able to visit you easily.'

He talked, and the whirlwind howled.

'WHO'S THIS?' Aunt Annie said. 'Kate? Who's this coming down the drive?'

'Miss Carrington.'

'And who is Miss Carrington?'

'My teacher.'

'Oh,' Aunt Annie said, sounding interested. 'She looks young to be a teacher.'

We were sitting on the verandah, topping beans. Aunt Annie was of the school which believed that useful work was the best remedy for any ill. She made me talk. She was better at it than Matt because she was more ruthless.

'Is she a good teacher? Do you like her?'

'Yes.'

'What do you like about her?'

Blank silence.

'Kate? What do you like about Miss Carrington?'

'She's nice.'

And then I was spared any more questions because Miss Carrington was too close.

'Hello,' Aunt Annie said, putting down her basket of beans and standing up to greet her. 'I understand you're Kate's teacher. I'm Annie Morrison.'

They shook hands, rather formally. Aunt Annie said, 'Would you like a cold drink? Or tea? You've walked from the village?'

'Yes,' Miss Carrington said. 'Thank you. I'd love some tea. Hello, Kate. I see you're hard at work.' She gave me a faint smile, and I saw that she was nervous. I wasn't noticing much, those days, but I noticed that because it was so unusual.

'Kate, do you think you could make us a pot of tea?' Aunt Annie asked. 'You could use the best china, don't you think? As it's Miss Carrington?' She smiled at Miss Carrington and said, 'Kate makes the best pot of tea of anyone I know.'

I got up and went into the house and put the kettle on. The house was very quiet. Bo was in our bedroom – Aunt Annie had put her there for her afternoon nap and Bo had roared her head off, but now she seemed to have gone to sleep.

While the kettle was boiling I climbed onto a chair and got down my mother's best teapot from the high shelf in the kitchen. The pot was round and smooth and a rich cream colour and had a branch of an apple tree painted on it, with several dark green leaves and two very red apples. The apples were not only painted but were raised, so that you could feel their roundness with your hands. There was a small cream jug and a covered sugar bowl to go with it, and six cups and six saucers and six little plates, all of them with apples on and none of them with chips. Aunt Annie had told me that the tea service was a wedding present to my parents from a lady in New Richmond and that it would be mine when I was older, but that I could use it now, if I liked, when especially important people came to call. I knew I was supposed to be pleased.

I warmed the pot and made the tea. I put the pot on the best tray and covered it with the tea cosy. I set out two cups and saucers, the milk and sugar, and carried it carefully to the door. I could see Miss Carrington and Aunt Annie through the screen door. Miss Carrington was saying, 'I hope you won't mind, Miss Morrison. I hope you won't take it amiss.'

Aunt Annie saw me and got up to open the door for me.

She said, 'Thank you, Kate. You've set things out very nicely. Now then, Miss Carrington and I have things to discuss – do you think you could take the beans into the kitchen and finish them for me? Or take them to the beach, if you prefer. Which would you prefer?'

'The beach,' I said, not caring one way or the other. I gathered up the beans and the pot and the knife and walked down the verandah steps and around the corner of the house. Just around the corner I dropped the knife. It must have been right at my feet, but the grass was long and I couldn't see it. I carefully combed the grass with my toes, holding the beans and their pot out to the side, and heard Miss Carrington say, 'I realize it's none of my business, but I felt I had to speak. They're all bright children, of course, but Matt is more than that. He has a love of learning . . . he is a scholar, Miss Morrison. A natural scholar. He is the cleverest child I have ever taught. *Much* the cleverest. And he has only the one year of high school left . . .'

57

'Two years, surely,' Aunt Annie said.

'No, just one. He skipped a grade, you see. So although he's two years younger than Luke, he's only one year behind. He'll sit his exams next spring. And he will win a scholarship to university. Certainly. Beyond any question.'

There was silence. My toes came up against something cool and hard. I bent down and picked up the knife.

Aunt Annie said, 'Would it cover everything? All of his living expenses? His lodgings?'

'Well no. But it would cover his tuition. And something could be sorted out about his lodgings. I'm sure it could. I'm sure some way could be found. Miss Morrison, I do apologize for pressing this, but you must understand – it would be a tragedy if Matt did not go to university. Genuinely, it would be a tragedy.'

After a minute Aunt Annie said gently, 'Miss Carrington, a worse tragedy than that has already taken place here.'

'I know! Oh my goodness, I realize that! But that is why it seems so wrong that this double blow should fall on Matt!'

Silence. A sigh from Aunt Annie. Finally, her tone still gentle, she said, 'I don't think you quite understand the position. We would help Matt if we possibly could. We would help all the children. But there is no money. I realize that sounds unlikely, but that is the case. The last five years – six years – have been very hard for all the farms in the Gaspé. Both of my brothers are in debt. My father is in debt. At the end of his life, he is in debt, and he has never owed a penny before.'

'But this house . . .'

'The money from this house, together with what Robert left, will see Luke through teachers' college and provide a very small sum to give to each of the others when they reach twenty-one. A very small sum. We could not in all conscience deprive the girls of that in order that Matt go to university. And in any case there would not be enough.'

'But surely . . .'

'Miss Carrington, please listen. I should not tell you this, it is most . . . inappropriate . . . But I want you to understand. I appreciate your concern for Matt and I want you to understand how . . . painful this is for the family. The reason Robert left so little is that he has been helping out the rest of us. He felt he was beholden to us, you see. My brothers sacrificed so that he could have his chance, and he took the chance and he did very well, so of course when things went badly for us he felt he had to help out. Which was very generous of him . . . And of course he could not know that his children . . . he would have assumed a good salary coming in for years to come.'

There was silence. I prodded the beans with my knife.

Miss Carrington said bleakly, 'A tragedy then. As you say.'

'I'm afraid so.'

'You couldn't . . . you couldn't at least let him finish high school. Miss Morrison, he *deserves* at *least* to finish high school.'

'My dear, my sister − not the one who is taking Kate and Elizabeth − has four sons, all of whom deserved to finish high school, all of whom deserved to go to university, come to that. They are clever boys. It is, I believe, a clever family. But they are all on the fishing boats now. There is no future for them even on the farm. And you might well call it a tragedy, but it is one that most of the world is familiar with. To be honest with you, I feel far worse about having to split up those children than I do about Matt not finishing high school. He has more education than most already.'

More silence. I imagined Miss Carrington, her mouth gone thin as it did in class when she was cross.

Aunt Annie said, 'We should count our blessings, you know. The children could have been in that car.'

I MADE my way down to the beach. When I had finished topping the beans, I sat for a bit, watching the waves, listening to their steady swish. Their sound, in all its variety, had been the background to my life. From the moment of my birth, I had never been without it.

After a while I picked up the knife again and pressed the point against my finger. It dented the skin, and then a small drop of dark glistening blood welled out. It hardly hurt at all.

Six

OH THE chances, the fragile little incidents which determine the course of our lives. If I say my life took a certain course because my parents died, well, that is understandable, that is a major event, that would shape anyone's future. But if I say my life took a certain course because Miss Carrington came that day, and I dropped a knife, and Matt, a few hours later, still wretchedly trying to help me, persisted in asking me questions, and Luke happened to be there at the time, trying to read the paper, and Bo was screaming . . .

'You've cut your finger,' Matt said.

We were sitting on the sofa. Supper was over and I'd finished drying the dishes for Aunt Annie, who now, persisting grimly in her efforts to get us accustomed to a new order, was putting Bo to bed. You could hear Bo raging through two closed doors. 'Not!' she was yelling. 'Not! Not! Not!'

What she meant was not Aunt Annie. We all knew that, Aunt Annie best of all.

Luke was on his knees and elbows on the floor,

pretending to read the paper. His hands were clenched against his jaw.

'How did you cut your finger?' Matt said.

'On a knife.'

'What were you doing with a knife?'

'Topping beans.'

'You should be more careful.'

He leaned back, waggled his shoulder blades, and groaned. 'My back's killing me. You'd rather be topping beans than doing what Luke and I were doing, I can tell you.'

He wanted me to ask him what they'd been doing. I knew that, but the words seemed to be so far down inside me that I couldn't drag them out.

He told me anyway.

'Today we were pitching straw. And I tell you, that is one awful job. The dust gets up your nose and in your mouth and the straw gets in your shirt and down your pants and the sweat and the dust turn into this sort of glue between your toes and Old Man Pye stands there leaning on his fork like some old troll, just hoping you'll slacken off so he'll have an excuse to eat you.'

He wanted me to laugh, but that was more than I could manage. I smiled at him though. He smiled back and said, 'Now tell me about your day. What exciting things happened today, apart from beans?'

I couldn't think of anything. Thinking had become as difficult as speaking. My mind seemed to have been swallowed up like a boat in a fog.

'Come on, Katie. What did you do? Did anyone come to visit?'

'Miss Carrington.'

'Miss Carrington? That's nice. What did Miss Carrington have to say?'

I dredged around in the fog. 'She said you were clever.'

Matt laughed. 'Did she?'

But I was remembering now. She'd been nervous. She'd been scared of Aunt Annie and she'd had to force herself to say what she wanted to say, and it had made her voice funny.

'She said you were the cleverest child she'd ever taught. She said it would be a . . . tradegy . . . a *tragedy* . . . if you didn't go to university.'

There was a moment's silence. Matt said, 'Good old Miss Carrington. It always pays to suck up to a teacher, Kate. Take it from me.'

His voice was funny now. I looked at him, but he was looking at Luke and his face was red. Luke had looked up from his paper and they were staring at each other. Then Luke, speaking to me but with his eyes still on Matt, said, 'What did Aunt Annie say?'

I tried to remember. 'She said there wasn't enough money.' She'd said more, but I couldn't remember what.

Luke nodded. He was still looking at Matt.

After a minute Matt said, 'Well she's right. Anyway, it doesn't matter.'

Luke didn't say anything.

Out of the blue, Matt seemed to be angry. He said, 'If you want to spend your life feeling guilty because you were born first that's up to you, but don't waste it on me.'

Luke didn't reply. He turned away and started reading his paper again. Matt bent forward and picked up another bit of the paper. He looked at it and then tossed it on the floor again. He looked at his watch and said, 'We should go to the pond. It'll be light for another hour,' but neither of us moved.

In the background we could hear Bo, still screaming.

Luke abruptly heaved himself to his feet and left the room, and we heard him going into Bo's and my room. We heard voices, his angry and Aunt Annie's very firm, and Bo's, heartbroken now, really sobbing; you could almost see her arms reaching out for Luke. Then, surprisingly clear and sharp, Aunt Annie saying, 'You're not helping her, Luke. Not one bit.'

Then we heard Luke's footsteps, loud and angry, and the door slamming as he left the house.

HERE'S THE thing about Luke. Up until the very day our parents died, I don't remember him ever picking Bo up. Not once. Matt would pick her up, but not Luke. I also don't remember ever having a proper conversation with him. Thousands with Matt, none with Luke. Apart from the occasional row or bit of bantering between him and Matt, I don't recall Luke ever showing that he knew — or cared — that the rest of us existed.

IN THE morning he wasn't there.

His bed had been slept in and there was a cereal bowl on the kitchen counter but there was no sign of him. He and Matt were supposed to be working on the farm.

'Maybe he's gone already,' Aunt Annie said. 'Making an early start.'

'Not a chance,' Matt said. He was very angry. He was pulling on his work boots by the door, tying the laces savagely, yanking the cuffs of his jeans down over the tops of them to stop the straw getting in.

'Where's he gone?' I said.

'I don't know, Kate. If he'd left a note, I'd know, but he hasn't. Which is typical. The day Luke bothers to tell anyone what he's doing will be a great, great day.'

This was true. Luke, the old Luke, the Luke of two months ago, had infuriated our parents by failing to keep them informed of his comings and goings. In those days Matt hadn't cared much, because it didn't affect him.

I started gnawing at my finger where I'd cut it. I was afraid Luke had left us. Run away or died.

'But where do you think he's gone?'

'Kate, I don't know. It doesn't matter. What matters is unless he's back in about two minutes we're going to be late for work.'

'You'll just have to go without him,' Aunt Annie said. She was making sandwiches for their lunch – farm-worker's sandwiches, great hunks of bread with slabs of ham half an inch thick. 'He'll have to make his own excuses. Could he have gone to town for some reason? Would he have any way of getting to town?'

'He could have gone in with the milk. Mr Janie leaves about four in the morning – he could have got a lift on the milk truck with him.'

'Will he come back?' My voice was starting to shake. After all, our parents had gone to town.

'Of course he'll come back. All I'm worried about is what I'm going to tell Old Man Pye. He's going to go up in smoke.'

'But how do you *know* he'll come back?'

'Kate, I know. Leave your finger alone.' He pulled my hand away from my mouth. 'I know, OK? I know.'

I SPENT the morning doing chores and most of the afternoon on the beach with Bo. Bo had declared war on

Aunt Annie. I guess as she saw it, Aunt Annie was responsible for everything that had gone wrong with her life, and the only solution was to fight her to the death. I think she would have won, too. I suspect Aunt Annie thought so as well.

So we were exiled from the house to give Aunt Annie a chance to marshal her defences. I can picture the two of us on the path to the beach, hand in hand, me dragging myself along, Bo stomping so hard little puffs of dust shot out from under her feet at every step. My hair would be hanging limp and lifeless, hers would be standing out from her head, radiating rage like a heat wave. A lovely pair of sisters.

We sat on the hot sand and watched the lake. It was dead calm. You could just see it breathing, slow deep breaths under its flat, shining, silver skin. Bo sat beside me, pinching pebbles between her fingers and sighing every now and then around her thumb.

I tried to still the whirlwind inside me, but when I succeeded, when by force of will I managed to calm it so that individual thoughts could settle and be looked at, the thoughts themselves overwhelmed me. Being without Matt. Being without Luke. Leaving our home. Going to live with strangers. Aunt Annie had told me about them; she had said there were four children, three boys and one girl. They were all older than Bo and me, but she said they were nice. But she wouldn't really know if they were nice, you would only know that if you were a child yourself. Matt had said that I must look after Bo, but he must know that I couldn't. I was too afraid. I was much more afraid than Bo was.

I focused hard on a small boat out in the lake and made myself concentrate on it. I knew whose boat it was – Jim

Sumack's, a friend of Luke's who lived on the Indian Reservation.

'That's Big Jim Sumack,' I said loudly to Bo. I wanted to talk, to drown out the thoughts.

Bo sighed, and sucked harder. Nowadays her thumb looked all water-logged, and it was getting a big white callus on the top.

'He's going fishing,' I said. 'He's going to catch a fish for dinner. He's called Big Jim Sumack because he weighs more than two hundred pounds. He doesn't go to school any more, but Mary Sumack's in Grade Three. In the winter she didn't come to school and they went to see her Mum and it was because she didn't have any shoes. The Indians are really poor.'

My mother had said we should all be ashamed. I hadn't been sure what it was she thought we should be ashamed of, and I'd felt obscurely to blame. I thought of my mother. I tried to summon up her face, but I couldn't get it to come clear. Bo had already stopped asking for her.

A loon popped up out of nowhere twenty yards out from the shore. 'There's a loon,' I said.

Bo sighed again, and the loon disappeared.

'Uke?' Bo said suddenly, taking her thumb out and looking at me.

'He's not here.'

'Att?'

'He's not here either. They'll be home in a while.'

I looked around for something to distract her, to stop her winding herself up into a rage. A spider was heading towards us across the sand, dragging a dead deer fly. Or rather he was tailing towards us, moving backwards, holding the fly with his jaws and front legs and scrabbling hard with the rest. Once Matt and I had watched a small spider trying to drag a Mayfly three times his size out of a hollow in the sand. The sand was dry, and every time he got his burden halfway up the slope the sides of the hollow caved in and he slid to the bottom again. He tried again and again, never varying his route, never slackening his pace. Matt had said, 'Here's the question, Katie: is he very very determined, or is his memory so short that he forgets what happened two seconds ago, so he always thinks he's doing it for the first time? That's the question.'

We'd watched him for almost half an hour, and in the end, to our delight, he succeeded, so we decided he was not only very determined but also very smart.

'Look, Bo,' I said. 'See the spider? He's got a fly, and he's dragging him home to his nest, see? And when he gets him home he'll spin a cocoon around him and then later, when he's hungry, he'll eat him.'

I wasn't trying to share my fascination with her as Matt had shared his with me. My goal was less exalted. I merely hoped that she would be interested, instead of angry, because I didn't feel up to coping with one of her rages.

It didn't work, though. I thought it was working, because she leaned forward and watched the spider intently for a couple of seconds, but then she took her thumb out, got to her feet, staggered over to him and stamped on him.

Seven

Matt got home just before six. I was waiting for him on the steps of the verandah. He asked if Luke was home yet, and when I said no he didn't say anything. He just walked straight down to the beach, stripped off everything but his underpants and plunged into the lake.

I'd followed him down and I stood silently on the shore watching the ripples spreading out from where he had disappeared. When he broke through the water again he looked like a seal, wet and sleek. His body was broken into blocks of light and dark; dark face and neck and forearms, paler back and chest, white legs.

He said, 'Could you get me a bar of soap? I forgot it.' And I went up to the house and got one.

He washed savagely, scrubbing at his body with the soap, rubbing it into his hair. Then he tossed it onto the beach and plunged into the water again, making a milk-white cloud in the dark water. He swam a long way out.

You weren't supposed to throw the soap onto the beach because it was almost impossible to get the sand out of it. You were supposed to put it on a rock. I picked it up and dipped it into the water and started trying to clean it off, but the sand just sank in deeper.

Matt swam back and waded out of the water. He said, 'Don't bother, Kate,' and took the soap from me. He gave me a brief, tight smile as we walked up to the house but it wasn't a real smile, just a stretch of skin.

AUNT ANNIE delayed supper as long as she could, hoping that Luke would appear, but in the end she served up without him. She'd cooked a leg of pork and there was a big bowl of apple sauce, which I loved but found I couldn't eat. I couldn't eat anything. I couldn't seem to swallow. Spit kept gathering in my mouth and I had to squeeze it down.

Bo was having problems too. When Aunt Annie had put her supper in front of her she'd thrown it on the floor, so now, white with exhaustion and with dark purple shadows under her eyes, she was sitting in front of an empty place, gloomily sucking her thumb.

Matt ate in a steady, business-like way, as if he were stoking a boiler. He'd changed into clean jeans and a shirt, and his hair was combed straight back. It dripped steadily onto his collar. There were scratches on his hands and arms from the straw. They'd been black before his swim but now they were fiery red.

'More pork?' Aunt Annie said, grimly cheerful. If she was concerned about Luke she wasn't going to show it.

'Thanks,' Matt said. He handed her his plate.

'Potatoes? Carrots? Apple sauce?'

'Thanks.'

'The apple sauce is from a Mrs Lily Stanovich. Dropped by this afternoon. She was enquiring about you all. A weepy soul. Still, it was kind of her to bring the sauce – it saved me a lot of paring. I told her you were on the beach, Kate, and she was all for going down for a chat with you, but I told her you had your hands full with Bo and maybe another time. The vegetables are from Alice Pye. Now there's a strange woman. She'll be the wife of your employer, Matt.'

She paused in a way that required an answer, so Matt nodded.

'And what's he like?'

'Mr Pye?'

'Yes. What's he like? Nice person to work for?'

Matt chewed. 'He pays OK,' he said at last.

'That's not what I'd call a fulsome description,' Aunt Annie said. 'Put a little meat on it for us.'

She'd had enough drama for one day and we were going to have a proper dinner-table conversation if it killed her.

'You want me to describe Mr Pye?'

'I do. Tell us all about him. We want to be entertained.'

Matt cut up a potato and forked a chunk in. You could see him considering adjectives and rejecting them. 'I think he's probably insane,' he said at last.

'For goodness sake, Matt. An honest description.'

'That's an honest description. I think he's probably insane. That's my opinion.'

'Insane in what way?'

'He's mad all the time.'

'Mad isn't a proper word.'

'Furious. Raging mad. In a rage.'

'Have you been having words with him?'

'Not me. He doesn't get at Luke or me – he knows we'd just walk off. It's his kids he goes for. 'Specially

Laurie. You should have heard him this afternoon. Laurie'd left a gate open – you should have heard him.'

'It's a serious thing,' said Aunt Annie disapprovingly. She didn't care for Matt's description of his employer. 'You wouldn't know that, not being brought up on a farm, but a lot of damage can be done if cattle get into a field. A whole crop can go down.'

'I know that, Aunt Annie! I've been working on that farm for years! Laurie knows it too! There were no cattle in either field. Anyway, I'm not talking about just today, I'm talking all the time. Old Man Pye's after him every minute of the day.'

He was trying hard not to be snappy but I could hear edges in his voice. He was so mad at Luke he didn't feel like talking at all, far less about Mr Pye.

Aunt Annie sighed. 'Well it's too bad, but there's no need to go calling him insane. Most fathers and sons go through a bad patch from time to time.'

'This is some bad patch,' Matt said. 'This is a bad patch that's been going on for fourteen years, getting worse . . .'

He stopped. He'd noticed at the same time as I did that Bo was behaving strangely. She'd pulled out her thumb and her hands were half-raised and her eyes were stretched wide. She looked like a cartoon of somebody listening.

'What in heaven's name's she up to now?' Aunt Annie said crossly, and Bo said, 'Uke!' and twisted round, and sure enough, there he was, coming down the drive.

'Right,' Matt said, putting down his knife and fork and pushing out his chair. 'Now I'm going to kill him.'

'You sit where you are, Matt. We don't need any of that.'

He didn't seem to have heard her. He headed for the door.

72

'You sit down, Matthew James Morrison! Sit down in your seat and hear what he has to say!'

'I don't care what he has to say.'

'Sit down!'

Her voice was shaking, and when I looked at her, her chin was wobbling and her eyes were strained and red. Matt looked at her too. He flushed. He said, 'Sorry,' and sat down.

Luke came in. He stopped in the doorway and looked at us. 'Hi,' he said.

Bo crowed and held her arms out, and he picked her up. She buried her face in his neck and kissed him passionately. He said, 'Am I too late for supper?'

Aunt Annie's chin was still wobbling. She swallowed, and said, 'There's some left. It's cold though,' without looking at him.

Luke was looking at Matt, who was staring at him. 'That's OK,' he said absently. 'I don't mind it cold.'

He sat down and dumped Bo on his lap.

Matt said, 'Where. Have. You. Been,' in the most deadly level tone.

'In town,' Luke said. 'I went to see Mr Levinson, Dad's lawyer. I had some things to sort out. Some things I needed to know. I can eat all those potatoes, if no one else wants them.'

'And you couldn't have told us you were going.' Matt's voice was flat and hard and thin as a fish-knife.

'I wanted to get things sorted out before I mentioned anything. Why?' He looked around. 'Has there been a problem?'

Matt made a sound in his throat.

Aunt Annie said, 'Never mind, Luke. Just tell us now.'

'Can I eat my supper first? I haven't eaten all day.'

'No,' Matt said.

'What's eating you anyway? OK! OK! Calm down! I'll tell you – it's not that complicated. Basically, I'm not going to teachers' college. I'm staying here. The four of us are staying here. I'm looking after you guys. It's all legal, I'm old enough and everything. We'll have the money I would have used to go to college – not from the house, obviously, because we won't sell it, but the rest of it. We'll need more than that, but I can get a job. I can work nights – from when you get home from school, Matt, so's you can look after Kate and Bo. It'd probably be in town though, so we'd need a car, so we'll have to spend some money on that, but Mr Levinson says he'll keep his eyes open for an old one for us. I told him you wanted to go to university and he said we should talk to Dad's bank about a loan, they might be sympathetic. Obviously you'd have to win a scholarship but since you're a genius that's no problem, right? Anyway, we don't have to worry about that yet. The main thing is, we're all staying here. So thank you very much for all your plans and everything, Aunt Annie, but we won't be needing them. But thank everyone for us, OK?'

There was silence.

Bo pointed at the apple sauce. 'Dat,' she said, and smacked her lips. No one paid any attention.

Matt said, 'You're not going to college.'

'Right.'

'You're staying here. You're giving up teaching.'

'I didn't want to be a teacher all that much. It was Mum and Dad who wanted it.'

He stood up from his chair, dumped Bo down on it, took a plate and started to help himself to the pork. My head felt funny, as if there were bees humming inside of it.

Aunt Annie was sitting very still with her hands clasped in her lap, looking at the table. Her eyes were still red.

'Dat!' Bo said, bouncing up and down on Luke's chair and craning her neck to see into the bowl of apple sauce. 'Dat!'

Matt said, 'No thanks.'

Luke looked at him. 'What?'

'I know why you're doing this. I don't want it, thanks.'

'What are you talking about?'

'How would you feel?' Matt said. He was white as a sheet. 'If I gave up a sure place at university so that you could try for a place – how would you feel? Your whole life, how would you feel?'

Luke said, 'I'm not doing this for you. I'm doing it for Bo and Kate. And because I want to.'

'I don't believe you. You're doing it because of what Kate said last night.'

'I don't give a bear's ass whether you believe me or not. Soon as you're eighteen you can take your share of the money and go off to Timbuktu for all I care.'

He finished loading his plate, plucked Bo off his chair and set her on the floor, sat down and started to eat.

'Dat!' Bo yelled. 'Dat . . . pudding!'

Luke lifted the bowl of apple sauce off the table and set it on the floor beside her.

Matt said, 'Aunt Annie, tell him he can't.'

I was staring at him incredulously. Luke was offering us salvation and Matt was turning it down. I couldn't believe it. I couldn't understand it. In fact, it was to be years before I understood it. Years before I realized how desperately he wanted what Luke was offering, for Bo and me as well as for himself, and how sick and enraged he was because he felt he had to turn it down.

He said again, 'Aunt Annie! Tell him!'

Aunt Annie had been studying the meat platter. She drew a breath and said, 'Luke, I'm afraid Matt is right. It's very generous of you, *very* generous, but I'm afraid it wouldn't do.'

Luke glanced at her but carried on eating. From under the table came the sound of Bo smacking her lips.

'I'm sorry your parents can't hear you make the offer,' Aunt Annie said. She smiled at him. Her face was stiff and white like Matt's. Another thing I didn't realize for years was how hard it all must have been for Aunt Annie. She wanted so much to do what was best for us – for her brother's sake and also, I think, because in spite of everything we'd put her through she had become fond of us all – and the options open to her were so limited. She must have seen how perfectly Luke's sacrifice seemed to solve everyone's problems, and she must also have understood Matt's agony. Most of all, she must have known that Luke could not really know what he was suggesting.

'The thing is, Luke, it wouldn't work. I'm surprised that Mr Levinson couldn't see that. But of course he's a man.'

Luke looked at her, chewing his pork. 'So what?'

'He wouldn't realize what hard work it is, bringing up a family. It's a full-time job. You cannot do both that and earn money to support you all. And the rest of us couldn't send enough to keep you. Not as a regular thing, to rely on.'

'Matt will help. He'll be able to work during the holidays.'

'Even with Matt's help, you couldn't do it. You have no idea what's involved, Luke. You can't have. It's been

76

all I could do to cope with the girls the past few weeks and I've been running a house for thirty years.'

'Yeah, but you're not used to kids,' Luke said. 'I'm used to them.'

'You are not, Luke. Living with them is not the same as being responsible for them. Caring for them. Looking after every single need they have, for years and years and years. It's never-ending hard work. Heavens, Bo on her own is a full-time job.'

'Yeah, but she likes me,' Luke said. He flushed. 'I didn't mean she doesn't like you. I mean she's easier with me. I know I can do it. I know it wouldn't be easy, but neighbours would help and everything. We'd work it out. I know I can do it.'

Aunt Annie straightened a bit in her chair. She looked full at Luke. Suddenly I saw our father in her – he'd had just that expression when he'd decided that an argument had gone far enough and it was time to bring it to an end. When she spoke she sounded like him too.

'Luke, you cannot know. For a while you would cope all right, but it would get harder. The neighbours wouldn't help for ever. Matt would be gone, you'd be on your own with two small children. You'd find that you'd given up your own life . . .'

'It's my life,' Luke said. 'I can do what I want with it and this is what I want.'

He sounded dogged, defiant, determined, but he put down his fork and ran both hands through his hair. He'd seen our father in her too.

Aunt Annie said, 'It's what you want *now*. In a year's time it may well not be, but you'd have lost your chance. I'm sorry, Luke. I cannot allow you . . .'

There was another sound. High-pitched. A wail. It was

coming from me. I found that my mouth was open, strained open, and my eyes were strained wide and I was wailing, wailing. The others were staring at me, and my mouth was trying to form a word, quivering and straining and trying to shape around a word.

'Please . . . Please . . . Please . . . Please . . . Please . . .'

PART TWO

Eight

THE NIGHT after the party invitation arrived from Matt's son, I did not sleep well. I had a number of vague incoherent dreams, some of them concerned with home, some with work, and then, towards morning, a very vivid one which stayed with me the rest of the day. Matt and I – our adult selves – were lying on our stomachs at the edge of the pond, watching a slim, streamlined little water bug called a pond skater skim across the surface, hunting for prey. He came to a stop right under our noses and we could clearly see the dimples his feet made on the surface of the water. Matt said, 'The water has kind of a skin on top, Kate. It's called surface tension. That's why he doesn't sink.'

I was astonished that he thought he had to tell me something so absurdly elementary. I am working on surfactants – compounds which reduce surface tension – at the moment. It is part of my field of research. 'I know,' I said gently. 'And the surface tension is caused by the fact that water has such high cohesion. The molecules are polar; the positive hydrogen atoms of one molecule are attracted to the negative oxygen atom of another. It's called the hydrogen bond.'

I looked at Matt to check that he had understood, but he was looking into the water. I waited for a long time, but he didn't say anything more. And then the alarm went off.

It was a Saturday. I was due to go to an exhibition with Daniel in the afternoon, after which we were meeting his parents downtown for a meal. I had a great pile of lab reports to mark which I was determined to finish first, so I got up and showered and made myself a pot of coffee, aware all the time of an unpleasant feeling left over from the dream. I ate a bowl of cornflakes standing at the kitchen window, with its splendid view of the kitchen window of the apartment across the light-well, and then took my coffee into my poky little dining-cum-living room where the reports were heaped on the table. The marking of lab reports is one of the most depressing activities known to man. They are written immediately after a lab experiment, when everything the student has learned should be fresh in his mind, and they therefore reveal exactly how much he or she has failed to understand. It is enough to make you weep. This is only my first year of assistant-professorship, but already the teaching part of it is getting me down. Why do kids come to university if they aren't interested in learning? Evidently because they think it's an easy option. They come for the beer and the parties; any facts they happen to pick up en route are strictly by the way.

I read the first report. It made no sense, so I read it again. The third time I realized that, dismal though it was, the fault lay not with it but with me. I put the report down and tried to identify just what it was, this emotion I was feeling, this hangover from the dream, and realized abruptly that it was shame.

It was totally illogical – feeling ashamed of something you did in a dream. In reality I would never lecture Matt. I've always been very careful about that sort of thing. I never even talk about my work with him because I'd have to simplify it and it seems to me that that would be an insult to him. Possibly he wouldn't see it that way, but I do.

I turned back to the reports. One or two showed some effort at accuracy, some awareness of scientific method. Half a dozen were so depressing that I had to restrain myself from writing 'drop the course' at the bottom. The door buzzer went when I still had two to go. I got up and pressed the door release and sat down again.

'I'm nearly finished,' I said when Daniel walked in, panting from the stairs. Considering that he's only thirty-four, he's very unfit. He has the kind of lean build that never runs to fat, but thin isn't necessarily healthy. I nag him about it and he nods seriously and agrees that he must get more exercise/eat more sensibly/get a decent amount of sleep. I imagine that tactic – solemnly agreeing with criticism – was learned early. His mother (Professor Crane of the Fine Art Department) has what you could call a dominant personality, and his father (Professor Crane of the History Department) is worse. Daniel handles them both very deftly, by agreeing with and then ignoring everything they say.

'There's coffee,' I said. 'Help yourself.'

He went into the kitchen and came out with a mug of coffee and stood beside me, reading the reports over my shoulder.

'I can't believe how bad they are,' I said. 'They're absolutely tragic.'

He nodded. 'They always are. Why are you doing them yourself? That's what teaching assistants are for.'

'How else am I going to know how the students are doing?'

'Why do you want to know how they're doing? Think of them as elephants, passing through.' He waved vaguely at a vanishing herd.

That is all pretence, of course. Daniel is at least as conscientious as I am. He says I take everything too seriously, implying that he just lets his students shift for themselves. In fact he spends more time on the teaching side of things than I do. The difference is that it doesn't seem to drive him mad.

I continued marking. Daniel wandered around the room sipping coffee and picking things up, turning them over and putting them down again. He is a 'fiddler' – his mother's word. He fiddles with things. His mother has collected some very beautiful objects over the years and has had to resort to locking them away behind glass doors to keep Daniel from fiddling with them.

'This has to be a relation.'

I looked up. He was holding a photograph in his hand. Simon. I'd forgotten I'd left it on the sofa.

I said, 'It's my nephew.'

'He looks a bit like the grand old dame hanging in your bedroom. Your great-great-great-great grandmother or whatever.'

'Just one great.'

I felt tense, all at once. I couldn't remember where I'd put the invitation. It had Matt's scribbled note on it, *Bring someone if you want to*. Was it with the photograph? Had Daniel seen it?

'Do you all have the same amazing hair?'

'It's just blond.'

There must have been something in my voice, because he looked at me curiously and put the photo down. 'Sorry. It was just lying there. I couldn't help noticing the family resemblance.'

'Sure,' I said casually. 'I know. Everyone says we all look alike.'

Had he seen the invitation or not?

I SHOULD say here that Daniel introduced me to his parents within a month of our first going out. We went to dinner with them. They live exactly where you would expect to find distinguished academics living, in a fine old 'century home' with a plaque on the wall in an area known as the Annex, near the university. There were paintings on the walls – originals, not prints – and several weighty bits of sculpture lying around. The furniture looked old, and good, and had a lustre to it which I imagine you get only with something that's been polished lovingly once a week for at least a hundred years. Where I come from such conspicuous good taste would be viewed with vague disapproval, hinting as it does at a love of material things. But I know that this is a kind of snobbishness and to be honest I found their home interesting rather than ostentatious.

Nonetheless, it was an uncomfortable evening. Quite apart from the surroundings – the four of us ate in a dining room with dark red wallpaper and an oval table big enough to seat at least a dozen people – I found Daniel's parents alarming. They are both extremely articulate and extremely opinionated and they contradict each other constantly, so that the air is thick with interruptions and denials and barbed remarks all flying at great speed. Every now and then one or other of them would suddenly remember that we were there and would pause mid-attack and look concerned and say something like, 'Daniel, do give Katherine some more wine,' and then instantly resume battle.

Daniel's mother said things like, 'Daniel's father would have you believe so and so, Katherine.' She would raise an elegant eyebrow at me, requiring that I snigger at the absurdity of so and so. She is tall and gaunt and striking to look at, with hair which is going silver rather than grey, cut short at the back and falling with razor-like precision at an angle across her face.

Daniel's father, who is shorter than she but gives an impression of power and mass and ferocious, barely contained energy, would smile, and dab his mouth with his napkin in a way that somehow made you think of a marksman calmly taking aim. He referred to his wife as 'the honourable doctor'. 'The honourable doctor is trying to recruit you to her cause, Katherine. Don't be deceived. She does not have logic on her side . . .'

I sat and listened to them, replying nervously when a reply was required, wondering by what genetic fluke the two of them had managed to produce someone as peaceful and non-competitive as Daniel.

Daniel was tucking in to venison stew, paying no attention to either of them. I was impressed by his courage in daring to show them to anyone – if they'd been my parents I would have denied that I knew them – and I expected him to apologize for them afterwards. But he didn't. He seemed to think they were perfectly normal.

He took it for granted that I would like them, or if I couldn't manage that, at least tolerate them for his sake. And in fact, once I got to know them better, I did like them, more or less, provided I could take them in small doses. They were both very welcoming to me and I do find them interesting. Besides, whether by fluke or not they did produce Daniel, so they can't be all bad.

But the point is, Daniel took it for granted that I would get to know them. As far as he was concerned, that was what you did when you became close to someone – you drew them into your family circle. After that first meeting we got together with them at fairly frequent intervals, once every month or so. Sometimes we went to their house, sometimes we met in a restaurant downtown. They would phone Daniel or he would say, time to see the War Department, which was what he called them. He assumed that I would want to see them too. And I did.

But of course, he expected me to do the same. The situation was different because of the distances but still, I knew that he was puzzled – more than puzzled – that I had not taken him home before. I knew it for a fact, because only a month or so before the invitation arrived from Simon, he had virtually said as much.

We had been out with friends for the evening, a colleague from the department and his new wife, who had been describing their first Christmas with their families. They had spent Christmas Eve with his family and Christmas Day with hers; the arrangement had pleased nobody and they'd had a one-hundred-mile trip in a snow storm in between. They made it sound funny but I found the tale depressing. Daniel was unusually quiet on the way home and I assumed he'd found it depressing too. I said something like, Oh well, at least they can laugh about it, and Daniel said, Hmmm. And then, after a minute's silence, he said, 'Kate, where are we going?'

I thought he meant his place or mine. He rents the top floor of a dilapidated old house about half a mile from the university. It's dark and shambling with small windows and vast, squat, overactive radiators which belt out heat in such quantities that he has to leave the windows open all year round, but there's room to turn around in it, which is more than can be said for my tacky little box, so we spend most of our time there. I said, 'Yours?'

He was driving. I have always liked Daniel's profile – like a friendly hawk – but now, lit up intermittently by the lights of oncoming cars, he looked uncharacteristically serious. He glanced at me and said, 'That's not what I mean.'

Something in his voice made my heart give a slight lurch. Daniel doesn't dramatize anything. He has a humorous take on life, or would like you to think he has, and regardless of the subject being discussed his tone is almost always light and vaguely amused. And it was now, but underneath it you could detect something else, though I wasn't sure what. I said, 'Sorry. What did you mean?'

He hesitated and then said, 'Do you realize that we've been going out more than a year?'

'Yes. Yes, I know.'

'The thing is, I'm not sure that we're . . . getting anywhere. I have no idea what you feel about . . . well, anything, really. Whether the relationship's even important to you.'

'It is,' I said quickly, looking at him.

'How important? Somewhat important? Quite important? Very important? Tick one.'

'Very. Very important.'

'Well, that's a relief.'

He was silent for a bit. I didn't say anything. I sat tightly, my hands gripped in my lap.

He said, 'But there's nothing to actually . . . show that, you know? That the relationship's important to you. I honestly didn't know. I mean, what do we talk about? Work. Friends and colleagues, mostly in relation to their work. We go to bed together, which is great – really great – but then we roll over and talk about what we're going to do tomorrow at work. Work's important. Absolutely. But it's not the only thing, is it?'

He stopped at a red light and sat staring at it as if it had the answer to something. I stared at it too.

'I still feel I know almost nothing about you.' He glanced at me and tried to smile. 'I'd like to get to know you. We've been going out for over a year and I think it's time I got to know you. Do you . . . I don't know if I'm explaining this properly . . . there seems to be some-thing . . .' he took his hand off the steering wheel and gestured, a flat movement, palm outwards as if against a wall, '. . . some barrier. Something in the way. As if you're only letting a small part of yourself . . . I don't know. I don't know how to put it.'

After a moment he looked at me again and attempted another smile. 'But it's a problem. I think you should know it's a problem.'

The light turned green. We moved on.

I was frightened. I'd had no idea he felt like that. I was appalled at the possibility that he was saying things were over, and shocked by how much that mattered to me.

You must understand: I had never thought that I would really love anyone. It hadn't been on the cards, as far as I was concerned. To be honest, I had thought that such intensity of feeling was beyond me. When I 'discovered' Daniel, if I can put it like that, I think I was somewhat dazed by the mere fact of his existence. I did not analyse my feelings too deeply, or let myself agonize about his, maybe because I was afraid that if I found I loved and needed him too much he would be bound to disappear. People I love and need have a habit of disappearing from my life. For the same reason I didn't let myself think too much about the future – *our* future. I just hoped for the best.

It's only with hindsight that I'm able to say all this. I wasn't aware of any of it at the time. I hadn't thought in terms of our relationship growing or evolving – it had never occurred to me that that was necessary or even desirable. I was fatalistic; I thought that it would work or it wouldn't, and there was very little I could do about it. Hoping for the best. I suppose it's like driving with your eyes closed.

I didn't know what to say to him. How to make him understand. I was very upset. I said, 'Daniel, I'm just not good at . . . talking about that sort of thing. Love and so on. But it doesn't mean I don't feel it.'

'I know that. But it's more than that, Kate.'

'What then?'

He didn't say anything for a moment. Then he said, 'You could involve me in other aspects of your life. Other things that are important to you.'

He didn't actually say, You could introduce me to your family, but I knew that was what he meant, or part of it. He meant that for starters I should take him home and introduce him to Luke and Bo. And to Matt.

The thing was, that was the one thing I couldn't even imagine doing. I had no idea why. I still can hardly understand it. I knew that he would like them, I knew that they would like him, and yet I found the idea absolutely impossible to deal with. It was ridiculous. I told myself it was ridiculous.

He had turned down a side street and pulled over to the kerb. I didn't know how long we'd been there, the engine running, snow hissing down on the windshield.

I said to him, 'I'll try, Daniel. I'll really try.'

He nodded. I wished that he would say something – say that he understood – but he did not; he put the car in gear, and drove me home to my flat. And since then a month had passed and we had not referred to it. But it was there between us. It hadn't gone away.

So I knew what he would feel, if he had seen the invitation from Matt. He would see it as the perfect opportunity, which of course it was.

He put the photograph of Simon down on the table, carefully, as if he guessed that it had some special significance for me. And because of his care I almost managed to invite him, right then. Almost managed to force myself to overcome whatever it was. But Matt was very much in my mind because of the dream, and suddenly I had a vivid mental image of the two of them meeting. Smiling and shaking hands. I saw it quite clearly; Matt enquiring about the trip, Daniel saying, It was great. Nice scenery. The two of them moving towards the house. Matt saying, 'You're at the university aren't you? Microbiology, Kate was saying...' And all at once resentment welled up in me so strongly that it took my breath away. I looked down at the report in front of me, tasting bitterness like metal in my mouth.

'Kate?'

I looked up at him reluctantly. He was frowning at me,

looking puzzled. Daniel Crane, youngest full professor in the Zoology Department, standing in the middle of my living room looking puzzled, because there was one detail in his life that wasn't quite perfect.

I wanted to say, You have had it so easy. So *easy*. You may have worked hard but luck has been with you all the way, and I bet you don't even know it. You're a clever man, I know that, I'm not denying that, but I have to say that compared to him, you're nothing out of the ordinary. Not really. Not compared to Matt.

'Is something wrong?'

'No,' I said. 'Why?'

'You look . . .'

I waited for him to go on, but he didn't. He picked up his coffee and sipped at it, still watching me. I thought, I can't do it. I just can't. If he's seen it – well, too bad. So be it.

I said, 'I'm nearly finished,' and went on with the marking.

Nine

N OT LONG ago I attended a conference in Edmonton to give a paper on the effect of pesticides on the life of still-water ponds. It wasn't a particularly brilliant conference but on the way back we flew very low over northern Ontario, and that in itself made the trip worthwhile. I was staggered by the vastness of it. The emptiness. We flew over miles and miles of nothing, of rocks and trees and lakes, beautiful and desolate and remote as the moon. And then below us I suddenly saw a thin grey-white line, weaving about in the middle of all that nothingness, finding its way around lakes and swamps and granite outcrops. And up ahead, as if it were a balloon and that fragile line a piece of string attached to it, a small clearing appeared at the side of a lake. There were fields marked out in the clearing, and a scattering of houses and several more grey-white lines knitting them all together. More or less at the centre, identifiable by its squat little spire and by the neat square of graveyard surrounding it, was the church, and beside that, in the middle of a battered patch of playground, the school.

It wasn't Crow Lake, but it might as well have been. I thought, Home.

And then I thought, Weren't we brave!

I didn't mean us in particular; I meant all those who dared to live remote from their fellows in such a vast and silent land.

Anyway, since then, when I think of home I often seem to see it from the air. I home in on it, so to speak, circling lower and lower so that more and more details become clear, until finally I see us, the four of us. Generally we seem to be in church, for some reason. There we are, two boys and two girls, sitting in a row, Bo not quite as well behaved as she would have been if our mother had been there, but not too bad, considering, and the rest of us quiet and attentive. It is possible that our clothes aren't too clean and that our shoes aren't polished, but I don't get low enough to see that.

It is odd that I always see the four of us, because we were four only for the first year. After that Matt was no longer with us. But of course that was the most significant year. It seems to me that more happened in that year than in all the other years of my childhood put together.

*

AUNT ANNIE stayed with us until the middle of September. Having been brought forcibly to the conclusion that I might not survive the break-up of the family, she was obliged to accept Luke's plan to give up his career in order to 'bring up the girls'. She wasn't happy about it, but there was no option, so she stayed until we were all safely settled into term-time and then took her leave.

I remember taking her to the station in our new (old) car. There would have been no need to go all that way –

we could have flagged down the train as it passed the Northern Side Road – but I suppose Matt and Luke felt that wasn't a sufficiently dignified send-off. I remember the train, how huge it was and how black, and the way it panted in the heat like a dog. I remember how amazed by it Bo was. Luke was carrying her and she kept taking his face in her hands and turning his head to look at it, insisting that he be amazed too.

Aunt Annie didn't say goodbye. When the time came to board she said for the second time that she was appointing me letter-writer-in-chief, and for the third time that we were to phone if there were problems, and then she climbed quite nimbly onto the box-step the conductor had put down for her and up into the train. We watched her make her way down inside the car, the conductor behind her carrying her bag. She sat down in a seat by the window and waved to us. It was a cheerful, childish wave, a folding and unfolding of the fingers. I remember it because both it and her smile contrasted oddly with the fact that there were tears running down her cheeks. Take no notice of the tears, her smile and her fingers said. So we took no notice of them, as if they were nothing to do with Aunt Annie, and waved gravely back.

I REMEMBER the drive home; all four of us sat in the front, Matt driving, Luke holding Bo on his lap, myself between them. No one said a word. When we turned into the driveway Luke looked across at Matt and said, 'Here we are then.'

Matt said, 'Yeah.'

'You OK about everything?'

'Sure.'

He looked worried though, and not very happy.

95

And Luke? Luke looked fiercely happy. Luke looked like a man going gloriously into battle, knowing that God was on his side.

ONE OTHER thing occurred that day; an incident unconnected to Aunt Annie's departure. At the time, none of us thought anything of it, and in fact it was a long time before I even thought of it again, and longer still before I realized that it might have had some significance.

It took place in the evening, after supper, while Matt and I were doing the dishes and Luke was getting Bo ready for bed.

Aunt Annie had left the house in almost painfully good order. In the final days before her departure she had scoured every surface, washed every window, and laundered every scrap of material in the house from the curtains on down. No doubt she knew Luke well enough by then to know that this was the last contact with soap and water many of the items would ever have, but I imagine in her concern over us she was also making a bargain with God: if she did everything in her power to get us off to a good start, He would be obliged to do everything in His to make sure that we came to no harm. A bargain is a bargain.

So Matt and I were standing in our gleaming kitchen, washing our shining saucepans and drying them with tea towels which had been washed, boiled, starched and ironed until they looked and felt like sheets of polished paper. Bo and Luke came in, Bo wearing preternaturally clean pyjamas and demanding a drink. Luke got her a glass of juice from the refrigerator, waited for her to drink it, and then picked her up and instructed her to say goodnight. He was being firm, letting her know right from the word go that now he was the boss, and Bo was in such good spirits at having — as she saw it — vanquished Aunt Annie that she let him think he was getting away with it.

'Say goodnight to the galley slaves,' Luke said.

Bo was looking out of the window. She turned her head and beamed obediently at Matt and me but then she pointed out into the dusk and said, 'Dat man!'

It was just getting dark. We had the lights on in the kitchen, but you could still make out the shapes of individual trees. And if you looked hard you could also see a dark shape standing far enough back that it almost merged into the woods which seemed to draw in around the house at night. We all looked out and the shadow moved, slid a little further back.

Matt frowned. 'Looks like Laurie Pye.'

Luke nodded. He went to the door and opened it and called, 'Hey, Laurie!'

The shadow hesitated, and then came slowly forward. Luke shifted Bo to his other arm and held the door open. 'How're you doin', Laurie? Come on in.'

Laurie stopped a few feet from the door. 'Naw,' he said. 'It's OK.'

'Come in,' Luke repeated. 'Come have a glass of juice or something. What can we do for you?'

Matt and I had come to the door too and Laurie looked briefly at us, dark eyes just flicking over us. He shook his head and said, 'Naw, it's OK. It doesn't matter.' And he turned and left.

That was all.

We watched him fade back into the woods. Matt and Luke looked at each other. Luke let the door close gently.

'Odd,' Matt said.

'You think something's wrong?'

'No idea.'

We thought no more about it. Matt and I went back to the dishes and Luke put Bo to bed, and that was that.

Looking back, I think he must have come hoping to talk to either Luke or Matt. I can't think what else he could have come for. He knew both of them better than almost anyone outside his own family – they'd been working side by side with him in his father's fields for years – and if he trusted anyone he probably trusted them.

Against that, I can't actually imagine Laurie Pye talking to anyone. I can't see that stark white face, those disturbing eyes, and imagine him uttering the words that he must have so badly needed to say.

The only other possibility I can think of is that he came almost accidentally. He'd gone out for a walk and suddenly found himself outside our house – though even that suggests that, consciously or unconsciously, he was looking for someone to talk to.

Whatever the reason, he stood outside in the gradually increasing darkness, looking in. Watching. I can imagine how it looked to him. The stress and anxiety Matt and Luke were still labouring under, Bo's vulnerability, my own still-traumatized state – none of that would have been visible to him. What he would have seen was the clean, orderly house, the quiet, cheerful domestic scene, the four of us getting on with our lives, helping each other, the eldest carrying the youngest in his arms. It must have looked idyllic. It must have made the idea of coming in and talking about what was going on in his own home seem impossible, completely out of the question. If Bo had been screaming or Matt and Luke arguing or even if we hadn't all been together in that shining kitchen, it might have been possible. He'd just picked a bad night.

*

No jobs turned up in town that would take Luke for the peculiar hours he wanted to work, but he got himself a job working at the McLeans' store. I have my doubts, thinking about it now, that Mr and Mrs McLean really needed help. They'd been running the store for twenty years and had always managed just fine. Still, they let on that they could use Luke for a couple of hours a day and it didn't occur to any of us that perhaps it was another act of charity.

They were a strange family. Strange individually and stranger still as a family group. If you took any group of children and set them on one side of a room and any group of parents and set them on the other, and then were told to match them up, Sally would have been positively the last child you would have matched with Mr and Mrs McLean. For a start, they were small and mousy, both of them, while Sally was quite tall and had that startling hair. Then there was the fact that Mr and Mrs McLean were famous for being shy, while Sally, particularly in her teens, was famous for being the reverse. Her body language, for example; the way she stood, pelvis forward, breasts lifted, chin delicately raised . . . I am sure that was not a language Mrs McLean ever spoke, or Mr McLean ever understood.

The other thing they were famous for was loving children. They would stand together behind the long dark counter that ran half the length of the store and if a child walked in, those shy smiles would change to beams of purest pleasure. They should have had a dozen of their own but Sally was their only one. They must have been well into their forties when she arrived – they were quite elderly compared to other parents I knew. I imagine they 'tried' for years, and for years nothing happened, and then in the way of such things, long after they'd accepted that it was God's will that they be childless, along came Sally. A surprise, as they say. And I imagine she continued to surprise them too.

So, Luke went to work for Mr and Mrs McLean. I don't remember what I thought of the arrangement. I imagine I didn't think about it much. I liked the store, though, or had liked it in the old days, when I had accompanied my mother on her weekly shopping expeditions. It was a big old barn of a building, made of unfinished planking and lined with rough wooden shelves, and it was crammed to the rafters with everything you could think of – fruit and vegetables in quart or bushel baskets, sliced bread, tins of beans, packets of raisins, pitchforks, soap, knitting wool, mousetraps, rubber boots, long johns, toilet paper, rolling pins, shotgun cartridges, writing paper, Ex-Lax. My mother would give me part of her list (with the items printed very neatly so that I could read them), and I would wander up and down the aisles until I found whatever it was, and put it in my basket. Frequently my mother and I would pass each other, and we would both smile, and she would ask me how I was making out or if I had happened to notice raisins, say, or tinned peaches, on my travels. When we had both gathered our purchases we would take them up to the counter, where Mr McLean would put them in bags for us while Mrs McLean wrote down the prices in thick black pencil, both of them beaming at me all the while.

I love the memories of those expeditions. They are among the few I have of the two of us alone together.

Now Luke was installed behind the counter too, though beaming wasn't something that came naturally to him. His hours were Monday to Friday from four in the afternoon when Matt got home from school until the store closed at six. On Monday evenings he worked later, driving the McLeans' truck into town to pick up the week's supplies and then stacking the shelves.

Sometimes Sally went with him on those trips. In the light of what transpired later, I expect she sat closer to him than was necessary and steadied herself, when they lurched over bumps and into potholes, by placing a hand on his thigh. What Luke felt about that I can only guess at. All the usual things, no doubt, plus the confusion that came from an awareness of his circumstances.

On Saturdays he worked mornings at Calvin Pye's farm and Matt worked afternoons. As far as I know, nothing further was said about Laurie's strange appearance at our door. Calvin could have used Luke six days a week, but Luke was restricted by his determination to look after Bo and me himself. More than one neighbour had offered to take us for a few hours each afternoon, but neither he nor Matt wanted that. Bo had taken against strangers in a big way and I was giving them cause for concern as well. Apparently I was still very withdrawn, and they felt the less disruption I had to deal with the better.

Matt's idea of baby-sitting, of course, was to take Bo and me back to the ponds, and as long as the fine weather lasted – and it lasted well into October that year – we went almost every afternoon. I recommend it, by the way – pond watching – as therapy. There is something about water, even if you have no particular interest in the life forms within it. It is the medium we came from, after all. We were all rocked by water at our beginnings.

The only fly in the ointment of those afternoons, as far as I was concerned, was that we often met Marie Pye on our way back. I was always tired by that stage, and hungry, and ready to go home, and I would circle around Matt, kicking impatiently at the railroad ties while he and Marie chatted. I couldn't think what they had to talk about that they couldn't talk about on Saturdays when Matt was at the farm. Both of them were weighed down, Marie with shopping, Matt with Bo sitting like a sandbag on his shoulders; you would have thought both of them would want to get home as quickly as possible. And yet there they stood, shifting about under their loads, talking about things that didn't matter. Minutes would drag by and I would dig holes in the dust with my shoe and chew my finger fretfully. Finally Matt would say, 'Guess I'd better go,' and Marie would say, 'Yes,' and they'd continue talking for another ten minutes.

Once she said to him hesitantly, 'How are you, Matt? Are you . . . OK?'

Everyone asked us that all the time, and what you had to say was, Yes, thanks, we're doing fine. This time though, Matt didn't reply straight away. I glanced up at him and saw that he was looking away, looking off into the woods beyond the tracks. Then his gaze came back to Marie and he smiled at her and said, 'Just about.'

She made a sort of gesture, an involuntary movement of her arms, despite their being full of groceries. Matt shrugged, and smiled again, and said, 'Anyway. I'd better go.'

I WONDER, now, if Matt was hit harder by our parents' death than any of us. Everyone assumed that I was the one most affected, but I wonder if that was so. I had Matt to turn to. He had nobody. He'd turned eighteen at the beginning of September, and it was assumed – by him as well as everyone else – that he was adult and would cope.

I hope Bo and I were of some comfort to him. I'm sure the ponds themselves were. I'm sure he drew comfort from the continuity of life there. The fact that the loss of one life did not destroy the community. The fact that the ending of life was part of the pattern.

As for Marie . . . I see now that he may also have found comfort in those brief meetings with Marie.

Ten

I SHOULD TELL you about the Pyes. Most of what I know
I learned from old Miss Vernon, during my high-school
years, when I was doing her vegetable garden. It's possible
that her memory wasn't too reliable, but on the other
hand she was actually there, she saw the family at virtually
every stage from Jackson Pye on down, so as sources go
she's pretty good. It wasn't only the Pyes she told me
about, of course; the entire history of Crow Lake and its
early inhabitants came rolling out over those rows of
carrots and beans. She'd talk while I worked and as I
progressed further and further down a row, so she'd raise
her voice to follow me, until suddenly she'd shout, 'Well
come and help me move, for goodness sake! How'm I
supposed to talk with you way over there?' And I'd go and
help her out of her kitchen chair and move it further
down the path beside the patch until I reached a place
where she could talk comfortably again.

According to her, Jackson Pye was quite a clever man. I
remember her asking me if I'd ever noticed the Pyes'
house. I didn't know what she was talking about – I'd seen
the Pyes' house about a million times – but afterwards I

went and looked at it again. It was a big wooden structure, set well back from the road. The front of the house was what Miss Vernon called 'handsome' in its proportions. It had very large sash windows on both sides of the front door and a wide, graceful verandah wrapping itself around three sides of the house. Jackson had left several large birches standing, fairly close, which provided shade in the summer and a bit of a wind-break in the winter. You could imagine sitting out on that verandah on a summer evening, listening to the breeze in the birches, relaxing after the labours of the day. That must surely have been what Jackson had in mind when he built it, though I can't quite imagine him sitting there. In fact, I don't recall ever seeing anyone sitting there. Relaxing wasn't something the Pyes went in for.

But as Miss Vernon said, it was a better than average house, particularly considering that it was designed and built by a man with no education of any kind. He designed the Janies' and the Vernons' houses as well and made a good job of them too. 'He had a picture in his head of how he wanted a place to look,' Miss Vernon said. 'And he could figure out how to make it come out just like the picture. Oh he was clever though. And a good farmer too. He chose his land well. The Pye farm's the best of the lot, you know. Well drained. Good soil, for these parts. It's better'n ours. Better'n Janie's. He could've had a real good place there, if only he hadn't fought with all his boys. Farmer needs sons, you know. Girls aren't worth as much. Well, some of them's all right, but most just don't have the muscle. Farming's hard work. You wouldn't know that, but it's hard work.' This when I'd been hoeing her garden for two hours in the blazing July sun.

'How many children did he have?' I asked. A lot of her stories about the old days didn't interest me much back then – kids aren't interested in the past, it's the future they're focused on – but the Pyes were an exception. Everyone's interested in catastrophe, and I had personal reasons as well for wanting to know about them by then.

'Seven. You carry on hoeing. You hoe and I'll talk, that way we're both doing what we're good at. Seven kids, five boys and two girls. The girls were twins, but both of them died when they were babies. I don't know what of, I was just little myself. Maybe scarlet fever. Anyways they both died.

'The boys, now let's see. Norman was the oldest. He was older than me by quite a bit. He ran away. I told you about that, didn't I? Went through the ice out on the lake one winter and was too scared of his daddy to go home. Next to him was Edward. Edward was a bit on the slow side. Mrs Pye'd had a hard time bringing him into the world and maybe it had something to do with that, I don't know. But he never did learn to read or write and his slowness just drove his daddy wild. Used to scream at him, Edward standin' there no more idea what was goin' on than a sheep.

'One day he just wandered off, right in the middle of being yelled at. Just turned around and walked off, as if all those years he'd been tryin' to put two and two together and he finally managed it, and the answer was, things weren't ever going to get any better. So off he went.

'That was two. Number three was Pete. You ever hear such a name? Peter Pye. Everyone called him Peter Piper, of course, always kept askin' how many pints of pickled peppers he could pick, must've nearly drove him crazy. But I guess that wasn't his biggest worry. No.'

She rattled her teeth, hunching over in her chair, staring into the past. I remember thinking how big her past was. Such a lot of it.

'You want some lemonade?' she said abruptly.

I nodded.

'Go get some then.'

My first task each afternoon that I came to her was to make a quart of lemonade and stick it in her smelly old refrigerator. Every few rows I'd be sent to get glasses for both of us, and every few glasses I'd have to help Miss Vernon get to her bathroom with a certain amount of urgency.

'What were we talking about?' she asked when we'd finished the lemonade, and I'd moved her chair down to the radishes.

'Jackson Pye's sons.'

'Oh yes. Where'd I get to?'

'You were just starting on Pete.'

'Pete,' she said, nodding. 'That's right.' She looked at me keenly. Her eyes were pale and milky, but even so I always got the impression she saw more than most people.

'I liked Pete. Really liked him. He liked me too.' She gave me a sly look. 'You probably won't believe that, being young. You think I was always like this.' The long jaw moved, ruminating. She reminded me of a horse – a very old horse, with sagging skin and whiskers, and almost no eyelashes left.

'He was a nice boy. Sweet, like his mother. She was a nice woman, poor soul. Funny thing, the Pye men always had good taste in women. You wouldn't think it. But Pete was like her. Quiet and sweet. Smart, too. He'd've done well in school if he'd been allowed to go. But he figured out sooner than the rest of 'em that the smart thing to do was move on. Told me he was going to go. Said he was goin' to Toronto. Wanted me to go with him. I didn't know what to do.'

She paused again, remembering. Watching her, I almost saw her young. Almost saw her fresh and pretty, looking into the face of this boy, wanting to go with him, wanting to stay at home. Torn. Trying to imagine what her life would turn out like if she went, what it would be like if she stayed.

'I didn't go. I was afraid to. I was only fifteen. My sister Nellie – she was a year younger than me – we were awful close, and I just couldn't see leavin' her, even for Pete.'

She sat for a while. Finally she stirred herself and looked at me.

'How old are you?'

'Fifteen.'

'Maybe you know what I mean then. Would you go off with some boy if you liked him? Right now, I mean. Just up and go.'

I shook my head. Privately I knew that I would never go off with some boy. I would go on my own, when I was ready. I knew that. I was working towards it. That was where the money Miss Vernon paid me went – into a special account, my 'university' account. Luke had arranged it for me, and I was grateful to him because I knew he could have used the extra cash. I worked very hard at school – harder than anyone I knew. I didn't much enjoy the social side of things – I was never 'one of the girls' – but I did enjoy working. The arts – languages and history, art and music – did not come easily to me, but I worked at them anyway. The sciences I loved, particularly biology. How could it have been otherwise? All of my grades were good. Luke studied my report cards carefully, looking bemused. 'You're just like Matt,' he said once. But he was wrong. I knew I was nothing like as clever as Matt.

'You can give me one of them radishes,' Miss Vernon said. 'I could just do with a radish.'

I picked a large radish and took it to her.

'Looks a good one. Have one yourself, if you like.'

I declined. Radishes on top of lemonade didn't tempt me.

'We all have choices. Sometimes you never know if you made the right one or not. Not much point in worryin' about it now. Anyways, that was Pete. Three gone, two left. Think of that poor woman watchin' her family trickle away. Brought seven children into the world and now she's down to two. I don't expect the ones that left ever wrote to her. They weren't given to that sort of thing. They just vanished off the face of the earth.

'OK. The two that's left are Arthur and Henry. They have an understanding between them that they're going to stick around no matter what, so's they both inherit the farm. It's plenty big enough for two and they reckon they've put so much work into it they're going to get it, no matter what.

'All this while, of course, time's moving on, and Nellie and me and the Pye boys are all in our late teens – maybe Arthur's twenty. And their future has become kind of important to Nellie and me because we've decided we're going to marry them.'

She gave a sharp cackle of laughter. 'Guess you think that's peculiar, 'specially seein' as I just said I liked Pete. But I waited a long time for Pete, hopin' he'd come back even though I knew deep down he wouldn't, and by the time I was nineteen I thought time was getting kinda short. As far as young men went, there wasn't what you'd call a whole lot of choice in Crow Lake back then. You probably think there isn't a whole lot of choice now, but it was a lot worse then. We were just the three families, and Struan was a good day's trip away, you didn't get to go there much. Frank Janie had a whole pack of boys but the Janies were an awful plain family. Not a very nice thing to say, but it's true. They were all scrawny and pasty faced. They were nice enough, but when you're young you're lookin' for more than nice. Or Nellie and I were anyway. To tell you the truth, we didn't give too much thought to what the Pye boys were actually like. We had this picture in our minds of the two of us, Nellie and me, settin' up home in that nice big farmhouse old Jackson had built. We saw ourselves chattin' and gigglin' away in the kitchen while we prepared their dinners, makin' apple pies at five o'clock in the morning so's we wouldn't be standin' over the stove in the heat of the day, doin' the garden and the chickens and the pigs, cleanin' the house – all the things our mother did only it'd be fun because Nellie and me would do it together. And we'd have children the same age as each other and the children would grow up together and never have a very clear idea who was their mother and who was their aunt. Oh we had the whole thing worked out. We saw ourselves sitting on that nice big verandah in the evenings with the mending on our laps, chatting away to each other while our men talked about this and that . . .'

She paused, looking at the picture in her mind, and then gave a snort. 'Two silly young girls, that's all we were. Playing at being grown up. We didn't have one sensible idea in our heads.' She ran the clawed fingers of one hand peevishly over the big swollen knuckles of the other. Seventy years on, the foolishness of her youth still annoyed her. She glared across the vegetable patch at me and said crossly, 'Unlike you, young Miss Morrison. My guess is you've got nothin' but sensible ideas in that head of yours. Too many sensible ideas. You want to try being young for a bit, while you still can. There's more to life than good grades, you know. More to life than being brainy.'

I didn't reply. I hated it when she told me things about myself. The previous week she had told me that I looked angry all the time, and that it was time I forgave whoever it was who'd made me so mad and got on with my life. I was so angry at her for saying it that I left without taking my money or saying goodbye.

Now she muttered to herself, watching me as I scratched out the weeds from round the roots of the radishes. It was extremely hot. I was barefoot, and the dark soil scorched the soles of my feet unless I scooped out little hollows to stand in. In the bushes behind us the cicadas sang their hymn of praise to the sun.

'You go and get us some more lemonade now,' Miss Vernon said, her voice still sharp. 'Get some cookies too. Then come and sit down here while you eat. It's a hot day.'

I went up to the house. I didn't much like Miss Vernon's house, for all that it had been well designed by Jackson Pye. It was too dark and too quiet and it smelled of old age and mice. I rinsed out our glasses and filled them again with lemonade, then got out the cookie tin and checked its contents. Cinnamon cookies. Cinnamon cookies meant Mrs Stanovich. Sour-cream cookies meant Mrs Mitchell. Date and raisin squares meant Mrs Tadworth. We Morrison children were not the only ones on

111

the consciences of the Good Women of Crow Lake. I balanced the glasses on top of the cookie tin and carried them back to the vegetable garden. I sat on the scorched grass beside Miss Vernon's chair and we munched cinnamon cookies and listened to the cicadas for a while, until we stopped being annoyed with the past and with each other.

'Where'd I get to?' Miss Vernon said at last.

'You and your sister had decided to marry Henry and Arthur Pye.'

'Ha!' she said. 'That's right! That's exactly right.'

She straightened herself in her chair, eyes narrowed, gazing off across her vegetable patch to the woods beyond and beyond the woods into her past. Facing it squarely and sternly now, the romantic notions of her girlhood long gone.

'We got this idea in our heads, Nellie and me. No sense to it at all – they hadn't courted us or anything. The odd bit of flirting here and there, nothin' more. Truth was, we didn't even know those two boys all that well. Sounds funny, since we grew up so close, with no one else to know. But they'd worked on that farm dawn till dusk almost since they could walk, they didn't ever have much in the way of free time. And they weren't ones for talkin'. Pete had been the only one given to talkin' and thinkin' about things. All Nellie and me really knew about Henry and Arthur Pye was that they were single and they were handsome. The Pye men were all handsome, every last one of 'em. Well, you know that yourself. Every one of 'em, once they'd got over the weedy stage, turned out tall and lean with that thick dark hair and those eyes of theirs. Nellie used to say their eyes were as dark as God's. Particularly Arthur and Henry – wonderful dark eyes.

They were big, husky boys too, bigger than their daddy. Bigger than our brothers.'

She sighed. 'Anyways, that was our plan, Nellie's and mine. We were going to marry the Pye boys. So we were glad to know that they were set on inheriting the farm. But of course, we all reckoned without old Jackson. You'd've thought he'd of learned his lesson, wouldn't you? He'd driven away three of his sons – more than half his labour force – you'd've thought any man would have realized he had to change, treat the ones he had left with some respect. But that seemed to be somethin' he couldn't learn.

'This particular winter he set them clearin' more land – choppin' down trees, clearin' away the undergrowth, diggin' out the tree roots. Awful hard work. My brothers were helping – all the families helped each other out – and they said when they arrived in the mornings the Pye boys were already hard at it and when they left at night they'd be hard at it still, and old Jackson wouldn't have let up cursing at them for a single minute the entire day. Until this one day, along towards dusk, Jackson yelled at Henry about somethin' and Henry stopped what he was doing; stood stock still for a moment, looking at the ground. And then he put down his axe and walked over to his father – you remember I said they were big boys? Well, he picked Jackson up by his neck.'

Miss Vernon clasped an arthritic old hand to her neck, close up under her chin.

'Like this. Lifted him right off the ground. He held him hard up against a tree for a minute or two, Jackson's legs danglin' and kickin' and his voice squeakin' out. My brothers said it would've been funny if it hadn't been so scary. And then Henry looked across at Arthur, who was standin' there with my brothers, not doin' anything to help his father, and said, "The farm's all yours, Art." And he lets his father drop, and walks off. Collects his stuff from the house and sets off down the road that very night.'

She sighed again and dropped her hands in her lap.

I picked a cinnamon cookie out of the tin and handed it to her, but she shook her head so I ate it myself. I chewed quietly, hoping that if I didn't disturb her she would go on, and eventually she did. She sounded tired, though, as if the memories themselves had taken their toll.

'Henry was to have been mine,' she said. 'I don't recall how Nellie and I worked out whose was whose, but I know Henry was to have been mine. But maybe he didn't know that, 'cause he didn't come to say goodbye. I thought of him, walking down that road; imagined his footprints exactly fitting the footprints of Pete, who'd gone before him. Edward and Norman too, of course – four sets of Pye footprints, all headed south, none of them ever coming back – but it was Pete I was thinking of. I remember thinking, There goes my last chance.'

She was silent for a while. Then she snorted again, but this time, rather than contempt, she seemed to be expressing wry acceptance.

'So Arthur got the farm,' she said.

She stopped again and began mumbling her teeth. I started to worry that she wasn't going to go on, so finally I prompted her. 'How about Nellie? Did Arthur marry her?'

'I'm comin' to that.' She gave me a sharp look. 'Have a little patience. It's a long story and it's wearin' me out.'

That was what I was afraid of – that she'd get worn out before she got to the end. I felt I needed to know everything that happened on that stricken farm. I didn't want to wait until the next day. What if she died in the night or had a stroke and lost the power of speech? I would never learn the rest of the story. For some reason it seemed to me that that would be a calamity. I almost felt that if I knew the whole of the past, if I knew exactly what had happened to previous generations of Pyes, I could slip back in time and straighten out their story, set it on a different course so that it couldn't collide with our own.

So I had difficulty restraining my impatience. I had to resist the urge to prod her, to nag at her to keep going. Both of us had forgotten that I was supposed to be weeding her garden. We sat on, she in her chair, me on the grass beside her, while the heat gradually faded out of the day.

'So, what happened next . . .' She rattled her teeth, scrolling back and forth through time. 'What happened next is Mrs Pye died. That's right. Pneumonia. Quite soon after Henry left. And about a couple of months after that Arthur asked Nellie to marry him. I remember watching them through the kitchen window. They were outside, out by the barn. I knew what he was askin' because of the way Nellie was squirmin' inside her clothes. You could see how pleased she was even from behind. She had an expressive seat, that girl. She said yes, of course. But our father said no. He said he had nothin' against Arthur personally but some day someone was going to get killed on that farm and he didn't want any daughter of his to be there when it happened. So that was that. Nellie went off with an itinerant preacher a year later. I'll tell you about that some other time, that's a story all on its own, and it served her right.

'Jackson and Arthur carried on alone. Some said Arthur didn't speak to his daddy the last three years of his life, but

115

I don't know how they'd know that for sure – what about at supper? How'd they know Arthur didn't say, "Pass the salt" or "What'd you do with the bread knife"? Anyway, one thing's for sure, Arthur was a happy man the day old Jackson was laid to rest. That I know, 'cause I was at the funeral. He just couldn't stop grinnin'. Smirked the whole way through the service. Wouldn't've surprised me one bit if you told me he'd come back after everyone else had gone and danced barefoot on the grave.

'Next day he saddles up and heads off down the road, and six weeks later back he comes with a wife.'

I looked at her uneasily. I was starting to feel a sense of foreboding – almost a premonition, as if unknown to myself I had always known the path this story was to take. As if the knowledge had been born in me and merely remained buried until now.

Miss Vernon was nodding at me as if she knew what I was feeling and agreed with it all. 'So that was the next Mrs Pye,' she said. 'Nice little thing. Big blue eyes. Looked quite a bit like Arthur's mother, as a matter of fact.

'She and Arthur set up home in that big grey farmhouse. Had it all to themselves, a fresh start, you might say. A year later, she had a baby. Next year she had another. Six kids in all, three boys and three girls, a nice-sized family. Things should have been fine. But guess what? Arthur quarrelled with all of them. Every single one. Girls got married when they were hardly even into their teens – anything to get away, see. I don't know where they went to but none of them ever came back. And two of the boys went too. Followed their uncles down that road . . .'

She shook her head and made a tutting sound, her tongue against her teeth.

'My, but the Pye women must've hated that road. Must've seemed like it had a "One Way" sign on it. Like in those fairy stories they tell you when you're little. That big mountain that swallowed up all the children – you know, the story with the rats.'

I nodded.

'Well what was it? I keep forgetting names of things. Makes me so mad.'

'The Pied Piper.'

'That's the one. Children all got swallowed up by that mountain. That's how it must've seemed to Mrs Pye. To all the Mrs Pyes. Off they all go, down that road . . .'

I thought of the road. White, dusty, unremarkable. The way out. I wanted to go down it myself, but even then – and I think I was at my bitterest and most resentful at that time, poor Miss Vernon saw the worst of me – I knew that I didn't want it as badly as those Pye children must have.

'Anyways, there was still one son left. Know who he was?'

I sorted through the generations, trying to tie in what she'd told me with what I'd known before, and then realized that there was only one person it could have been.

'Calvin?'

'Right. Calvin Pye. He was the one that stayed. My opinion is he hated his daddy worse than any of them. And he was scareder of him too. But he was still the one that stayed. Stubborn. Must have been tough for him. Skinny little kid, small for his age. Didn't come into his strength till he was about eighteen or so – so the work must have been real hard. And all the while, Arthur screamin' at him . . .'

All the way through her story I had had a picture in my mind, at every stage, of whichever one she was talking

117

about, but now I found that I couldn't picture Calvin as a boy. I kept seeing Laurie instead. Laurie, a skinny little kid, small for his age, labouring day after day in the fields, accompanied always – *always* – by his father's abuse.

'He never answered back,' Miss Vernon was saying, and I was confused until I remembered it was Calvin she was talking about. 'Even when he was fully grown. Never dared to. Too scared. He just stood there and took it, just swallowed whatever he was feelin'. Must've just about scalded out his insides.'

So there was a difference, after all. As a child, Laurie too had burned bright with swallowed rage, but when he was older he did answer back. Oh, definitely, he did answer back.

Miss Vernon was rambling on. 'And then his mother died. Let me see . . . how old would Calvin have been . . . about twenty-one, twenty-two. She died standin' at the kitchen stove, makin' gravy. Never was one to make a fuss. Got the whole dinner cooked, all bar the gravy. I know that 'cause I helped lay her out. Gravy was all stuck on the bottom of the pan – the men never thought to take it off the stove. I had an awful job to get it clean.

'We couldn't any of us understand why Calvin stayed after that. Thought surely he'd go. Couldn't imagine him wantin' the farm that bad. But he stayed. Maybe he thought his daddy was goin' to pass on soon, but he was wrong about that. Arthur was a fit man, he lasted another eighteen years. Imagine it. Livin' and workin' together every day for eighteen years, hatin' each other's guts. It's enough to curdle your blood just thinkin' about it.'

She shook her head and clicked her tongue against her teeth again. 'Families,' she said. She shifted about in her chair, easing herself this way and that. I hoped she wasn't

118

going to say she needed the bathroom. I was afraid she'd lose the thread, now, at the last minute, so close to the point where my own knowledge took over. But it was all right, she carried on.

'Where was I?'

'Arthur and Calvin were left together.'

'That's right. That's right. Just the two of them in that big old house, busy hating each other. They must've been good at it by the end. Practice makes perfect. Finally Arthur had a stroke. He was roarin' at Calvin about somethin' across a field of sugar beets and he just dropped dead. Killed by rage, you might say, and a blessed relief for everybody.'

She paused again. 'So how old's that make Calvin by the time he's finally free? You work it out. I never could add up.'

'Thirty-nine or forty.'

'That's about right. A middle-aged man. But never mind, he's free at last and he's got a good farm. What do you think happens next? You tell me.'

I swallowed. The apprehension I'd felt earlier had congealed now in the pit of my stomach. I said, 'He went to New Liskeard and found a wife?'

She nodded. 'That's right. You figured it out. Spotted the pattern.'

We sat for a bit, listening to the silence. The cicadas had stopped singing. For years I had tried to catch them in the act of stopping – to hear the very last cicada sound the very last note of the day – but I'd never managed it. Now the woods were eerily quiet, waiting for the creatures of the night to begin their shift.

'I could do with another cookie now,' Miss Vernon said.

I passed her one and she ate it slowly, mumbling crumbs down the front of her dress. Mouth still full she said, 'She was a nice woman, too, only I forget her name. Pye men always had good taste in women. What was her name, then? You should remember it.'

'Alice,' I said.

'That's right. Alice. She was a nice woman. Started off full of life, like they all did. Bakin' for the church functions, joinin' the sewing bee. Think she even played the organ in church for a while. That's right. She did. But then Calvin said the practisin' took up too much time so she had to give it up. Joyce Tadworth took over, she didn't know one note from another. It was pure torture listenin' to her . . .'

She gazed off into the darkness of the woods, remembering discords. After a minute she said vaguely, 'Alice had a lot of miscarriages. Must've had about two miscarriages for every live birth, poor woman. So she ended up with just the three. I never did get a proper hold on their names. You'd know them, though. You don't need me to tell you about them.'

I thought of Rosie. She'd been like some poor seedling accidentally sown outside somebody's back door – spindle-thin, pale and weedy, trodden on every time she raised her head. I had a sudden vivid memory of her standing beside her desk – our desks had been next to each other so she'd also been standing beside mine. We'd both have been about six at the time, in Grade One. Miss Carrington must have asked her a question; you had to stand to answer questions. But Rosie couldn't answer it. She'd stood there, silent, and after a minute I'd noticed that her whole body was shaking. Miss Carrington said, quite kindly, 'I'm sure you know this, Rosie. Give it a try.' And there was a faint trickling noise, and the smell of urine, and I'd suddenly seen a little puddle growing on the floor around Rosie's shoes. Miss Carrington didn't ask her any questions after that.

That was Rosie. And then there was Marie. The way she always stood, when she wasn't carrying things, with her arms wrapped round herself, hugging her elbows as if she were cold, even on a hot day. Her voice always so soft and timid – too soft and too timid. It had irritated me. I remembered listening to her talking with Matt, and being irritated by the sound of it.

And Laurie, who'd taken by far the lion's share of Calvin's wrath. I'd had no idea, at the time, of what his life was like. Such things were completely beyond my imagining. All I was aware of was that he almost never met your eyes, and that when he did, there was something in his own eyes that obliged you to look away.

Miss Vernon stirred and sighed. She said, 'You tell me something now. You're supposed to be smart, so they tell me. How come all the Pye men took such a dislike to their own kids? How could that happen, three generations running? Is it somethin' in their blood? Or is it just 'cause that's the only way they know to behave? 'Cause it doesn't seem natural, to me. Doesn't make any sense.'

'I don't know,' I said.

'No. Didn't think you would. You're not that smart. Nobody knows.'

We sat in silence. Shade was spreading out from the woods, moving stealthily, creeping up on us. I slapped a mosquito and the skin of my arm felt cool.

'Anyways,' Miss Vernon said. 'Guess you know the rest. Probably know it better than I do.'

I nodded. I knew the rest.

She brushed crumbs off her lap with her twisted old hand.

'Do you want me to pick some vegetables for your supper?' I said.

'Beans. But first you've got to get me to the bathroom. I've left it kinda late.'

So we shuffled off to her bathroom, Miss Vernon and I, and left the history of the Pyes to be absorbed once more, slowly, like mist off the lake, into the cool evening air.

Eleven

I WAS FIFTEEN when Miss Vernon told me the Pyes' story. At that age I was capable, though only just, of fully comprehending all that she said, of wondering at it and seeing the relevance it had to what had taken place in my own generation. I wouldn't go so far as to say that it made me any more sympathetic or understanding, but at least it helped me put things in context. If I'd heard the story at the age of seven, I'm sure it would have meant nothing to me at all. For a start, the very young are necessarily self-centred. What do they care for the tragic or untidy lives of their neighbours? Their primary business is survival, and their preoccupation is with those who help them to survive. Of course their business is also learning about the world around them – hence the boundless curiosity of young animals – but survival comes first, and for me that year, survival – at least in the emotional sense – was as much as I could manage.

That awful year, as every year, I walked to school each day along the railroad tracks. It was the shortest route; the road meandered around, while the railroad tracks ran straight. In fact the straightness of them amazes me now, though I never gave it a thought as a child. When the crew building the railroad came to an obstacle they blasted their way through it or hacked it down or filled it in or built a bridge over it, whatever was called for.

I have seen old photographs of those men and they don't look like heroes. They are leaning on their picks, their hats shoved back on their heads, grinning at the camera with mouthfuls of bad teeth. Most of them look to be on the small side, lean to the point of skinniness, their muscles corded and stringy rather than bulging out of their shirts. Quite a few look as if they didn't have enough to eat when they were growing up. But they must have had huge stamina and endurance, no doubt about that.

The path they cut was three or four times wider than the tracks themselves and over the years it had filled itself with wildflowers and grasses — fireweed and milkweed, golden rod and Queen Anne's lace, harebell and goat's beard — so that I walked along the rails each morning as if walking through a meadow. By September everything was in seed. The seed heads shook their contents over you as you passed and the burrs clung to your clothes. Some days thousands of milkweed pods would burst open together, triggered by the heat of the sun; thousands and thousands of small silent explosions repeating themselves in salvos down the miles of tracks. On those days I walked through clouds of silken down drifting about like smoke in the morning breeze.

I passed through all of this as if I were sleep-walking. I was conscious of it but I did not really see it. At school it was the same; Miss Carrington would lecture us on arithmetic or grammar or history or geography and I would sit, politely attentive, and take in not a single word. I would be watching the dust-motes, perhaps, as they hung in the broad bands of sunlight that slanted through the classroom windows. Or I'd be listening to the thunder of the sugar beets as they were loaded into hopper-cars, ready for their trip south. The railroad tracks ran past the bottom of the school yard and the siding where the hopper-cars waited their turn to be loaded was directly opposite the school. The weigh-scales were there, and the hopper itself – a dilapidated wooden structure shaped like an inverted pyramid – and the long metal and rubber arm of the conveyor belt, which stuck up into the air at an angle and could be swung out over the hopper-cars. All through September trucks from the farms would jolt along the rutted path beside the tracks and dump their loads of beets into the hopper with a roar which brought Miss Carrington to a standstill. And then the conveyor belt would be switched on and the beets would start to drop, first one at a time and then in a steady rumble, into the huge hollow drum of a hopper-car. In other years, after the first week or so back at school I hadn't noticed the noise much; we all grew up with that roar and like the sound of the waves it took its place as part of the background to our lives. That September though, there seemed to be something hypnotic about it. I listened, fascinated, and the dull, heavy rumble seemed to sink into my soul.

Miss Carrington came home with me. She said, 'May I walk home with you, Kate? It's been a while since I saw those handsome brothers of yours. Do you suppose they'd mind if I dropped in?'

It must have been early October by then. The days were still warm but the evenings were cool and the dark came quickly.

125

I didn't take Miss Carrington along the railroad tracks because she was wearing a long skirt and I thought she'd never get the burrs out of it. We walked home the proper way, along the road, though it took longer and was very dusty. She talked about her home, which was another farming community, though larger and not as remote as ours. She'd lived in a big farmhouse and they'd had a horse.

She said, 'I have brothers too – in fact I have three. But no sister. You're ahead of me there.'

She smiled down at me. Her hair was pulled back loosely and tied with a plain blue ribbon. She was tall and thin and her face was too long to be called pretty, but she had nice eyes. They were large and very dark brown, and her hair was brown too, and on sunny days it had red and gold lights in it.

Luke and Bo were out at the side of the house when we came down the drive, hanging out laundry, though it was late and the sun was already losing its heat. Matt was not home yet – the bus dropped him off at the end of the road about four o'clock. Luke stopped when he saw Miss Carrington. He left a diaper hanging by one peg, picked Bo up and came to meet us. The diaper didn't look very clean. There were stains on it and it was a long way off white.

Miss Carrington said, 'Hello, Luke. I hope you don't mind. I just came to see how you were getting on.'

Luke looked embarrassed. He didn't like Miss Carrington seeing him doing diapers. He said, 'Um, fine, thanks. I'm a bit behind . . .' He gestured at the laundry. 'I meant to get it out this morning but Bo was into everything.'

He was always late hanging out the diapers. They were his least favourite job and he put off doing them all day.

He put Bo down but she whined and started climbing his trouser leg so he picked her up again. He ran his free hand through his hair and said, 'Anyway, would you like a drink or something?' He looked vaguely towards the house.

'No no,' Miss Carrington said. 'I'm not staying . . . I just wondered how you were making out.'

Luke nodded. 'Fine thanks. It's going OK.' He hesitated. 'But look, come in and sit down for a bit. It's hot out here. You must want a drink of something. There's um . . . tea . . .'

'A glass of water,' Miss Carrington said. 'A glass of water would be lovely. But I won't come in. I only wanted to see how you were doing and to have a quick word about something . . .'

'Oh,' Luke said, looking at her. 'Oh. Right. Um, Kate, would you get Miss Carrington a glass of water? You . . . um . . . might have to wash a glass.'

I went up to the house. It was a mess. The kitchen was the worst; there were dirty plates and cups all over the counter and bits of food lying around. At some stage Bo had pulled all the pots and pans out of the bottom cupboards and you had to pick your way through them to get at anything. I found a glass and washed it under the tap and then filled it with cold water and took it back out. Milk had dried in it and there was still a white circle at the bottom, but I hoped Miss Carrington wouldn't notice.

She and Luke were talking. Luke was still holding Bo; she was sucking her thumb and clutching a clothes peg in the same hand. The clothes peg was digging into her cheek, but she didn't seem to notice. She was giving Miss Carrington her narrow-eyed look, but Miss Carrington was concentrating on what Luke was saying. He was

127

asking her a question. Something about Dr Christopherson.

'I don't think so,' Miss Carrington said. 'I doubt there's much he could do, quite honestly. I think it's probably just a matter of time. I just think we should keep in touch. You know, monitor the progress . . .'

She saw me coming with her glass of water and smiled at me. 'Thank you, Kate. That's just the ticket.'

'Joos,' Bo said, reaching for the glass.

'Could you take her, Kate?' Luke said. 'Could you get her a drink and a piece of bread or something? She didn't have much lunch.'

He passed Bo down to me, and I staggered under her weight. She took her thumb out and grinned at me. 'KatieKatieKate,' she said, and showed me her clothes peg.

I carried her into the house and got her some juice. Then I got some bread out of the bread tin and cut a slice.

'Here's some bread, Bo.'

She took the bread and examined it suspiciously. I went over to the window. Luke and Miss Carrington were still talking. It was after four, but Matt still wasn't home. Whenever the school bus was late I started imagining accidents – another logging truck, the bus on its side, bodies, Matt lying dead. But suddenly, there he was, coming down the drive, his books under his arm. He'd seen Luke and Miss Carrington and went over to join them. I saw Miss Carrington turn and smile at him and wait for him to come up. She looked strange beside them. It was hard to believe she'd been their teacher; they were both much bigger than she was, especially Luke, and she didn't look all that much older than they were.

She said something to Matt and he nodded. He watched her face while she spoke and then looked at the ground.

He shifted his books to his other arm, nodding slowly, head down. Miss Carrington made a little gesture with her hands and he looked at her and gave a faint smile. Matt's face was the most familiar thing in my universe; it was the hint of anxiety in his smile that made me suspect that they were talking about me. What were they saying? Had I done something wrong in class? My stomach contracted with dread. Miss Carrington had reproved me, gently, several times, for not paying attention. Was that it? Luke wouldn't care – he'd never been a great one for paying attention himself. But Matt . . . I wasn't afraid that he would be cross with me, but I was very afraid of disappointing him, or of not being as clever as he wanted me to be.

Miss Carrington said something else and they both looked at her and then both said something in reply, and she smiled and turned and walked off up the drive. Matt and Luke came towards the house, talking, their heads down.

'Anyway, I'd better get to the store. I'm late already,' Luke said as they came in. 'Could you finish hanging out the diapers? She caught me in the middle of it.'

'Yeah, OK.' Matt dropped his books on the table and smiled at me and Bo. 'Hi ladies,' he said. 'How was the day?'

Bo was breaking chunks off the bread and pushing them into her mouth. Her chin worked up and down, chewing busily, but she beamed at Matt and waved a crust at him. Crumbs of bread trickled down her front onto the floor.

'I'm off,' Luke said. He took the car keys from the window sill and went out, letting the door bang behind him.

Matt leaned against the door frame, surveying the mess.

After a minute he said, 'I'll tell you what the problem is, ladies. The problem is that Bo here is better at making a mess than Luke is at cleaning it up. That is the problem in a nutshell.'

He made it sound like a joke, but the chaos bothered him. I think he saw it as symbolic; the mess the house was in reflected the mess our lives were in. It gave weight to his fear that Luke's grand plan wasn't going to work. Luke didn't see it like that. As far as he was concerned, a mess was a mess and so what?

But I didn't care about any of that at the moment.

I said, 'What did Miss Carrington want?'

'Oh she just wondered how we were doing. You know, like everyone does. It was nice of her to come all this way, wasn't it?'

He started picking up the saucepans, wiping the dirt off their bases with his hand before stacking them inside each other.

'Did she talk about me?'

'Sure. She talked about all of us.'

'Yes, but specially about me? What did she say about me?'

My mouth was quivering. I tried to press my lips together, but still it quivered. Matt looked at me carefully, put the saucepans down on the counter, stepped over to me – circumventing Bo who was mashing crumbs into the floor with her toe – and tugged reprovingly on one of my braids.

'Hey. What are you getting upset for? She didn't say anything bad about you.'

'But what?'

He suppressed a sigh, and I was afraid that on top of

everything else I was making him more tired and more unhappy than he already was.

'She said you were kind of quiet sometimes, Katie. That was all, OK? And that's not bad. There's nothing wrong with being quiet. In fact it's good. I like quiet women.' He frowned at Bo. 'Are you listening, Bo? I like quiet women. It's the loud ones that drive you crazy.'

AT NIGHT I lay in bed and listened to the cries of the snow-geese as they passed overhead. Day and night they flew, tens of thousands of them, trailing their long ragged V-shapes across the sky, urging each other on with their harsh, sad cries. Leaving us for the winter.

*

I THINK it was around that time that there was a fight in the school yard. There were frequently fights in the school yard, boys being boys, but this one was more savage than usual.

It took place in the belt of trees that formed the boundary of the school property, out beyond the sand-burr-studded dust the boys used as a baseball pitch. If it had been out in the open Miss Carrington would have spotted it sooner and put a stop to it. As it was, awareness spread slowly. The boys were playing baseball at the time; several of them noticed that something was going on and sloped off to watch. Their movement was noticed by the older girls, who had been clustered together at the corner of the school, watching the boys from a distance, and who stopped talking and stood looking towards the trees. They in turn were noticed by a few of the younger girls, who were playing double-dutch on the small paved area at the bottom of the school steps, and finally by Miss Carrington, who was sitting on the steps marking spellings and was suddenly arrested by the silence.

She stood up and looked over at the trees for a moment and then began walking quickly towards them. A boy emerged, running. We saw him gesturing and Miss Carrington broke into a run, her long skirt flapping. And then she disappeared into the trees and we all stood, waiting, not knowing what was going on.

Then Miss Carrington reappeared, striding towards the school, accompanied by two boys who were half-carrying, half-dragging a third. The third was covered in blood. It was running from his nose, from his mouth, from his ear, running down his neck, soaking his shirt. Miss Carrington strode past us, white-faced. She said, 'Bring him in,' to the boys, and went into the school. The injured boy was Alex Kirby, a farm boy and a prize bully.

The rest of the boys arrived, glancing back over their shoulders at a straggler, who walked slowly, stiffly, and who also had blood on him. Their expressions were slightly awed, slightly alarmed. The straggler was Laurie Pye.

The other boys crowded around the steps with the girls. Laurie stopped a little way off. I watched him. I was standing by the wall, where I'd been all along, watching the other girls skip. (Watching was all I did that year. Rosie Pye had been standing by the wall too – watching was all Rosie had ever done, but our isolation had not formed a bond between us.)

Laurie's nose was bloody and the knuckles of his right hand were split. He stood for a minute or two, looking at the crowd around the step without any expression. Rosie was looking at him, her face as expressionless as his, but he didn't notice her.

Then he must have become aware of his hand because he looked at it, and in doing so caught sight of his shirt, which was practically hanging off him. It had torn right down the side seam and part way across the back. He lifted it out from himself, turning slightly, examining the damage, and I saw his back and side, his ribs like a washboard. There were marks on his back. Small curved marks like little horseshoes. Some were bluish-red and stood out from the skin and some were white and faded and flat. His back was covered with them, all the same shape, like a U on its side. Then Laurie pieced the edges of the seam together and tucked the shirt into his jeans, awkwardly, not using his right hand, and you couldn't see the marks any more.

He'd just finished when Miss Carrington appeared. She stood in the doorway, looking at him, and then seemed to become aware of the rest of us. 'You're dismissed,' she said to us. 'You can go home. Alex is all right – the doctor's coming. You can all go home.'

Then she looked past us at Laurie again. She looked worried. I don't imagine Laurie had been involved in a fight before. He was not popular with the other boys but they'd avoided him rather than picking on him. As I say, there was something about his eyes.

Miss Carrington said, 'Come in, Laurie. I want to talk to you.'

Laurie turned around and walked away.

I DON'T know what the fight was about, though I've no doubt Alex Kirby started it. He suffered a broken nose and his left ear was partly torn off. He was back at school the next day, with gruesome black stitches holding his ear on.

Laurie didn't come back at all.

133

As for what I had seen – well, I didn't know what they were, those small horseshoes. They had no meaning, no significance. Even if I'd known what was going on at the Pyes' farm that autumn, I doubt if I'd have put two and two together. I wasn't taking much in, that year.

So I didn't mention the marks to anyone. And of course there's no way of knowing if it would have made any difference if I had.

Twelve

SUNDAY 11TH October
    Dear Aunt Annie,
    How are you? I hope you are well. We are all well. Bo is well.
Miss Carrington came. Mrs Mitchell came she brot stew. Mrs
Stanovich came she brot pie.
    Love, Kate

    Sunday 18th October
    Dear Aunt Annie,
    How are you? I hope you are well. We are all well. Mrs
Stanovich came she brot a chicken. Mrs Tadworth came she brot
ham.
    Love, Kate

I have those letters now. Aunt Annie died a year ago of
cancer and after her death Uncle William sent them to me.
I was touched that she had kept them, particularly given
their remarkably consistent lack of style and content.
There was a whole box of them, covering a period of
several years, and when I read through the early ones I
thought, good God, they say absolutely *nothing*. Looking

through them again though, trying to imagine Aunt Annie reading them, picturing her unfolding the ragged little scraps of paper, adjusting her spectacles and peering at my scrawl, I realized that if she looked hard – and she would have looked hard – she probably found a certain amount of comfort between the lines.

For a start, she would know that we were not starving and that we had not been forgotten by the community. She would know that I was in good enough shape to sit down and write a letter and that Luke and Matt were organized enough to see that I did. The fact that I invariably wrote on a Sunday implied that we had a routine, and Aunt Annie was of the school which set great store by routines. And every now and then there would be a scrap of genuine news:

Sunday 15th November
Dear Aunt Annie
How are you? I hope you are well. We are all well. Bo is well. Mr Turtle brok his leg he fell off the school roof there was a ded crow in the chimny and he klimed up to get it out. Mrs Stanovich came she brot rice puding she said Miss Carrington said Laurie had to come back to school and Mr Pye was rood. Mrs Lucas came she brot pikles and beens. Last night it snowed.
Love, Kate

WITH REGARD to all the food: I don't know if the church women had established a rota or if it was just left to each individual conscience, but every few days a major meal would arrive. Either we would find it sitting on the doorstep in the morning or a farm truck would come bounding down the driveway and any one of a dozen farmers' wives would climb out with a stewpot tucked under her arm. 'Here you are, dear, just passing. Put it on the stove for twenty minutes, it should do two meals. How is everyone? My goodness look at Bo! How she's grown!'

They didn't linger long. I think they didn't know quite how to deal with Luke. Had he been a girl, or younger, or less obviously determined to manage everything himself, they might have sat down for a chat and in the chatting have passed on much useful advice. But Luke was Luke, so they would hand over their offerings, tactfully not looking around them at the chaos, and leave.

There was one exception to the tact. Mrs Stanovich arrived at least twice a week, heaving her bulk out from behind the steering wheel of her husband's battered truck and puffing up the steps to the front door with two loaves of bread balancing on the top of a bushel basket of corn, or a leg of pork tucked under one arm and a sack of potatoes under the other. She would stand amidst the chaos of the kitchen, legs planted wide, bosoms heaving together under her cardigan in a great round agitated mass, hair raked back into a bun as if she knew Jesus didn't care what she looked like, and gaze around her, chins wobbling with distress.

She couldn't actually bring herself to say anything to Luke, she had enough sensitivity for that, but her face said it for her. And if she caught sight of Bo or myself, the distress welled up and spilled over.

'My darling, my sweetie' (dragging me to her bosoms. Only me – after the first time she knew better than to try to smother Bo). 'We must try to accept the will of our blessed Lord, but it is *hard* sometimes, it is *hard* to see the sense in it, it is *hard* to see the point.'

Sometimes I thought I detected an edge to her voice, as

if she were actually speaking not to me but to someone out of sight but within earshot. She aimed the words at me, but she intended the Lord to get the message. She was angry with Him. She thought that in taking our parents away from us, especially our mother, whom I think she had truly loved, He'd been guilty of a quite disgraceful error of judgement.

'How LONG's it going to go on?' Matt asked. 'For ever? Week in, week out, for the next thirty years?'

Luke looked at a half-demolished ham from the Tadworths' pigs sitting on the counter. 'It's damn good ham,' he said thoughtfully. 'You gotta admit it.'

We'd finished dinner and he'd put Bo to bed. I was sitting at the kitchen table, theoretically learning my spellings.

'That's not the point, is it?' Matt said. 'The point is we can't go on taking this stuff.'

'Why not?'

'Come on, Luke! We can't live off charity all our lives! You can't go on expecting other people to look after us. They've got families of their own. They're not exactly rich, you know, the people around here.'

'They're not exactly poor,' Luke said.

'Where'd that pike come from last week? You telling me the Sumacks aren't poor?'

'They can only eat so many fish,' Luke said, ''specially pike.'

'They *sell* the rest, Luke. They *sell* the rest because they need the money!'

'Yeah, well what am I supposed to say? Hey, Jim, thanks buddy but I can't accept it 'cause you guys are poor? He came for a chat, for God's sake, and he'd been

fishing so he gave me a fish! You go on about it like it's
going to be for ever! It's just until we get ourselves sorted
out. Get ourselves some proper work. Then they'll stop
because they'll see we don't need it any more.'

'Yeah, well when's that going to be? When's this proper
job going to appear?'

'Something will turn up,' Luke said equably.

'Well I'm glad you're so sure of that, Luke. It must be
useful, having inside knowledge.'

Luke said, 'You like to worry, don't you? You've
always just loved worrying.'

Matt sighed and started unloading his schoolbag onto
the table.

'They like bringing us things,' Luke said, pressing his
point. 'Makes them feel holy. Anyway, you're not the one
who has to thank them. You're off at school. I'm the one
who has to think up what to say for the millionth time,
one lady after another standing at the door. Some days
there's a steady stream of ladies all day long.'

Matt looked at him. You could see him considering
something in his mind. He sat down at the table beside me
and selected one of the books from the stack he'd brought
home. The arrangement was that I could sit across from
him and learn my spellings and he'd test me in between
doing bits of his own homework. When I'd learned them
to his satisfaction (or more likely when he'd given up
hope) I was allowed to sit on beside him and draw pictures
while he worked.

Now though, he didn't get down to work straight
away. He unzipped his pencil case and spilled out the
contents onto the table and then, looking at me out of the
corner of his eye, said in a loud whisper, 'Do you think

Luke's good looking, Kate? Give me your honest opinion. I need a woman's view.'

He was teasing, and I was glad because it meant he'd dropped the argument. I hated it when they argued.

Luke snorted. He was scraping scraps off the plates into the garbage pail. He didn't empty it often enough and it smelled. His housekeeping was on the basic side. All the vegetables were cooked in one pot and banged out onto our plates in a heap to save washing up. Clothes were washed only when they reached Luke's definition of dirty. My school lunches consisted of an apple and a couple of slices of bread with a hunk of cheese between them. But I don't remember him ever failing to make me a lunch and you could always find something to wear if you looked hard enough. We didn't go without anything important.

'I mean, he has a point,' Matt said, still whispering. 'Something must bring all those women to our door. Is it Luke himself, d'you think? His beautiful body?'

Luke thumped him. In the old days, when everything was normal, he used to thump Matt a lot – whenever, in fact, he couldn't think of a reply to one of his smart remarks. There was no heat behind it, it wasn't like one of their rare but terrifying fights. It was just his way of saying, Watch it, little brother, or I'll wipe you out. Matt never retaliated, which was his way of saying that it would be beneath him to stoop so low. He just rubbed whatever bit of him had been thumped and carried on.

'All day long, you see, there's this queue of fabulous, sexy women; Mrs Lucas, Mrs Tadworth, Mrs Stanovich. All lined up at the door, panting, tongues hanging out, tails wagging.'

'Piss off,' Luke said. He'd started washing the dishes in a

140

haphazard sort of way. Matt's chair was right behind him so they had their backs to each other.

'Don't talk like him, OK?' Matt said, still whispering. 'Only inarticulate people use language like that. Like the way they resort to physical violence when they see they're losing an argument.'

'Yeah, well, they're about to resort to it again,' Luke said. 'Any minute now.'

I was giggling. I hadn't giggled in a long time. Matt was looking deadly earnest.

'The thing is,' he said, frowning gravely at me, 'rumour has it that several women and one in particular, I could name names but I won't, but she has red hair, find Luke absolutely irresistible. So irresistible that they just can't leave him alone. Seems crazy to me, but then I'm a man. You're a woman. What do you think? Is Luke irresistible?'

'Matt?' Luke said, 'Shut up.'

He still had his hands in the sink but he'd stopped washing things and had gone still.

'I really want to know,' Matt said. 'Whadya think? Do you think he's irresistible?'

'No,' I said, still giggling.

'Matt,' Luke said quietly.

'That's what I thought. So why is it that a certain red-head . . . Ow! Hey! What's up with you!'

He swung round in his chair, clutching his shoulder. Luke's punch had nearly flattened him. Luke wasn't smiling. He was standing with his hands by his sides, dripping dishwater.

Matt stared at him, and after a minute Luke said seriously, 'I said, shut up.'

I KNOW why now. I pieced it together years later.

Something had taken place that Matt didn't know about, and it made the subject of Sally McLean a touchy one as far as Luke was concerned, and definitely not a good one for jokes.

It had happened the previous Saturday afternoon while Matt was doing his stint at the Pyes' farm. The fall ploughing was long over but there were fences to repair and Calvin Pye wanted the floor of a shed concreted, so Matt was out and Luke and Bo and I were at home – we were outside, working on the woodpile.

It had snowed on and off in the previous weeks and though the snow hadn't settled, winter was definitely on its way. There was a stillness in the air that you don't get at any other time of year. The lake was still, too. There was a rim of ice along the shore, thin and lacy and gritty with sand; sometimes it melted in the afternoon but it was always back the next morning, and it was thicker every day.

So the woodpile had become a priority and that afternoon we were all working on it. Luke was splitting logs, I was gathering kindling and Bo was busily taking off the pile everything that Luke put on it and putting it down somewhere else. It was fairly late, about four o'clock, and the light was starting to fade. I went off into the woods to where an old tree had blown down to get some more branches to break up for kindling, and when I got back, dragging the branches behind me, Sally McLean was leaning against the woodpile, talking to Luke.

She was wearing a dark-green heavy-knitted sweater which made her skin seem even paler than usual and her hair even redder, and she had painted a line of black stuff around her eyes, which made them look huge. She kept toying with her hair as she talked to Luke, winding it round her fingers. Now and then she'd put a tail of it in her mouth and draw it smoothly through her lips.

Luke was fiddling with the axe. First he'd drop it head down on the ground, holding onto the end of the haft, and then he'd swing it upright again and rub his thumb across the blade as if testing its sharpness. Then he'd drop it down again and thump it thoughtfully up and down.

Sally had been saying something but she stopped when I came up. For a moment she looked irritated, but then she recovered herself and smiled at me. She turned to Luke and said, 'Your little sisters are so cute. You're really good with them, you know. Everybody says so.'

'Yeah?' Luke said. He automatically looked across at Bo. She'd started making a woodpile of her own about ten feet from the real one. She kept dumping bits of wood on top of one another and they kept rolling off. You could tell she was starting to get mad; she was saying, 'Dat one, an' *dat* one, an' *dat* one,' and the 'dat' was getting louder every time.

'Yes,' Sally said. 'Everyone thinks it's really amazing. You do everything for them, don't you?'

'Most things, I guess,' Luke said, still watching Bo.

Sally watched her for a moment too, her head tipped to one side, her mouth curving in a smile. There was something odd about the smile. It was as if she were trying it on in front of a mirror, like a dress.

Still smiling she said, 'She's just adorable, isn't she?'

'*Bo*?' Luke said. He thought she must mean someone else.

'*Dat* one,' Bo said severely, dropping a log as big as she was on top of her woodpile. The whole thing collapsed.

'Bad stick!' Bo yelled. 'Bad bad stick!'

'Here,' Luke said. He leaned the axe up against the

143

woodpile and went over to her. 'Stack them like this, OK? Put a big one at each end, then lay the little ones in between, like this.'

Bo stuck her thumb in her mouth and leaned against his leg.

'Do you even give them their baths and everything?' Sally asked. She looked shyly at Luke under her eyelashes.

'Me or Matt,' Luke said. 'Are you tired, Bo? Do you want a nap?'

Bo nodded.

Luke looked around and saw me with my branch. He said, 'Take her in, OK Kate? Bo, you go with Kate. I've got to finish here.'

Bo stomped over to me and we walked up to the house together. I waited to hear the whack of the axe but I didn't hear anything. When we got to the door I turned around and looked back. Luke was just standing there, talking to Sally.

Bo and I went in and I took her coat off for her. You had to unplug her thumb to get it off and it made a popping sound, which made her smile, though she stuck it back in right away.

'Do you want a drink or anything?' I said.

A shake of the head.

'Do you want me to read to you for a minute?'

A nod.

She led the way to our bedroom. I cleared a space in the pile of our clothes that no one ever got around to putting away, and sat on the floor beside her cot and started reading *The Three Billy Goats Gruff*, but before we even got to the First Little Billy Goat going trit trot trit trot across the bridge she was asleep. I stopped reading and just turned the pages, looking at the pictures, but I'd seen them too many times. I closed the book and put on my coat again and went back outside.

Luke and Sally had vanished. I wandered back to the woodpile, looking for them. The axe was still there. The ground all around was very soft and spongy from absorbing years and years of sawdust and my feet didn't make a sound. It was getting dark and the cold was creeping in with the night. Matt had told me that cold was just the absence of heat, but it didn't feel like that. It felt like a presence. It felt stealthy, like a thief. You had to wrap your clothes tight around you or it would steal your warmth, and when all your warmth was gone you'd just be a shell, empty and brittle as a dead beetle.

I went around the end of the woodpile, wondering if Sally had gone home and Luke had gone to the shed for something, and then I saw them. Sally was leaning against a tree and Luke was standing in front of her, very close. It was dark under the trees and I could barely make out their faces. I could tell Sally was smiling though – I could see her teeth.

Luke had his arms either side of her, hands resting on the trunk of the tree, but as I watched she took hold of one wrist and then took his hand in hers. She made an exclamation – his hand must have been cold – and rubbed it for a moment between both of hers. Then she smiled at him again, and took his hand, and slid it up under her sweater. I saw the white gleam of her bare skin, and she gave a sort of gasp and then laughed and pushed his hand further up.

Luke went very still. It seemed to me he wasn't even breathing. He dropped his head and I got the impression that his eyes were closed. He stayed like that for about a minute; Sally was watching him, her eyes wide. Then, very slowly, he withdrew his hand. For a minute he didn't move any other part of him; he stayed as he was, head down, one arm braced against the tree. And then – and the thing was, even in that light I could see the effort in it, as if a huge magnetic force was drawing him towards Sally and it took every ounce of strength he had to withstand it – he pushed himself away.

I saw the effort. It didn't mean anything to me at the time of course, but later, when I had reason to think of such things again, I remembered it clearly. The hand that had touched her breast was hanging down at his side as if it were useless, and the other arm did all the work. It braced itself against the rough, dark, bark of the tree and *pushed*.

And then he was upright, free-standing, both arms at his sides. He looked at Sally but he didn't say anything. He just turned around and walked away.

THAT WAS what I saw, and what Matt didn't know. That was why Luke found Matt's teasing so un-funny. Because Sally McLean wasn't just any girl, she was the daughter of his employers, and Luke was scared. He was afraid that if Sally decided that she was offended, if she felt herself to be a woman scorned, she would see to it that he lost his job.

PART THREE

Thirteen

I DON'T UNDERSTAND people. I don't mean that in an arrogant sense – I'm not saying people are incomprehensible because they don't act as I do. I mean it as a statement of fact. I know that no one can truly claim to understand anyone else, but it's a matter of degree. Many people are a complete mystery to me. I just can't see how their minds work at all. It's a fault, I guess.

Daniel said once in his mild way, 'Does the word empathy mean anything to you, Kate?'

We'd been discussing a colleague who had conducted a highly unprofessional piece of research. He hadn't exactly falsified the data but he'd been, shall we say, 'selective' in the way he'd reported it. That sort of thing doesn't do the reputation of the department any good and his contract was not renewed the following year. I thought that was entirely appropriate. Daniel did as well, I was sure, but he seemed reluctant to say so, which annoyed me.

'I'm not trying to justify it,' he said. 'I'm just saying you can understand the temptation.'

I said I couldn't understand how anyone could want

glory which they knew they'd gained under false pretences.

Daniel said, 'Look, he'd been slogging away for years, he knew others were slogging away in the same field and might well get there first, he was sure that in the end he'd be proved right anyway . . .'

I said that was a pretty paltry excuse, if you asked me. And after a pause, Daniel said, 'Does the word empathy mean anything to you, Kate?'

It was our first quarrel. Except that we didn't quarrel, we withdrew, and were polite and distant with each other for several days.

Daniel is naive in some ways. He hasn't had to struggle for anything in life and that has made him easy-going. Undemanding. Not so much of himself as of other people. He is generous and fair and tolerant, all of which are qualities I admire, but sometimes I think he carries them too far. Sometimes he makes excuses for people in a way which almost denies them responsibility for themselves. I believe in free will. I do not deny the influence of genetics or environment − what biologist could? − and I'm aware that we are biologically programmed to do many of the things we do. But within those constraints, I believe we have choice. The idea that we are carried along by fate, unable to resist or change direction, sounds suspiciously like an excuse to me.

But I'm getting off the subject. What I wanted to say was, I thought at the time that Daniel's comment about empathy was very unfair, but it kept coming back to me, irritatingly, whenever someone did something really off the wall. And when I started thinking about Luke and Sally again, back in February when all this family business came up, I found myself trying to imagine what Sally had thought she was doing, all those years ago. What could have been in her mind? How could any girl want to become involved with someone as encumbered as Luke?

The only explanation I could think of was that she failed to realize that Luke's situation was for real. I think she was highly sexed, and not very bright and therefore more than usually at the mercy of her hormones, and something about Luke's situation appealed to her. Big brother looking after two little sisters – did she find some illicit sexual thrill in the idea? Or was it more innocent? Maybe Sally looked at us and saw a pretty picture and simply wanted to paint herself into it. Handsome boy, pretty girl, two ready-made children – maybe inside her head Sally McLean was playing house. But then Luke took his hand away and spoiled the game.

I can imagine the story she told her parents. She'd be a great story teller. She'd have worked it out on her way home that evening and by the time she got there she would have believed it herself. She would have burst into the small living room the McLeans had at the back of the store, her hair dishevelled and her cheeks flaming with injured pride disguised as distress. Her parents would have looked up in alarm and stared at her, and she'd have stared back for a second or two and then burst into sobs.

She'd have said, 'Daddy . . . Daddy . . .' in a broken voice, and poor wordless old Mr McLean would have found words and said, 'What, baby?' (Or 'sweetheart'. He would have called her something like that.) 'What is it?'

And Sally would have sobbed, 'Daddy, you know Luke . . .'

'Luke? Yes. Yes?'

'Well he . . . he tried . . .'

You can just see it, can't you?

151

It's possible that they didn't believe her – however much they loved her they must have had some knowledge of their own daughter. But it wouldn't have made any difference. They would have known that if Sally had taken against him, it would be impossible to keep Luke on.

They didn't tell him straight away. They must have agonized about it for a week or so, while Sally raged in the background and Luke allowed himself to hope. I can't imagine how they finally broke it to him, both of them being at a loss for words at the best of times. In the end, Luke probably made it easy for them. Probably when they were locking up one night Mr McLean cleared this throat half a dozen times and finally said, 'Uh, Luke . . .'

And Luke waited for a minute, hoping against hope that it wasn't what he thought it was. And then the silence would have gone on until he knew it had to be what he thought it was, so he would have said, 'OK. Yeah. I know.'

Mr McLean would have looked ashamed. He'd have said in a whisper, 'Sorry, Luke.'

Though maybe I'm underestimating the extent to which even parental love is blind. Maybe they did believe Sally, and were disgusted by Luke, and felt that he had betrayed their kindness in the vilest way.

I doubt it though. We still used their store, there being no alternative, and they still beamed at me whenever I came in, and when I got home I always discovered that little extras had somehow found their way into the shopping bag; a couple of blackballs, a twist of liquorice – the odd little treat that they knew we couldn't afford.

*

As I said, it was back in February, when the invitation to

Matt's son's birthday party arrived, that I started thinking about all this again. Normally when I'm about to go home for a visit the memories start drifting in, but this time they came in a real flood. Partly, I guess, it was the significance of Simon turning eighteen. But part of it, I'm sure, was due to the 'problem' of Daniel.

Daniel had indeed seen the invitation. He had read it. He knew that he could have been included in it if I had chosen to include him.

That realization came to me slowly, but I got my first serious hint at an exhibition we went to the afternoon after the invitation arrived. The exhibition had the inspiring title 'Microscopes Through the Ages', and unsurprisingly we were the only people there. In fact it wasn't as bad as it sounded; there was everything from a collection of little flea-glasses from about 1600 to a magnificent and completely useless instrument that had been made for King George III, which was too tall to use if it was mounted on a table and too short to use if it stood on the floor, and had lenses which were incorrectly positioned. Apart from that, as Daniel said, it was perfect in every way. Fit for a king.

What told me that Daniel had something on his mind, though, was that a number of the more robust instruments had been set out so that you could play with them, and yet he didn't. Daniel the great fiddler, Daniel the microbiologist. He stood in front of them, one after another, staring at them thoughtfully but hardly touching them. Then he stood for a ridiculously long time staring at a century-old micrograph of the proboscis of a Victorian house fly, and then he looked at his watch and said that it was time we headed downtown to meet his parents for dinner.

Normally, I was happy enough to get together from time to time with the Professors Crane. I had to be feeling fairly strong to cope with a whole evening in their company, but they had accepted me without reservation from the first time we met, which had impressed me, considering the difference in our backgrounds, and biased me in their favour. In the early days I had found their battles at the dinner table stressful, but I think that was because I expected one or other of them to win. When I realized how well matched they were I was able to relax a little. I was still sometimes enlisted or used as ammunition by one or the other of them, or even by both at the same time, but I was learning how to handle that.

That evening, though, they were both on particularly prickly form. I had difficulty concentrating on what they were saying because I was so conscious of Daniel's abstraction, and throughout the evening I could feel the levels of tension within me rising like mercury in a barometer. The restaurant was one of their favourites, small, expensive and airless, or so it seemed that night. Daniel's mother spent most of the evening reminiscing about his childhood, which was something she hadn't done before, and for the first time in my life I realized that there are advantages in having your parents safely dead.

'He was the most placid child, Katherine. From when he was still in diapers – I might say he was in diapers for an inordinately long time, but even so – you could take him anywhere, plonk him down in the middle of a cocktail party, an art gallery, a lecture theatre . . .'

'This happened, did it?' Daniel's father said, sounding intrigued. 'I don't recall seeing Daniel in diapers in a lecture theatre. Or at a cocktail party, come to that.'

'You wouldn't recall it, Hugo. By definition, you can only recall what you have taken in in the first place. Your mind was on higher things, dear. You were very seldom "with us" in the mental sense. Physically very much so, but mentally, no. We did quite a lot of entertaining, Katherine, faculty get-togethers or dinners for visiting professors, you know the sort of thing, and so of course Daniel was very used to strangers. And he would come into the living room, dressed in his pyjamas, to say goodnight to the guests and an hour later you would suddenly notice that he was still there, wide-eyed, taking in all that was being said, whatever the topic of conversation happened to be, politics, art, anthropology . . .'

'Astrophysics,' Daniel's father said, droning as if reading from a list, 'economics – particularly Keynesian, took that in like nobody's business – philosophy – at the age of two he was taking in three philosophers a week. You were particularly smitten with the works of Descartes, weren't you Daniel?'

Daniel was engrossed in the menu, but after a moment the silence reached him and he looked up. 'Pardon?'

'I said that at the age of two you were smitten with Descartes. That's correct, isn't it?'

'Oh,' Daniel said. He nodded. 'Right. Smitten's the word.' He returned to the menu.

'He was a very, very rewarding child,' his mother continued smoothly. 'But of course he did benefit from being exposed to such a range of ideas and opinions from such an early age. It was a huge advantage, there's no doubt about it. Most children suffer from a crippling lack of stimulation. The brain is like any other muscle; use it and it develops. Ignore it and it atrophies.'

Daniel heard that. 'Just a small detail,' he said mildly, laying down the menu, 'but the brain is not a muscle. It's a shade more complex than that. I think I'm going to have the beef.' He looked around for a waiter and found one.

'Is the pepper sauce very hot? Like, is it very peppery, or more creamy?'

'I think it's more creamy,' the waiter said doubtfully. 'I'm not sure.'

'I'll risk it. And I'll have a baked potato. And carrots.'

'And especially when we were abroad, Katherine. Especially when we were in England. And when we were in Rome! Daniel was six. Was it six? Maybe seven. Anyway, within a month of our arriving in Rome his Italian was better than mine.'

I said, 'I didn't know you spoke Italian, Daniel.'

'I don't,' Daniel said. 'The waiter is waiting to take the order. What does everyone want?'

'But then neither does his mother,' his father said.

'The chicken,' his mother said. She smiled at the waiter and he quailed visibly. 'No potatoes. Salad – please make sure it's very fresh. No dressing with it. Mineral water to drink, no lemon, no ice.'

The waiter nodded, scribbling furiously. I found myself trying to picture Daniel's mother in Crow Lake. It couldn't be done. I tried to imagine her in the McLeans' store, buying potatoes, or toilet paper, and I simply couldn't do it. I tried to imagine introducing her to Mrs Stanovich and found that I couldn't get the two of them into the same frame of my mind at the same time. Even Miss Carrington's image slid nervously out of the picture if I tried to bring Daniel's mother into it.

For a moment – and with a feeling of relief, because it would have been such a neat and simple explanation – I wondered if my reluctance to take Daniel home with me might be related to this gulf between my two worlds. Maybe that was the problem – they were simply too different. But I knew even as I had the thought that it was not the answer. I might not be able to imagine Daniel's mother in Crow Lake but I had no trouble at all imagining Daniel there. He would look out of place – if ever there was a born city slicker, it's Daniel – but no one would mind. He is the most open and least judgemental of men.

They were all looking at me. 'Oh,' I said. 'Sorry. I'll have the chicken. And a baked potato and salad.'

'Steak,' Daniel's father said. 'Extremely rare. Fries. No vegetables whatsoever. Everyone all right with red wine?' He swivelled his head around looking for dissent. 'Good. A bottle of the Bordeaux.'

Daniel's mother said, 'You cannot deny, Daniel, that the experiences of early childhood are hugely important to a child's intellectual development. That's why the parental role is so crucial. What you will be in adult life is set in childhood. "The child is father of the man" and so on.'

Daniel nodded slowly. I wanted to catch his eye, to have him indicate by some small gesture that he knew the evening wasn't a success and that we would go as soon as possible, but he did not look in my direction.

His father was talking to me, bending towards me confidentially and speaking out of the corner of his mouth so that his wife wouldn't hear. 'I've never had the faintest bloody idea what that expression means,' he said. ' "The child is father of the man." You happen to know?'

'I think it just means that the characteristics you show as a child you'll also show as an adult. Something like that.'

'Oh. So Einstein was Einstein while he was still a babe in arms?' He paused and narrowed his eyes, trying to visualize it. 'And Daniel was Daniel and was always going to be, no matter whether his mother took him to dinner parties in a diaper or not?'

'I think quite a lot is pre-set. Though I think circumstances have some effect.'

He nodded. 'In other words, it means the precise opposite of what the honourable Doctor thinks it means. Which is what you'd expect, but it's nice to have it confirmed by someone who actually knows what she's talking about.'

'I'm not sure . . .' I said.

Daniel's mother leaned in my direction. 'Pay no attention to him, Katherine. I'm not denying that there are other influences than parental. Teachers, for instance, can play a critical role. For instance, in your own case. It is enormously to your credit that you have done so well having lost your parents so young, but I imagine you had at least one extremely good teacher, somewhere along the way?'

Matt's face came to me. I thought of the thousands of hours we had spent together. 'Yes,' I said. 'Yes I did.'

Daniel's mother smoothed her hair back with a long fine-fingered hand. A practised gesture of triumph. 'And would I also be right in imagining that you had her at quite an early age? At public school, rather than at high school?'

Daniel was studying the menu again. I would have worried less if he had looked bored or fed up or irritated, but he looked none of those things. He looked . . . absent. As if he had unhooked himself from us, and moved away. I gathered my thoughts with difficulty. 'It was a him, actually. But yes, it was up until I was eight. Though I had pretty good teaching all the way through.'

'Unusual for a man to inspire a young child. Men are usually hopeless with children. Daniel's father being a case in point. Hugo was completely unaware of Daniel's existence until Daniel was made a full professor. An envelope arrived from the university one morning addressed to Professor D. A. Crane – Daniel was moving house and had re-routed his mail to us in the interim – and Hugo said, quite seriously, 'Who the hell is Professor D. A. Crane? We've been at that bloody university twenty years and they still don't know our names!' I informed him that he had a son of that name and he was thrilled to bits. Said we should invite him to dinner. Thank you, waiter. That looks lovely, apart from the potato. I said no potatoes. No, never mind, my husband will eat it. But of course there are exceptions to every rule. For instance Daniel was telling us that you and your sister were brought up by an older brother? I think that is wonderful. I take my hat off to your mother. It absolutely proves my point. She must have been a wonderful person to have produced such a son.'

Daniel's father blinked. He said, 'I think that takes the prize for the most convoluted bit of reasoning I've heard this year. Ever, maybe. Did you take that in, Daniel?'

Daniel looked at him blankly. 'Pardon? Oh. Sorry, no. I missed it. I was thinking about something else.'

'Good man,' his father said approvingly. 'Have some wine.'

ON THE way home I tried to tell myself I'd been imagining things. Daniel had seemed to recover himself when we got up from the meal, as if the problem had been one of circulation and he'd just needed to be shaken up. We said goodbye to his parents and hurried through an icy drizzle to the car. On the way home we talked about the evening and the waiter and the fact that his parents scare the living daylights out of everyone they meet, which somehow, incredibly, Daniel had failed to notice. I said something about him having had a remarkable childhood and he smiled his usual wry smile and said that was one way of putting it. I analysed his answer and decided it was standard Daniel. I said that not many children got an opportunity to travel like that at an early age and he said that was true, and then added that an opportunity to stay somewhere long enough to make friends or settle in a school would have been nice, but you couldn't have everything. I said that at least he had met some very interesting people and he nodded gravely.

'But what?' I said.

'Nothing. Just that you aren't interested in interesting people when you're a kid. I'd have settled for the odd bit of attention from my parents. That business about my standing around for hours listening to guests? That was because I wanted to speak to my mother and she kept saying, "Wait a minute." But I'm making it sound as if I had a miserable childhood. It wasn't miserable. Lonely, but not miserable.'

I looked at him and he glanced at me and smiled. 'Anyway, I imagine you've had about enough of my family for one night. I certainly have.'

I said that actually I'd found it fascinating. He inclined his head, as if acknowledging a polite remark. There was something about the gesture . . . that and the negative tone of his last remark. I can't quite describe it, except to say that it was a flatness. An emptiness. As if none of it mattered – as if nothing mattered.

It was so untypical of Daniel that I knew right then, for certain, that he had seen the invitation. And with that knowledge came two revelations; firstly that my failure to invite him mattered very much to him – even more than I had feared it would. He thought it said something about my commitment to our relationship. It didn't, but he thought it did, and it was what he thought that counted. Secondly, that we had arrived at one of those turning points in a relationship where if you take the wrong course you drift apart like boats in a fog. I hadn't really believed it would come to this. I guess I had been hoping, in spite of what he'd said earlier, that we could carry on as we were.

He turned into the potholed entrance to the parking lot behind my apartment block, parked in a space near the door and switched off the engine. We sat for a minute in silence while I came to terms with the fact that now that the moment of choice had arrived, I had no choice at all. Sometime in the previous year, without my being aware of it, Daniel had become fundamental to my life.

I said, 'You know the conference in Montreal in April?'

'The pollution one?'

'I won't be able to go. Something's come up. It's my nephew's eighteenth birthday that weekend and there's a big family bash I have to go to. I just found out about it yesterday.'

'Oh,' Daniel said. 'Right. Well, you can get transcripts of the papers, if there's anything interesting.'

Cold was seeping in through the seams of the car, thin insidious streams of freezing air. Daniel switched on the engine and boosted the heat. It roared for a moment and then he turned it down.

I said, 'They told me to bring someone if I want to. I thought of asking you but then I thought, it'll be nothing but reminiscing all weekend. You'd probably be bored out of your mind.'

Daniel was looking out of the window, which was rapidly steaming up. He said, 'I'd be fascinated.'

'Would you really?' Knowing full well that he really would.

He turned and looked at me, both hands still on the steering wheel. He was trying to look casual, but relief was written all over his face. 'Yes,' he said, 'Really. I'd love to come.'

'Good.'

I didn't know what I was feeling – relief, despair, confusion, the whole shooting match. I'd have liked to be able to tell him the truth – unburden myself by explaining why I hadn't wanted him to come. But how do you explain what you don't understand?

Fourteen

IN A year of bad times, I think that winter must have been one of the worst for Matt. Not *the* worst — that came later — but one of them. To me he often seemed much older than Luke; he saw problems more clearly and was more realistic about the chances of solving them. In many ways he was easy-going but it wasn't in his nature to set trouble to one side in the hope that it would go away. If a problem arose Matt worked at it until it was solved. It was one of his strengths academically, but the problems we faced that winter were not within his power to solve. And always in the background there would have been guilt about the fact that Luke was giving up his chance while he, Matt, was carrying on with his studies. The fact that he would soon be escaping from our problems must have made all of them seem worse.

Luke losing his job, for instance; I know that worried Matt a lot more than it did Luke. Not that Luke wasn't concerned, but ever since the day he'd decided to stay at home and look after us, he seemed to have an unshakeable faith that everything would work out all right. No doubt the more religious in the community would have approved – remember the lilies of the field – but I think that calm certainty of his drove Matt mad, and was a major cause of the increasing friction between them.

'It'll be OK,' I heard Luke say, one night towards the end of November.

It was late. I'd been asleep for several hours and had wakened, needing the toilet, so I'd padded down the hall in my bare feet and then stood listening to their voices, my toes curling up from the cold linoleum of the bathroom floor. Small hard grains of snow were hissing against the bathroom window; if you pressed your face against the glass it looked as if the night had a million holes in it.

'Something will turn up,' Luke said.

'Like what?' said Matt.

'I dunno. But it'll work out.'

'How do you know?'

Silence from Luke – probably a shrug.

'Come on, Luke. How do you know? How do you know everything's going to work out? What makes you so sure?'

'It just will.'

'Jesus Christ!' Matt said. 'Jesus Christ!'

I had never heard him use those words in that way before.

CHRISTMAS WAS approaching – that family time, that worst of all times for the newly bereaved, that unrivalled time for magnifying tensions.

'What are we going to do about presents for the Mitchells' kids?' Matt said.

We were in the kitchen. Matt was cleaning spark plugs in readiness for another vain attempt to start the car. It was a hard winter, one of the coldest on record, and the car had been an early casualty. In the unlikely event of a job with the right hours turning up in town, Luke would need a car to get there.

Luke was scraping carrots for supper. Long ribbony shreds of carrot peel were piled on the counter. Some hung limply over the edge and Bo was playing with half a dozen that had made it to the floor.

Luke looked blankly at Matt. 'What?'

'The Mitchells' kids,' Matt said. 'There are two of them. The Mitchells are sure to give Kate and Bo something – maybe us too – so we'll have to give their kids something.'

Rev. Mitchell and his wife had invited us to spend Christmas Day with them. None of us wanted to go but there was no way out of it. The Tadworths had invited us for Boxing Day and we didn't want to go there either. I can imagine the church mothers anxiously working out who should have us, unable to bear the idea of our being on our own and unable to see that we would have preferred it.

Luke put the carrot down and turned around to look at Matt properly. 'Will they expect presents?'

'No, they won't *expect* presents. But we still have to give them something.'

Luke turned slowly back to the carrots. He'd managed to knock off quite a few more peelings which Bo was draping elegantly over her head.

'How old are their kids?' he said finally. 'And what sex?'

'How can you not know that?' Matt said. 'You've known them all your life.'

'I don't notice everybody's kids.'

'They're girls. They're about . . . ten.' He looked at me. 'Do you know how old they are, Kate?'

'There are three of them,' I said anxiously.

'There are?'

'How could you not know that?' Luke said. 'You've known them all your life.'

'Are there three, Kate? I only thought there were two.'

'The baby's pretty small.'

'Oh well, a baby,' Matt said.

'Oh right,' Luke said. 'A baby doesn't count.'

'Martha's ten and Janie's seven,' I said quickly.

Another pile of carrot peelings dribbled to the floor. Bo made a gobbling noise and scooped them up lavishly.

Matt said, 'For God's sake don't work so close to the edge! They're all going on the floor!'

'I'll pick them up later,' Luke said.

'If you didn't peel them so close to the edge you wouldn't *need* to pick them up later.'

Luke looked at him over his shoulder. 'Does it *matter*?'

'Yes it matters! It matters because you *won't* pick them up later, you'll forget, and walk all over them, and traipse them through the house where they'll join the rest of the crud! That's why this house is such a pigsty!'

Luke put down the carrot and the scraper and turned around. After a minute he said, 'If it bothers you so much, you could try cleaning it up yourself for a change.'

'That's rich,' Matt said quietly. He was leaning forward, his arms on his knees. 'That is really rich. I spend my whole damned life cleaning up after you. My whole damned life. And if you think . . .' He stopped. He looked at Bo and me, and then he got up and left the room.

Sunday 27th December
Dear Aunt Annie,
Thank you very much for the sweater. I really like it. Bo likes

166

hers to and Matt and Luke like theres. There going to write to you themselfs. Bo knew hers was a lamb and she liked it and I like the duck on mine. Thank you for the books, there really nice and the socks are nice to. And the hats. On Christmas we went to Rev Mitchell and I sat beside Janie and there was a big turky but I couldnt eat very much. Yestrday we went to the Tadworths and they had turky to. Mrs Mitchell gave me a brush and come set and a book and she gave Bo a doll and Janie gave me a pen. Mrs Tadworth gave me a doll. Matt gave me a book about insects and Luke gave me a book about frogs. Mrs Stanovich gave me and Bo dresses that match, and they fit. Mrs Tadworth gave us a whole ham with clovs on it its really good and Mrs Stanovich gave us a Christmas Cake and so did Mrs Pye and Dr Christopherson and Mrs Christopherson came out to see us and brot us some little wee oranges that are really nice . . .

It went on in that vein for about half a page. They were good people. You won't find better.

*

BY THE end of January the snow was piled up against the house in smooth curving drifts. In the night the house groaned with cold. There had been several storms before the lake froze over, and the waves, with arctic winds driving them on, had broken up the sheets of ice that had formed along the shore and tossed them up on their edges. For a week they stood like glistening shards of glass, jagged as shark's teeth. Then the wind picked up again, and the temperature dropped, and waves smashed against the shards and threw up spray which froze before it hit the ground. It fell with a rattle and piled up in pebbled heaps amongst the shards, finally covering them completely in hills of polished glass. And then the lake froze over and at night the only sound was the moaning of the wind.

Matt and Luke dug a trench through the snow from the front door to the driveway and then all the way up the driveway to the road, and took it in turns to shovel it out each morning. There was no need to shovel out the whole driveway because the car still wouldn't start. In places the walls of the trench were so high I couldn't see over them. Bo thought it was wonderful, but she didn't see much of it because Luke was afraid to let her out for long in case she froze.

I'd set off for school in the morning so bundled up I could hardly move; panties and an undershirt followed by long johns, followed by trousers under my skirt and a flannel blouse under my sweater, followed by snow leggings and a parka and a scarf pulled up over my nose and a hat pulled down to my eyes and two pairs of mitts and three pairs of socks and winter boots which had belonged to Matt after they'd belonged to Luke. I was worried that if I fell over I wouldn't be able to get up again. I'd just lie where I'd fallen until I froze straight through to my bones.

Sometimes in the morning when I got to the road I found Matt still waiting there for the school bus, stamping about and clapping his mittened hands together to keep warm. The bus might have broken down or got stuck in a drift or be grinding its way along a back road behind a snowplough – there was no way of knowing which. On those days Matt normally waited until I appeared and then walked along the road with me, hoping to meet the bus on the way.

'Is that you?' he'd say when I came up, bending down to peer at the gap between my scarf and my hat.

'Yes.' Muffled by the scarf.

'It could be anybody.'

'It's me.'

Already the scarf was wet on the inside from my breath. It smelled of wet wool and frost and air that would sear your lungs if you gave it half a chance.

'Guess I'll have to take your word for it. Would you like some company?'

'Yes.'

'Let's go then. Are you keeping your fingers moving?'

I'd wiggle my mittened fingers at him and he'd nod in approval and we'd set off, the snow creaking under our feet.

He still joked with me, still teased, but I could hear the effort in his voice. No part-time job had miraculously appeared in the village and it was too cold to attempt any of the tasks at the Pyes' farm, so neither he nor Luke had worked for two months.

Sunday 11th February

Dear Aunt Annie,

How are you? I hope you are well. Bo is sick she has meezles. Dr Christopherson says she will be fine but she's really spotty and really really crabby. Peeple at school have meezles too but Ive already had it. We did about Henry Hudson and the Northwest Passage. His men were really mean. We did about frakshons to. If you have two ½ apples you have one hole apple and if you have four ½ apples you have two apples and if you have three you have one and ½. Rosie Pye started crying at school.

Love Kate

We weren't the only ones having a hard winter. Old Miss Vernon nearly died that February from a cold which developed into pneumonia. Mrs Stanovich's eldest son's house burned down and he and his wife had to move back in with his parents. Jim Sumack got frostbite while he was out ice-fishing and only just escaped having to have his toes amputated. Dr Christopherson got stuck in snowdrifts on five separate occasions, on the last of which one of his patients had to deliver her own twins because her husband slipped on the ice outside the front door when he was running to fetch a neighbour for help and broke his leg.

And then there were the Pyes. Something was worrying Matt about the Pyes. I don't know for sure that it was the same thing that caused Rosie's distress at school, but the odds are that it was.

'SOMEBODY should do something,' Matt said.

It was evening. I was supposed to be getting ready for bed but I couldn't find my pyjamas and I'd come to ask Luke where they were. I paused behind the door to the dining room to listen to them, to reassure myself that they weren't arguing.

'Like what?' Luke said.

'Tell someone. Tell Rev. Mitchell or someone.'

'Tell him what, though? Like what do we actually know?'

'We know it's getting worse.'

'Do we?'

'I saw Marie yesterday. On the way home from school. I saw her walking so I got off the bus.'

'Yeah?'

'Yeah.'

'Did she say something?'

'Not exactly. Something's wrong, though.'

A pause. Luke said, 'It's partly his own fault.'

'Laurie's?'

'Yeah. He answers back.'

'Well wouldn't you?'

'Not if I got hit for it. He should get smart and shut up.'

Another pause. Matt said flatly, 'You think he hits him, then.'

A hesitation. 'Maybe.'

'I think so too. Not little taps either – he walks funny sometimes. That's why I think we should do something.'

'Like what?' Luke said.

'We could tell Rev. Mitchell.'

'What good would that do? What could he do?'

'He might talk to Old Man Pye or something,' Matt said. 'I don't know, but he might be able to think of something.'

'That might make it worse.'

'If he knew people knew about it, he might stop.'

'But what if he thought Mrs Pye or Marie had said something?' Luke said. 'He might start on them.'

'Are you saying we shouldn't do anything? Just sit here? Knowing about it but not doing anything?'

'We don't actually *know* anything.'

A series of thumps on the table – Matt angrily closing one textbook and taking out another. 'That's your philosophy of life, Luke. When in doubt, do nothing.'

They should have told Rev. Mitchell. But that's hindsight speaking. In their defence I can only say that they were preoccupied with their own problems, which must have felt pretty serious at the time; Bo's measles and my tremulous state and no work for three months, and the tension between them growing, like thunder you can feel before you can hear it, growing and swelling and gathering itself up day by day.

171

Fifteen

MARCH. The snow still in deep drifts, still white and smooth. To look at, the same as February. When you walked on it, though, you could feel the difference. There was a thin crust which broke under your weight and beneath it the snow sagged. Fresh falls lay like dust for a day or two and then developed a crust of their own. Underneath, the old snow lay heavily, like the flesh of a fat old woman.

I think it was sometime around March that Luke started trying to potty-train Bo. It was quite a dramatic episode in our lives, Bo being Bo, and the memory of it is still with me. I remember sitting at the kitchen table doing homework with Matt, and Bo stomping in, wearing about six layers on her top half but naked from the waist down, carrying her potty – empty – in both hands. She was looking grim. Luke was just behind her and he was looking grim too. He was saying something about did she want to wear diapers for the rest of her life, and how could she stand it, being soaking wet and stinking like a cesspit all the time, and Bo was ignoring him. She took the potty over to the garbage pail in the corner of the kitchen and crammed it in and then stomped out again.

I remember Luke sliding down the wall until he was sitting on the floor with his knees drawn up, putting his arms on his knees and his head on his arms and saying, 'I am so tired of her shit.' And I remember Bo, who had stopped in the doorway, turning and looking back at him. She looked uncertain for a minute, and then she came back and patted his head and said, 'Don't cry, Luke.' She didn't retrieve her potty though. She sympathized with him, but not that much.

And I remember Matt saying, 'Luke? That's her first complete sentence. "Don't cry Luke."' And they both laughed.

MAYBE I'VE got the timing wrong though. Maybe it wasn't March, because I don't think they were doing much laughing at that time. I think we'd reached the stage by then where, like all roads leading to Rome, every conversation, every incident, ended in an argument – and usually the same argument.

There was an afternoon – maybe a Sunday, when we all had a bit of free time – when Luke decided I should teach Bo some nursery rhymes. A peaceable occupation if ever there was one. He was concerned that she was going to grow up not knowing any and persuaded me to sing some to her. She was over the measles by then and back to her old noisy self, slinging saucepans about in the kitchen.

'Teach her some, Kate,' he said. 'Teach her the main ones.'

'What are the main ones?'

'*I* don't know. Teach her the ones you like best.'

I couldn't think of a single one. 'I don't remember any,' I said.

' "Hickory Dickory Dock",' Matt said. He was sitting at the kitchen table writing to Aunt Annie.

Self-consciously I said, 'Say "Hickory Dickory Dock", Bo.'

Bo paused in her work and looked at me suspiciously.

'She thinks you've flipped,' Matt said, scribbling away.

I tried again. 'Bo, say "Hickory Dickory Dock".'

'Icky Dicky Dock,' Bo said brusquely. She looked around her, searching for a particular saucepan.

'Good!' I said. 'That's good, Bo. Now say, "The mouse ran up the clock."'

'*Dis* pan,' Bo said. She seized the largest pan and started whamming the others into it in order of size. She was pretty good at it, too. She didn't make many mistakes.

'She's ignoring you,' Matt said in a pause in the din. 'She's decided you're nuts.'

'Come on, Bo,' I said. ' "The mouse ran up the clock."'

'Silly,' Bo said, sparing a moment to wave a stern finger at me.

'It is pretty dumb,' Luke said. 'Try another one. Sing her a whole one.'

I thought for a moment and then sang:

'Miss Polly had a dolly who was sick, sick, sick,
So she phoned for the doctor to come quick, quick, quick,
The doctor came with his bag and his hat
And he knocked on the door with a rat-a-tat-tat.'

Bo looked at me with narrow-eyed interest.

'You've got her,' Matt said in a stage whisper. 'She's hooked. Reel her in slowly.'

'Sick sick sick,' Bo said experimentally. 'La la la.'

'Good, Bo! Good! Listen:

'He looked at the dolly and he shook his head
And he said, 'Miss Polly, put her straight to bed.'
He wrote out a letter for a pill, pill, pill,
"I'll be back in the morning with my bill, bill, bill."'

'Pill pill pill,' Bo said, watching my lips closely and bending her knees in time to the rhythm.

'Good, Bo! That's really good!'

'Sick sick sick!' Bo chanted. 'Bill bill bill!'

'Good!'

'Have we had a bill from Dr Christopherson?' Matt asked.

Luke said, 'What?'

'For Bo's measles. Have we had a bill?'

Luke shrugged. 'Don't think so.' He went back to watching Bo.

'Sick sick sick!' Bo yelled, belting it out. 'La la la!'

'How much will it be, do you think?' Matt said.

'Haven't a clue.'

'Yeah, but roughly. He must have made four or five visits. It's bound to be quite a bit.'

'Let's worry about it when it arrives, OK? Sing it again, Kate. Take it a line at a time. She's really learning fast.'

But I was watching Matt, who'd got to his feet and gone over to the window. It was dark already and he couldn't have seen anything but his own reflection, but he just stood there, looking out.

There was silence for a moment and then Luke said,

'You just love to worry, don't you? You just can't exist without worrying. You can't let one single thing pass, you can't have one single afternoon, one single *minute* when you're not *stewing* away, *chewing* away at it. You can't just let things *go* for one single solitary minute . . . You have to ruin every Goddamned thing we do.'

Matt said quietly, 'We've got to do something, Luke. We're going through Dad's money so fast . . .'

'I keep telling you! Something will turn up!'

'Sure,' Matt said. 'Sure.'

I think that was probably the turning point for him – the point at which he decided things couldn't go on as they were. Which was absurd, really, because if he'd thought about it he would have known that Dr Christopherson would never have dreamed of sending them a bill.

*

THERE IS a three-week gap in my letters to Aunt Annie in March and I know why. That was when the friction between Matt and Luke finally came to a head, and the Eleventh Commandment was well and truly shattered and our small world very nearly fell apart.

Matt broke the news at dinner. That seems to have been the rule in our household – if you had anything earth-shattering to say you said it at the dinner table, preferably when everyone else had a mouthful.

'I've got something to tell you all,' he said, helping himself to Mrs Stanovich's stew. 'I've quit school.'

As it happened Luke did have a mouthful. He stopped chewing and looked down the table at Matt. At some stage during the preceding months they had changed the seating plan; Luke now sat at our mother's place, which was nearest the kitchen, and Matt at our father's. Bo and I were still side by side.

'I talked to Mr Stone today,' Matt continued. 'Told him I was leaving for financial reasons. I've got a full-time job at the Hudson's Bay store. Nine to five, Monday to Saturday. Obviously transport is a problem until we get the car going again, but I've got that sorted out. I'll go in on the school bus, and if I can't get back in the evenings they say I can sleep in the store room at the Bay. They've been really helpful. Mr Williams – he's the boss – he knew Dad, it turns out – he seems a good guy.'

Luke was still staring at him, his mouth full of meat. Matt looked back at him calmly and started to eat. Luke gave a couple of chews and swallowed. It wasn't very well chewed – you could see a big lump going down his throat, like when a snake swallows a frog. He swallowed again, twice, ducking his chin to help push the food down, and said, 'What are you talking about?'

'Work,' Matt said. 'I've got a job. I'm going to earn some money.'

Luke said, 'What the hell are you talking about?'

Matt looked at Bo and me and raised his eyebrows. 'Someone's not too swift today, ladies. Should I try again?' He wasn't needling Luke, he was trying to make a joke out of it, make it less of a big deal.

He turned back to Luke. 'A job, Luke. Work. What you do to earn money, so you can buy things.'

'What do you mean you've quit school?'

'I mean I've quit school. You know? "Quit" as in "stop"? I've stopped going to school. I'm not going to school any more.'

Luke pushed his chair back from the table. He didn't

look as if he thought it was a joke. He said, 'What the hell are you talking about. You've got exams in two months.'

'I'll probably sit the exams, get my Grade Thirteen. Mr Stone said I could do that. It won't matter that I'll have missed a couple of months – I've done enough to pass anyway.'

'Passing isn't good enough – you have to get a scholarship. You know that! How're you going to get to university if you don't get a scholarship?'

'I'm not going to university.'

Luke stared at him, bug-eyed.

Matt said gently, 'Look, what we're doing – trying to keep going with part-time jobs so one of us can always be with the girls – it's not going to work. How can it work? We must have been nuts to think it could.'

He studied Luke's face, which was going red, anger massing up under the skin, and glanced uneasily at Bo and me. He must have been regretting that he'd made his announcement while we were present. He couldn't have expected Luke to be pleased at the change of plan, but he obviously hadn't expected quite such a reaction.

'Look,' he said. 'Let's talk about it later, OK?'

'Oh no,' Luke said. 'Ohhh no. We're going to sort it out right now, because tomorrow you're going back to school.'

There was silence for the count of two or three. Matt said quietly, 'It's not your decision, Luke. Like I said, I've quit.'

'Well you can just un-quit! There's no Goddamned reason at all for you to take a full-time job. At most we've got another month before we can start back with Old Man Pye, and then . . .'

'That's no answer! Even if we make it through this year,

how are you going to manage when I leave? It's impossible! One of us has to work and one of us has to stay home – that's the only way.'

'Like hell it is! Like hell!' Luke's voice was rising in volume and pitch. 'We're not going to need to stay with the girls for ever! Next year Bo can go to someone in the afternoons – lots of people have offered – and Kate can join her there after school. They'll both be OK without us by then. I'll be able to work five afternoons a week. We can live on that! That plus what Aunt Annie sends.'

He drew a breath, and you could see the effort he was making to calm down and speak reasonably, rationally, because he knew that was the only way to influence Matt.

'You go to university, you study for three, four years . . .' He stabbed it out on the table with his finger, stabbed so hard with the effort to speak calmly that his finger shuddered. 'You work in the summers. You pay for yourself and if there's anything left over you send it home. You get your degree.' He looked up at Matt and stabbed out the last bit again. 'You *get* your *degree*. *Then* you get a job, because *then* you'll be able to get a *good* job. And *then* you can help, if we still need help.'

Matt was shaking his head. 'You're kidding yourself. What part-time job is going to crop up next year just so you can work afternoons? You're dreaming.'

'It'll work out,' Luke said, hanging onto his temper with his teeth. 'And anyway it isn't your problem. Winning a scholarship's your problem. Looking after the girls is mine.'

Matt went white. That was the funny thing about them; Luke's anger rose to his face, Matt's sank to his guts.

Matt said, 'Since when do you have sole responsibility for the girls? Since exactly when? What do you think I am? They're my sisters too, you know. Do you think I'm going to just abandon them to you when you can't even get a job?'

Luke took hold of the sides of the table with both hands and ducked his head down like a bull about to charge. Then he leaned forward over the table and roared, 'I'LL GET A JOB! SOMETHING WILL TURN UP!'

Matt stood up and walked out of the room.

For a moment Luke sat where he was, gripping the table. Then he scrambled to his feet and went after him.

I sat rigid, not breathing. There was a crash in the living room and they started shouting again.

Bo climbed down off her chair and went to the doorway and stood there, her thumb in her mouth, watching them. I went and stood beside her. An armchair was on its side and they were shouting across it. Luke said that Matt was going to ruin everything. Matt said, who did Luke think he was, God? Planning out everyone's life for them? Luke said that Matt just couldn't stand it, could he? Just couldn't stand the thought that he, Luke, was going to do something important for once, something really important. It always had to be Matt. Well too bad. Too Goddamned bad. *He* was the one who'd said he'd bring up the girls, it was *his* job and *he* was going to Goddamned well do it, and he certainly did not need any help from Matt.

Matt was white as a sheet by then. He said, that was what it was about, wasn't it? It was all about Luke. Saint Luke, carving out a role for himself as chief martyr and saviour of the family. It was nothing to do with the girls, really, was it? Nothing to do with what was really best for them. It was just Luke's Goddamned ego, all the way.

And there was more, and worse, months and months of

worry and frustration and grief all coming out together, all spilling out in a great rage of words, and it went on and on until Luke said the one final and unforgivable thing. He said that he'd given up his Goddamned future so that Matt could get a degree and if Matt threw that away now, he'd kill him.

I don't know how to describe what happened next. You see fights in movies and on television where people swing at each other and knock each other down or smash each other's jaws, but they are not real. The rage in them is not real. The fear in you, the watcher, is not real. You do not truly love the protagonists, you are not truly terrified that one of them will die. In times past, when they'd fought, I'd been afraid that Matt would be killed. Now I was certain of it, and certain that Luke would somehow die also. I thought the walls of the house would shatter and fall down around us. I thought the end of the world had come. And then I knew it had, because in the middle of all the uproar a movement beside me caught my eye and I looked down and saw Bo shaking so that even her hair seemed to vibrate. She'd gone rigid, her arms sticking down stiffly at her sides, fingers spread, and her mouth was open wide and tears were pouring down her face but she wasn't making a sound. It was the most frightening thing I'd ever seen. She was so brave, Bo. I had thought that nothing could frighten her.

It ended at last, though not by burning itself out. The last thing that happened was that Matt swung at Luke and Luke caught his arm and gave the most tremendous heave and wrenched Matt right off his feet. There was a curious sound, a kind of dull snap, and a terrific yell from Matt, and then he crashed into the wall and slid down it to the floor.

For a moment there was no sound at all.

Then Luke said, 'Get up.' He was panting, still furious.

Matt was lying at a funny angle up against the wall. He didn't answer. I could see his face; it was stiff and white, his eyes open wide.

'Get up,' Luke said again. When Matt still didn't reply he stepped towards him, and then Matt spoke.

He said, 'Stay back!' He seemed to force the words out through his teeth.

Luke stopped. 'Get up,' he said again, but he sounded uncertain.

Matt didn't reply. It was then that I saw that something had happened to his arm. It was twisted behind him, underneath him, and his shoulder was a huge hump and in the wrong place. I started screaming. I thought his arm had come off. Inside his shirt, his arm had come off at the shoulder. I was sure of it. Mr Tadworth's eldest son had had his arm cut off when he fell under a box-car and he had bled to death before anyone could help him.

Luke was shouting at someone, shouting at me. 'Shut up! Shut up, Kate!' He grabbed me and shook me and then I was quiet.

He looked at Matt and ran both his hands through his hair. 'What's wrong?' he said.

'Call the doctor,' Matt said. His voice was so tight it just scraped out.

'Why? What's wrong?' But he'd seen the arm too, and his voice was unsteady.

'Call the doctor.'

I REMEMBER the wait, Matt lying so still it seemed he wasn't breathing, his face grey and shiny with sweat. I remember Dr Christopherson coming into the room and looking at Matt where he lay, and then at Bo and myself, and finally at Luke, who was sitting, by then, with his head in his hands. He said, 'What happened?' and no one replied.

I remember that he knelt down beside Matt and unbuttoned his shirt and slid his hand up to feel the shoulder, and Matt drew his lips back over his teeth exactly like the fox I'd once seen caught in one of Mr Sumack's traps. Dr Christopherson said quietly, 'OK, Matt. It's OK. Your shoulder's dislocated, that's all. We'll have it right in no time.'

He stood up and gave Luke a look, flat and hard, and said, 'You're going to have to help,' and I remember Luke looking at him, and then looking at Matt and wiping his mouth with the back of his hand.

Dr Christopherson turned and looked thoughtfully at Bo and me. Bo had almost stopped shaking, though the tears were still rolling down. Every now and then a tremor would run through her and her breath would come out with a shudder. Dr Christopherson came over and put a hand on her head and smoothed her hair, and then did the same to me.

He said, 'I'm going to need your help too, Kate. Will you help me with something? Molly's alone in the car and she gets lonely if I leave her too long. I wonder if you'd help me get Bo into her snowsuit and then the two of you could go out and sit in the car and keep her company. The car's out at the road – I couldn't get it down your driveway – but I've left the engine running, so it's nice and warm.'

I remember walking behind him as he carried Bo along the snow tunnel up to the road, and I remember Molly's delight when he opened the car door and sat Bo and me down beside her on the back seat. Molly was the gentlest dog I've ever known. She was also a marvellous nurse. She washed Bo's tear-soaked face gently with her tongue, crooning to her all the while, and within a few minutes Bo was crooning back, burying herself in Molly's warm neck, wrapping herself in the silken ears.

As for me, I sat beside them and waited to be told that Matt was dead. I knew by then that when terrible things were about to happen an excuse was found to get Bo and me out of the way. I'd had plenty of opportunities to work that one out. So by the time Dr Christopherson came back for us I was deep in shock and he had another patient on his hands.

The irony of it all, of course, was that within weeks Luke was proved right. Something Turned Up.

Part Four

Sixteen

THERE WAS a time – quite a long time – when none of them seemed very real to me.

Perhaps 'real' isn't the right word. 'Relevant' is better. My family didn't seem relevant. It was while I was an undergraduate. Not the first year, when I was so homesick I thought I might die of it, but later, in the second and third years, when my horizons were expanding and Crow Lake seemed to shrink to the tiny insignificant dot that it appeared to be on the map.

I had discovered by then that Great Grandmother Morrison was more right than she knew about the power of education. She had seen it both as an ultimate good and as the key to escaping the poverty of farming, but she'd had no idea of the other doors it could open. I was studying zoology and I'd passed my first-year exams at the top of the class, and had been told that if I continued in the same vein I would be funded to do my PhD. I knew that if I acquitted myself well in that, jobs would be available, either at the university itself or elsewhere. I knew that if at some stage I wished to work abroad, it could probably be arranged. The world was spreading itself out before me; I felt that I could go anywhere, do anything. Be anyone.

Matt and Luke and Bo receded then into a small shadowed corner of my mind. At that time – in my second year I was not yet twenty, so Bo was only fourteen – Bo still had choices open to her, but Matt and Luke were where they had always been, and I knew they always would be. The distance between us seemed so huge and that part of my life so far in the past that I couldn't imagine that we had anything left in common at all.

Money was too tight for me to go home for short breaks, and as more and better-paid summer jobs were to be had in Toronto than at home I didn't go for summers either. There was a two-year gap when I didn't see them at all, and it would have been longer except that they came to my graduation. All three of them came, dressed in their best. I was touched, but I was embarrassed by them. I did not introduce them to my friends.

I had gone out a few times during those years with boys I met in classes, but none of the relationships took off. My failure in that regard didn't bother me. For one thing I was studying too hard to give much thought to it; for another, as I said earlier, I had never thought I would love anyone. I fancied myself as the eccentric academic, I suppose. Solitary and self-sufficient, in love with her work.

That was not just a fantasy – I was, genuinely, in love with my work. University life was an utter revelation to me – the books and resources, the labs with their dissecting scopes and wonderful compound microscopes, the tutors and professors, each with his or her own particular area of expertise – all there for the asking. By the middle of my third year I had decided definitely to go on to further study. By the end of that year, I had chosen the branch of zoology I would specialize in.

I made that decision as a consequence of a field trip to a small lake north of Toronto. The lake was popular with holiday makers, particularly those interested in boating and other water sports. We visited it in September, after the holiday makers had gone home. The purpose of the field trip was to try to assess the impact people had on the environment in the course of the summer months, and as part of our investigation we took samples of the water and collected specimens of the flora and fauna from the water's edge, to examine back in the laboratory. The aquatic creatures we carried back in jars or plastic bags filled with water and sitting in a cooler full of ice; the others travelled back to Toronto in boxes or jars. Once we got to the lab our task was to identify and document what we had collected, comment on its apparent state of health, and if it was dead, speculate on what had killed it.

I had collected most of my creatures from a small bay at one end of the lake, and in scooping them up I had also netted a bit of decaying organic matter from the bottom of the bay. Back at the lab, having safely transferred my creatures to tanks, I tipped the mud and debris into a dish and quickly sorted through it to see if it contained anything of interest. Mostly it was just dead leaves and twigs, but in amongst them there was a small, black, unidentifiable blob. I lifted it out with forceps, put it carefully on a wet paper towel to keep it from drying out, and slid it under the dissecting scope.

The blob had originally been a water boatman, *Notonecta*, a fierce little predator who spends a lot of his time hanging upside down from the surface of the water, monitoring vibrations for signs of prey. I knew *Notonecta* well from my years with Matt – he was the first indication we had of the fact that surface tension works upside down as well as right way up – and under normal circumstances I would have recognized him instantly. As it was, it took me several minutes to identify this specimen because he was covered – *caked* – in a sticky black coat of lubricating oil from one of the lake's many motor boats. He was *thick* with it, the delicate sensory hairs on his abdomen clogged, the breathing spiracles completely blocked.

I find it hard to explain now why I was so affected by it. All creatures die and most of the ways they meet their end are pretty horrible when viewed in human terms. And it wasn't that I hadn't known about pollution – it is a major topic in all of the life sciences. Perhaps it was because the victim in this case was so well known to me. I had been intrigued by water boatmen when I was a child – it had seemed to me that they were hanging from the ceiling, and I kept waiting for them to get tired and drop off.

Whatever the reason, what I felt, looking at that tiny blackened body, was a mixture of horror and actual . . . *grief.* I had not consciously thought about the ponds for some years, but now they came back to me, vividly. They were far too small for boating, of course, but there were countless other pollutants that could rain down on them or seep into them from the surrounding soil. I imagined myself, going back to them one day in the future, looking into their depths and seeing . . . nothing.

I decided right then that I was going to be an invertebrate ecologist and that my area of study would be the effects of pollution on the population of freshwater ponds. I suppose you could say that my choice was inevitable, and was set long before I came across that single, dead bug. Perhaps. All I know is, that little *Notonecta* re-awoke something in me, and gave me a purpose which I hadn't even known I was lacking.

For a long time after that, studying absorbed me so completely that I had very little time for anything else. The few boys I went out with seemed to be nothing like as interesting as my work. And the people of my past were, well, in the past. And seemed irrelevant.

It wasn't until I met Daniel that I realized I hadn't left my family behind after all. We were introduced when I joined the department, and after that we kept bumping into each other in the corridors – you know how it goes. And then one day I was working in my lab – I have what is called a wet lab, full of aquaria, where I can control the environment of my invertebrates and study their responses – and I turned to find him standing in the doorway. I hadn't known anyone was there and gave a slight start, and he said, 'Sorry. I shouldn't have disturbed you. You look engrossed.'

I said, 'No – it's fine. I was only watching a pond skater.'

'Watching him do what?' he said.

'Skate,' I said, and he smiled.

'Is he particularly good at it?'

I smiled back uncertainly. I'm not very good at casual chit-chat. It's not that I can't be bothered, it just seems to be a skill I can't quite get the hang of.

I said, rather lamely, 'He is, actually. I mean, pond skaters in general are amazingly good . . . skaters.'

'May I have a look?'

'Sure. Of course.'

He stepped in and peered into the tank, but he moved too quickly, and the pond skater was so startled it leapt about ten centimetres into the air. There is netting covering the tank to prevent creatures escaping, so I wasn't perturbed, but Daniel backed off hastily.

'Sorry,' he said. 'I seem to be startling everyone today.'

'It's all right,' I said. I was anxious that he not be put off. There was something about him that I liked – a seriousness which I thought I detected underneath his easy manner. I liked his face too. It is long and thin, like the rest of him, with that strong, rather hawkish nose and thinning, sandy hair. 'He's a bit nervous, that's all. I've been lowering the surface tension. I've lowered it by eight per cent so far, and he's getting edgy.'

'What are you working on?'

'Surfactants. The effect they have on surface dwellers.'

'You mean detergents? That sort of thing?'

'That's right. And other pollutants. Quite a few things can lower the surface tension. Or they stick onto the hydrophobic surfaces of the insects so they aren't water-proof any more. So they sink.'

'But not the pond skater?'

'Not yet. But he'll have his limit.'

'Sounds very cruel.'

'Oh I'll rescue him,' I said quickly. 'He'll be fine.'

He smiled, and I realized he'd been joking, and felt myself flush. There was a slight pause, and then he said, 'When you've rescued him, would you be interested in a coffee?'

So we went for a coffee, and talked about pond skaters, and the fact that they can glide 15 centimetres with a single stroke of their legs and reach the astonishing speed of 125 centimetres per second. And then we talked about pollution in general, and oil spills in particular, and the fact that snails have been known to eat oil and apparently enjoy it. And after that we talked about bacteria (Daniel's speciality) and their ability to change and adapt, and whether that means they are going to inherit the earth.

And then we started going out together.

He amazed me. The fact is — and I'm aware that this sounds a ridiculously cynical thing to say — I had never expected truly to admire anyone again, and I admired Daniel. I've said that I found him naive in some ways, and rather too easy-going, but I think that is partly a result of his generosity of mind. For a while I convinced myself that admiration and liking were all I felt. I made lists of his good points — his sense of humour, his curiosity, his intelligence, his attractiveness, his refusal to join in the back-stabbing and pettiness that seem to be part of the academic environment — as if that would render them emotionally neutral. I made lists of his bad points — his old-womanish dislike of getting his feet wet, his physical laziness, his tendency (though he would deny it) to think he's always right — as if they would cancel out the good points and mean I felt nothing at all. And then one day — I was in the shower at the time, soaping my feet, or some such emotionally neutral part of myself — it came to me that the feelings I had for him could only be described by the word 'love'. It was then, I think, that I unconsciously decided not to think about our relationship too much, not to analyse it or ask myself whether he returned my feelings, whether it would last. This, as I've said, led to problems between us, and my only excuse is that in the past, people I have loved have tended to disappear from my life, and I was afraid of that happening again.

Anyway, the point is that although the love I felt for Daniel was quite different from anything I had felt before, still there was a sort of *recognition* about it. Love goes deeper than anything else, I guess. It gets to the core of you, and when Daniel got to the core of me I found that Matt and Luke and Bo were there too. They were part of me. In spite of the years apart I still knew their faces better than my own. Anything I knew of love I had learned from them.

I began going home for holidays occasionally. I had the money by then. It felt strange – I was an oddity in the community, 'the one that got away'. They were all proud of me, of course, and teasingly addressed me as Dr Morrison, or 'the Professor'. Some were deferential, which should have been funny but somehow was painful instead. Luke played the proud father, which should have been painful but was funny. Bo was the one I felt easiest with. Bo takes you as you are.

Matt? Oh, Matt was proud of me. Matt was so proud of me I could hardly bear it.

*

SIMON's birthday party was at the end of April and I spent most of March trying to think of a suitable present for him. What do you give a boy on the occasion of his entry into manhood? More particularly, what does an aunt give to her only nephew? More particularly still, what was the appropriate present to give to Matt's son? To be honest, I was as concerned that Matt approve of the gift as I was that Simon like it.

I knew that Simon was hoping to come to the university to study physics in a year's time. (I might say that 'hoping' is unnecessary in Simon's case. He has inherited his father's brains and will walk through his exams.) So I prowled around the physics department on a couple of afternoons looking for inspiration. None came.

I left it for a week or two, thinking that something

would come to me, but nothing did. All the normal things – clothes and books and music – were insufficient for a milestone birthday, and in any case I wouldn't have dared to guess at Simon's taste in any of them. Very large things – a car, a trip to Europe – were beyond my means. Middle-sized things – music machines and so on – he either had already or would be given by his parents.

Days passed. April arrived. I am an organized person; I dislike leaving things to the last minute. Particularly important things.

In desperation I went downtown on two successive Saturdays, looking for ideas, wandering through the crowds, hopefully scanning the mountains of junk for something worthy of the occasion. On the second Saturday Daniel came with me, claiming that he loved shopping and always had good ideas. In fact he had ridiculous ideas. He loved everything he saw and made increasingly silly suggestions until I got cross and told him to go home.

'God but you take it seriously,' he complained. 'Is there anything in this world that you don't take seriously? This is about a birthday party, for God's sake! It's supposed to be *fun*!'

I pointed out that (a) as he was an only child and had no nieces or nephews he didn't know what he was talking about, and (b) anyone who thought shopping for important presents under a time constraint was *fun* needed his head read.

'Look,' he said, irritation starting to creep in round the edges, 'Over there is a phone. Why don't you phone your brother and ask him if he can think of anything this kid would like?'

'Daniel, I want to do this myself. Please go home.'

He went, looking peeved. But he'd been in such good spirits since I'd invited him to the party that I knew even my neurotic behaviour wouldn't bring him down for long.

Finally I decided to open an account for Simon at the university bookstore and pay into it enough to cover the cost of textbooks in the first year of his degree. In addition, so that he would have something to unwrap on the day, I bought him a small gyroscope – just a toy, really, but well made and nicely symbolic of the beauty and intricacy of the subject he had chosen to study.

Daniel redeemed himself, when I told him what I had decided, by saying that he thought they were great presents. Then he spoiled it, as only Daniel can, by saying that they were also very 'me'.

'What do you mean?' I said suspiciously.

'Well, textbooks. Does he have any other aunt who would give him textbooks for his eighteenth birthday?'

'When I think of the hours I spent in the library trying to get hold of textbooks that were out on loan, because I couldn't afford to buy my own . . .'

He grinned and said he was only teasing.

*

I DON'T know if it was because Matt was on my mind, but on the Tuesday of the week before Simon's party I had a bit of a crisis at work. Nothing like it had ever happened before and I can't think of anything else that it could have stemmed from – I hadn't received a critical review of a paper or hit a stumbling block in my research or anything like that. It had to be related to thoughts of home.

My job – Assistant Professor, Invertebrate Ecology – has a number of components: carrying out research, analysing and writing up my findings, writing papers for publication, giving papers at conferences, supervising graduate students, teaching undergraduates . . . plus a ridiculous amount of administration.

The research I love. It calls for patience, precision and a methodical approach, and all of those I have. That makes it sound dull, but it is far from dull. On a pure level, it allows you to feel that you have added your own tiny piece to the jigsaw of scientific knowledge. On a more basic level, an understanding of the environment is essential if we are to avoid destroying it. Research is the most important part of my job and I never have enough time for it.

The writing of papers and articles I don't mind. The exchange of ideas is vital and I'm prepared to do my bit.

I don't much care for giving papers at conferences because I know I don't speak terribly well. I'm clear enough, I can present a well-structured paper, but my delivery lacks zip.

Teaching I don't enjoy at all. This is primarily a research university and I only have four hours a week in front of a class, but it takes me almost a week to prepare each lecture and it eats great chunks out of my research time. Also, I find it hard to relate to the students. Daniel enjoys them. He pretends not to, in the same way that he pretends not to work – he works all the time, he just calls it something else. Secretly, he finds the students interesting and stimulating. Secretly, I do not. I don't understand them. They don't seem to take anything seriously.

Anyway, this 'crisis', if that isn't too dramatic a name for it, came in the middle of a lecture. It started as a minor hiccup. I'd been explaining the hydrophobic nature of the hair piles of specific arthropods to a lecture theatre filled with third years, and I suddenly had such a vivid flashback that I completely lost my train of thought. What I remembered was Matt and me, in our usual pose, flat on our bellies beside the pond, our heads hanging out over the water. We'd been watching damsel flies performing their delicate iridescent dances over the water when our attention had been caught by a very small beetle crawling down the stem of a bulrush. He was about six inches above the surface when we spotted him, trotting purposefully downwards. Where did he think he was going, we wondered, and what would he do when he reached the water? Did he realize it was there? Matt said insects didn't have noses as we do but they could smell and detect damp with their antennae, so probably he did. In which case, what was he after? A drink? Matt said he'd thought insects got all the liquid they needed from the plants they ate or the blood they sucked, but maybe he was wrong about that. I said maybe the beetle was a she and was going to lay her eggs in the water as the damsel flies did. Matt said he didn't think beetles did that, but he could be wrong about that too. I said maybe the beetle was just thinking of other things, like what to have for dinner, and wasn't looking where he was going, and Matt said in that case he was in for a surprise.

But we were the ones who got the surprise. When he reached the water the beetle didn't so much as pause. He just kept on walking. The surface of the water dimpled for a moment as his head butted into it, and then it wrapped itself around him and swallowed him up.

I was alarmed, I thought he'd drown, but Matt said, 'No – look! Look what he's done!'

I peered down into the water and saw that our beetle, still marching steadily downwards, was surrounded by a glistening silver bubble.

'It's air,' Matt said, craning forward, shading the surface of the pond with his hands to cut down on the reflection. 'He's got his own submarine, Katie. Isn't that something? I wonder how long he can stay down.'

I know how the beetle did it now of course – there's no mystery about it. Many of the creatures who live on the water–air boundary carry down an air bubble with them when they submerge. The air is trapped in a velvety pile of hairs so densely packed that they are completely waterproof. As oxygen is used up, more diffuses in from the surrounding water. As to the length of time our beetle could stay down, that would depend on the amount of oxygen dissolved in the water and how rapidly he was using up his supply. Generally, the more active the insect and the warmer the water, the less time he can remain submerged.

IT WAS the composition of the hair pile that I was explaining to my third-year students when the memory of that day suddenly floated across my mind, momentarily dispersing my thoughts and causing me to stumble and come to a halt. I pretended to study my notes while I got myself together, and carried on with the lecture. The third years, who had roused themselves briefly in the hope that something interesting was going to happen, settled back in their seats. In the front row a girl yawned so massively that she seemed in danger of dislocating her jaw.

It was the yawn that got me. I'd been yawned at before – all students are chronically short of sleep and most lecturers have had the experience of looking out over a sea of snoring bodies – but for some reason I suddenly found I couldn't go on.

I stood speechless, staring out over my audience. Inside

my head, my inner ear played back to me the sound of my voice. The drone of it. The flat, monotonal delivery. And overlaid on top of the drone, like a film joined up with the wrong soundtrack. I kept seeing my own introduction to this subject; Matt and I, side by side, with the sun beating down on our backs. The beetle sauntering along under the water, safe in his tiny submarine. Matt's amazement and delight.

Matt thought it was miraculous . . . no, there is more to it than that. Matt *saw that it was miraculous*. Without him I would not have seen that. I would never have realized that the lives which played themselves out in front of us every day were wonderful, in the original sense of the word. I would have *observed*, but I would not have *wondered*.

And now I was putting an entire class to sleep. How many of the students reclining in front of me would have had the opportunity to see what I had seen, let alone in the company of someone like Matt? Most of them were city kids; some had never seen a real pond in their lives until they went on one of our field trips. This lecture was their first introduction to this particular subject. And they were more unfortunate than they knew, because if things had turned out differently, it would have been Matt standing in front of them instead of me. If that had been the case not one of them would have been yawning. I am not exaggerating this. I am not glorifying him. It's a fact. If Matt had been speaking to them, they would have been riveted.

They had roused themselves again, curious now, aware that something was wrong. I looked down at my lecture notes, moved the pages around, looked up at them again.

I said, 'I'm sorry. I've been boring you.'

I packed up my notes and left the room.

'I SHOULDN'T be in this job,' I said to Daniel, later that night.

'Kate, it happens to everybody. No one is on top form all the time.'

'It isn't a question of form. It's a question of basic ability. I can't teach. I can't put it across. I'm killing the subject for them.'

I was sounding melodramatic, which I didn't intend but which was how I felt. I felt tearful and desperate and absurd. I'm not given to that sort of thing; normally I'm quite rational.

Daniel put both hands through his hair, what there was of it, in a way that reminded me of Luke. 'You are so *hard* on yourself! You give one sub-standard lecture . . . Most of the lecturers in most of the universities in most of the cities of the world are total *crap*. And most of them don't care.'

I said, 'The point is, Daniel, it isn't one sub-standard lecture. It's all of them. And what it means is I'm not doing my job properly. And I just don't think I can carry on, week after week, year after year, doing something so badly.'

'You're over-reacting, Kate.'

Silence for a moment.

Daniel said more gently, 'What did Prof. Kylie say?'

I shrugged. 'He's always nice. You know him.'

'Kylie? Nice? Well there we are – there's your answer. You're the only person in the department Kylie bothers to be nice to. Now why would that be? Ask yourself that.'

But I was thinking of Matt. I was thinking that I felt as if somehow I had betrayed him. That was how I felt. And I couldn't understand it, really, because the truth was, Matt betrayed himself.

Seventeen

A<small>LL THAT</small> winter, while we were preoccupied with our own problems, things must have been deteriorating for the Pyes. I imagine there were clues if we'd been on the look-out for them, but the Pyes' farm was quite isolated and the winter being such a hard one people weren't getting about much. The Pyes stopped going to church but for some weeks that didn't strike anyone as significant; the roads were snowed in half the time so the congregation was often pretty sparse anyway.

During the rest of the year Matt and Luke would have been the ones to know if anything unusual was happening, but there was no work at the farm during the winter months so they had no contact with the family either.

Laurie hadn't been to school since the fight with Alex Kirby in October. According to Mrs Stanovich, who lived on the Northern Side Road and therefore saw such traffic as there was to and from the Pye farm, Miss Carrington had called at the farm several times in the run-up to Christmas. Presumably she was reminding Calvin of his legal obligation to send his children to school until they were sixteen, but she obviously didn't get anywhere.

Laurie would have been nearly fifteen by then, and the school board was inclined to turn a blind eye to truancy among farm children because they knew they were needed at home.

At the end of March, when the thaw came, Matt and Luke resumed their work for Mr Pye. About that time Rosie started missing quite a bit of school. She'd always been sickly, inclined to catch every germ going, but maybe Miss Carrington suspected there was more to it this time, because the week after they went back to work she came to see Luke and Matt. (If she knew about our own little crisis she didn't let on. I don't imagine she did. Dr Christopherson was not a gossip.)

She came to ask, delicately, clearly aware that it was an uncomfortable question, if the boys thought everything was all right with the Pyes. I know that much because I was eavesdropping, but then Matt shut the door so I don't know what they said. Whatever it was, though, it wasn't enough.

I SUSPECT things would have been different if Laurie had been a carbon copy of his father in spirit as well as in looks. There would still have been conflict – from what Miss Vernon told me about the family history a certain amount of conflict was almost inevitable – but maybe it wouldn't have been as bad. Calvin had never stood up to his own father, according to Miss Vernon. Laurie did. Laurie would not be cowed. I imagine that was what really got Calvin going. To have lacked the courage to defy his own father, to have taken so much abuse, for so long, and then to be 'sassed' – I expect that was how he would have seen it – by his own son; that must have been the last straw.

This would explain why things got worse during that year. Laurie was well into adolescence by then. In childhood he would not have dared, but with all that testosterone coursing through his bloodstream, he did.

I can't think what it must have been like for Mrs Pye and Marie, watching, trying vainly to calm things down, trying to intervene. Mrs Pye broke her arm that winter. She had it in a cast for months. She said she slipped on the ice and hit it on the doorstep. Which is possible, I suppose.

She came to see us one day – it must have been at the beginning of the winter, when she was still getting out a bit. She'd brought us something, an offering of food, probably, and I remember her standing at the door asking Luke how we all were, and I remember that although she was looking at him you could tell she wasn't paying any attention to his reply. She seemed to be listening for something. Listening over her shoulder, so to speak. I suppose she was in a permanent state of waiting for the next crisis.

As for Rosie – I don't recall her ever being one-hundred-per-cent normal, but for most of that year, even while she was still going to school fairly regularly, she'd been as inarticulate as a stone. Fear must have rendered Rosie stupid. Feeling must have rendered her numb.

But it's Marie I find it hardest to think about. Empathy, as Daniel says, is not my strong point, and it is more difficult still to empathize with someone you don't like. I never liked Marie. I remember going out to look for Matt one afternoon; he was late and the fear I always felt at such times had reached the point where I couldn't bear it any longer, so I pulled on my coat and boots and went up to the road to look for him, imagining, as usual, the bus in a ditch and Matt lying dead beside it. And instead there he was, standing halfway up the bank of snow the snow-plough had left, talking to Marie. Her arms were wrapped around herself in that defensive pose of hers, and her eyes were red and her nose was red and she looked her normal pathetic self. I think I despised her. I suppose I blamed her for making Matt late.

But she must have been suffering too. I do realize that.

*

As FOR us, Matt and Bo and I, well, having hit rock bottom with something of a thump, things in the Morrison family finally started to look up.

Sunday March 30th

Dear Aunt Annie,

How are you? I hope you are well. Mr Turtle fell off the roof agen. He was shuvling snow off so the roof wodnt cave in and he fell off and brok his leg. Mrs Turtle says hes to dumm and to old so Miss Carrington said wod Luke like to be janitor.

Love, Kate

Sunday April 6th

Dear Aunt Annie

How are you? I hope you are well. Lukes our janitor now. He has to go to school really early in the morning and lite the furnas and shuvl snow and everything that needs doing, and he has to clean the toilets. But he says he dosnt mind. And in the summer he has to try to get rid of the poison ivy becasue Miss Carrington says its a menis.

Love, Kate

So there you are. It was just like Luke said: Something

205

Turned Up. As a matter of fact within the space of a few weeks, Several Things Turned Up.

BUT TO go back a bit: in the days following the 'incident' between Matt and Luke, Dr Christopherson had come out several times, ostensibly to check Matt's shoulder but probably to check on Bo and me as well. On the last visit he took both boys into the living room and read them the riot act. I know that because I listened at the door. He'd brought Molly into the house to entertain Bo and me but I was wise to that now, and I'd decided I wasn't going to be kept in the dark any more. I believe it was my first conscious act of defiance.

The riot act started deceptively. Dr Christopherson said that everyone admired what the boys were trying to do for me and Bo and everyone knew how hard they'd both tried to make things work.

There was a little silence. I imagine they both knew that wasn't the sum total of what he intended to say.

He went on. He said that it was hard to accept that sometimes, in spite of all your efforts, things just didn't work out. There was no shame in admitting it. In fact it was important to admit it. It was important to recognize when something wasn't working, because otherwise you placed yourself under an impossible strain. And then, of course, things tended to go seriously wrong.

There was another silence. Then Luke said, so quietly that I had to strain to hear, pressing my ear against the door, that they'd sorted everything out now and everything was fine.

Dr Christopherson said were they sure about that?

His voice was gentle, but there was an underlying gravity that even I could hear. He waited a while, his question hanging in the air between them. I imagined Luke's hand raking its way through his hair. Then the doctor said that it was Bo and me he was concerned about. What had happened in front of us must never happen again. We'd been through too much. We were too vulnerable.

There was a longer silence. Luke coughed.

Dr Christopherson said that much as he would hate to do it, if he ever had any reason to suspect a repeat occurrence he would have no choice but to contact Aunt Annie. Fortunately I didn't realize the implications of this. I assumed that he was threatening them with a telling-off by Aunt Annie, a prospect which pleased me no end. It didn't occur to me that he was saying that Bo and I would be sent out east.

This time the silence stretched out until Dr Christopherson broke it himself. He said that he needed their assurance on two counts. Firstly, that in future if there was friction they would resolve it peaceably. Secondly, that if they were encountering problems they would seek help. Their desire to be self-sufficient was admirable, but they should remember that too much pride was a weakness, some would say a sin. Many people in the community would like to help, out of respect for our parents. So, their assurances please. No more outbursts of violence, and from now on their own pride would take second place to the welfare of Bo and myself.

They answered him then, first Luke and then Matt, and gave their undertakings. Dr Christopherson put them to the test, instantly, by saying that he imagined money was a bit short at the moment and he would like to help out. They failed the test, instantly, by saying in strangled voices that they were fine, really, that there was lots of our father's money left, but thanks very much. He probably knew that they were lying, but decided that they'd eaten as much humble pie as they could reasonably be expected to swallow in one day, and he let it pass. There was the sound of chairs creaking and I shot back to the kitchen to where Bo and Molly were taking afternoon tea on the floor.

It was a couple of weeks afterwards that Mr Turtle fell off the roof.

Matt was back at school by then. I don't know how Luke persuaded him; certainly not by dislocating his shoulder. In fact, it occurred to me recently that it might not have been Luke at all. It could have been Marie. Anyway, Matt was back at school and working like a madman for his exams. He didn't have what you'd call ideal study conditions. Once Luke took the job of school janitor Matt had to baby-sit from the moment he got home from school, and Bo was not the easiest baby to sit. My students come to me from time to time with excuses for not having handed in an assignment. They were sick (hungover) or they couldn't get hold of a particular book at the library (had gone too late) or they had three other assignments due at the same time (all left to the last minute), and I think of Matt, squatting on the floor with his chemistry text on one side of him and Bo, who was on her potty and refused to stay there unless he sat with her, on the other, furiously scribbling notes into a pad on his knee.

There were still financial worries, of course. The duties of a janitor took up only a couple of hours a day. (Perfect hours, as it happened, because Luke could be back from his morning duties before Matt left for school and leave the after-school duties until Matt got back.) The previous janitors had always been farmers as well, so the job had merely provided a bit extra. I'm sure the school board was as generous as they could be, but they couldn't pay Luke a living wage for ten to fifteen hours' work a week. It was a help, but it wasn't enough.

Spring was well under way by then and there was plenty of farm work to be had, but Luke didn't take it because he still couldn't bring himself to leave Bo with neighbours. Mr Tadworth offered a job that was right up Luke's street. He had two acres, thickly wooded, that he wanted cleared; he wanted the trees felled and the roots dug out, the logs dragged back to the house by tractor, cut into lengths, split, and sold as firewood in town. Luke's kind of work, but it was a job that required daylight and Mr Tadworth wanted it done quickly. He couldn't hang about waiting for weekends, when Luke would be free.

There was a bit of what Dr Christopherson called 'friction' about that one. Matt maintained that Bo would be just fine now if she spent a couple of days a week with someone else. Luke refused to consider it. He'd said he was going to stay with her for a year and he was going to stay with her for a year.

I remember that argument. I remember Matt saying, '*Exactly* a year? Does it have to be *exactly* a year? How about a year minus a month? Would you consider that? How about a year minus a *week*?'

Silence from Luke.

'If the right job came along when there was still a day to go before the year was up, would you turn it down, Luke? Would you say that it was in Bo's best interests that you turn it down?'

Luke said, 'Shut up, OK Matt?'

I saw Matt's jaw go tight, but with Dr Christopherson's shadow hanging over him, he shut up.

And then, Something Else Turned Up.

I HEARD a debate once on the theme 'Character is Destiny'. It was an undergraduate affair and ended in disarray because the protagonists had failed to define their terms beforehand. They came unstuck on 'destiny'. Clearly, if a random hit by a meteorite is your destiny, your personality doesn't have much bearing on your fate.

Still, it's an interesting idea. Take Luke, for example. You could argue that his determination, his refusal to consider the possibility of failure, made things happen. Matt was far more rational, but Luke's irrationality paid off in the end, almost as if destiny were bending to his will.

Or take Calvin Pye. With hindsight, it seems that Calvin Pye's fate could have been predicted almost from the moment of his birth. Likewise Laurie's. But there, it seems to me, you have one of the weaknesses of the argument – namely that everyone's destiny is tied up, to a greater or lesser degree, with the destinies of everyone else.

And of course, you can just as easily turn the proposition on its head. In Luke's case, you could argue that without the loss of our parents he might never have developed that remarkable determination of his. He must have had it in him, but without the interference of destiny it might never have come out. He rose to the occasion, you might say, but the occasion came first.

And Matt? How would you explain Matt? But I have never been able to explain Matt. In any case, I have no wish to analyse him. It makes me too sad.

*

Dear Aunt Annie,

How are you? I hope you are well. Mrs Stanovich says Jesus says she can spare us two afternoons a week. She says her children are grone and we need her more than they do. Luke says we dont need her at all but Matt says yes we do and it woud be good because Bo and me woud be in our own home.

Love, Kate

'Mornings I'm busy,' Mrs Stanovich said. 'Mornings there's the men's breakfast and dinner to get and supper to be got started. Mondays and Fridays are busy all day. Monday's market day and Friday's chickens. Tuesdays, Wednesdays and Thursdays I can double up some things, so you choose which two you want.'

She looked defiantly at Matt and Luke. She was not blessed with beauty, Lily Stanovich, with her small, weak-looking eyes and large, fleshy face, but still, she had presence. And I think now that there was something close to nobility in her defiance. Raw courage. I'm sure she must have known what we thought of her — what everybody thought. I remember my father — even my father — saying that he bet the Lord's toes curled with embarrassment every time Lily Stanovich opened her mouth, and my mother saying staunchly that she had a heart of pure gold and that was all that mattered. And I remember my father replying (though under his breath) that it was one of the things that mattered, but it wasn't all.

In some communities she might have passed almost unnoticed, but in ours ... well, we were mostly Presbyterians, as I have said. Name-dropping the Father, Son and Holy Ghost was not the done thing. Likewise

emoting, and Mrs Stanovich emoted like nobody's business. Even her husband was embarrassed by her. Even her
sons.

Nonetheless, she stood four-square in front of Matt and
Luke, cheeks flushed, neck mottled, and defied them to
turn down her offer. Two afternoons a week. She could
look after the girls, do a bit of cooking, maybe a bit of
cleaning (she slipped the cleaning in as if it weren't
uppermost in her mind) and Luke could go do some of the
things that needed doing on the farms. The Lord had
spoken to her and she was going to do His will. I think
even Luke must have known that they had no choice but
to accept.

'She'll infect the girls,' he said later to Matt, in an
undertone, as if afraid that our parents, up there on their
clouds, would hear him and make him stand in the
kitchen.

'Infect?' Matt said uneasily, evidently imagining the
same thing. 'That's not a very nice way to put it.'

'You know what I mean. They have to testify or
something. Whatever it's called. Bear Witness. They have
to Bear Witness.'

'Not here, they don't,' Matt said.

'How're we going to stop her? We can't say, "Look,
you can clean our house but you can't Bear Witness."'

'We can say it nicely.'

'How do you say that nicely?'

'Say our parents would want Kate and Bo brought up in
our own religion. We could say that. She'd accept that.
She loved Mum.'

'You say it,' said Luke.

So Mrs Stanovich came on Tuesday and Thursday

afternoons and Luke chopped down Mr Tadworth's trees and cleared his field for him. Mrs Stanovich and Bo didn't see eye to eye on everything, but they worked things out. Mrs Stanovich let Bo hammer saucepans in the kitchen and Bo let Mrs Stanovich clean the rest of the house, and then Mrs Stanovich let Bo take the saucepans into the dining room and Bo let Mrs Stanovich clean the kitchen. And then Bo was allowed to choose any books she liked to take to bed with her so long as she stayed there for an hour, while Mrs Stanovich scoured the saucepans and cooked the evening meal. When I came home from school Bo was allowed up and we were both permitted to do whatever we liked as long as we let her 'get on with these windows', or whatever the project of the day happened to be. I've never known anyone who could pack more into an afternoon. The house was transformed.

She was easier to take than she had been, mostly because she was less distressed. For a while she galloped to the door and enveloped me when I got home, but that tailed off after a bit. I imagine she saw how I hated it. I imagine she couldn't help but see. It would have been like hugging a lizard.

I hope she knew we were grateful to her. No – I'll rephrase that. I hope we were grateful to her. I have an uneasy feeling we weren't, at the time. But maybe it didn't matter. She wasn't doing it only for us.

Eighteen

Laurie Pye left home on a Saturday afternoon in April. I'm not sure of the date because I didn't write to Aunt Annie about it, but I know it was in April because we'd had a spell of warm weather which fooled us all into thinking winter was over, and it was a Saturday afternoon because Matt was there and saw him go.

Matt didn't say much about it at the time. He said Old Man Pye and Laurie had had a row and Laurie'd lit off, and he left it at that. Both he and Luke had witnessed countless rows between Calvin and Laurie before, after all. And Laurie had run away a couple of times when he was small and had always come back of his own accord.

That night the weather revealed itself as the fraud it was and the temperature dropped to minus ten. Matt was uneasy. He said Laurie'd only been wearing a thin shirt when he left. But Luke said it would just persuade him to come home that bit sooner. In fact, probably he was home already and probably Mr Pye had calmed down a bit in the meantime. After thinking about it for a bit, Matt agreed.

On Sunday, though, none of the Pyes were at church and there was no snow to account for it. Matt was pretty quiet on the way home and that set off alarm bells in my head. If Matt was worried, so was I; trouble, as far as I was concerned, was bound to be our trouble. So I kept extra quiet and listened extra hard, and after lunch, when Matt and Luke were doing the dishes, I heard what had happened. And grim though the story was, I was relieved, because it wasn't our trouble after all.

On Saturday afternoon Mr Pye and Laurie and Matt had slaughtered a bullock. Of all the farm work, slaughtering was the job Matt hated most. He wasn't sentimental about animals but it sickened him nonetheless, particularly when, as in this case, the bullock got wise to what was about to happen and died in terror. It took all three of them to do the job and in the course of it Mr Pye got kicked, which didn't improve his temper.

Matt said Mr Pye started yelling at Laurie for not pulling his weight. He called him pathetic. Useless as a girl. He said in fifteen years Laurie hadn't learned one Goddamned thing about farming. Didn't try. Didn't listen. Dumb as the Goddamned bullock.

The bullock's blood was draining out of him while all this was going on. He was down on his side on the ground, heaving and thrashing while the life soaked out of him into the soil.

Laurie said, 'I must've got it from you.'

He'd been kneeling on the bullock's rump, Matt said, but he stood up as he spoke. The bullock had pretty much stopped thrashing. Shudders ran through it in waves, like ripples on a lake. Blood formed a thick dark pool around it. Matt was still crouched by its head, holding it by the horns, his full weight leaning on it. One horn had gouged a deep groove in the soil.

Calvin Pye had been wiping the knife off on an old bale

of straw. He looked at Laurie over the great shuddering body.

He said, 'What did you say?'

Laurie said, 'I said I must have got it from you. Dumbness. Stoopidness.'

Matt said there was a spell where nobody breathed. He himself stayed exactly as he was, holding the bullock's horns, looking down at it. He said its tongue was lying on the ground. It was spilling out of the bullock's mouth like a great clot of blood.

Calvin Pye said, 'Did I hear you right?'

Laurie said, 'Unless you've gone deaf.'

Matt said there was a small scraping noise and he looked up, but fortunately it was the sound of Calvin putting down the knife on a concrete block. If he'd been picking it up, Matt said, he didn't know what he would have done. It was plenty scary enough as it was.

Calvin walked over to the barn. He disappeared inside, and reappeared almost immediately with something hanging from one hand. It was a belt, Matt said.

He walked back towards them, his eyes on Laurie. Matt watched him. He was still kneeling by the bullock's head, still holding its horns. Laurie was watching his father too. He didn't look scared, Matt said. Matt was extremely scared.

Calvin Pye didn't say anything. He was circling the pool of blood around the bullock's body, and as he walked he was wrapping the end of the belt, the soft end, the non-buckle end, around his hand.

Matt got to his feet. He said, 'Mr Pye?' and he said his voice came out as a squawk.

Neither of them heard him. They were just looking at each other. The belt buckle was swinging loosely but

Laurie wasn't looking at it. His eyes were fixed on his father's.

Matt said time seemed to have slowed right down. Less than a dozen steps separated Calvin from his son, but each step took for ever. Laurie did nothing. Just stood there. It wasn't until his father got more or less to the animal's tail, so that there were only about three steps between them, that Laurie spoke.

He said, 'You're not hitting me ever again, you bastard. I'm going. But I hope you die. I hope you die like that bullock. I hope somebody stabs you through the throat.'

And then he turned and ran.

Matt said Calvin started after him but after only a few yards he stopped and came back. He didn't look at Matt. He just stood looking down at the bullock, no life left in it now, coiling the belt around his hand. Then he said, indifferently, as though nothing had happened, 'What are you waiting for? Start clearing up.'

NOTHING to do with us. That's what I thought. I didn't know that the Pyes' story was already starting to converge with our own. No one knew. We were all bumbling along, the Morrisons and the Pyes and the Mitchells and the Janies and the Stanoviches and all the others, side by side, week in, week out, our paths similar in some ways and different in others, all apparently running parallel. But parallel lines never meet.

Nineteen

A NOTHER THING I didn't know at the time was that that spring was to be the last I had with Matt. Our visits to the ponds, which had formed such a fundamental part of my life that I had imagined them to be without number and without end, were in fact almost over. By the following September the ponds themselves would have been desecrated twice over, as far as I was concerned, and for some years after that I did not visit them at all. And when I did, it was without Matt, and it was not the same.

Perhaps that is why our expeditions that spring stand out so clearly in my memory. Like the last meal with my parents, they have come to have a special significance. Also, of course, I was finally of an age to begin to understand what I was seeing and to begin to think about it. The interest which Matt had sparked in me had developed by then into a deeper curiosity, and that year I was noticing and wondering about things without being prompted.

Life cycles being as they are, spring is the best time for pond watching, and that spring every form of life seemed bent on revealing its secrets to us. I remember sliding down the path to 'our' pond in great excitement one evening, because the surface of the water appeared to be boiling. It bubbled and seethed like soup in a cauldron. We couldn't imagine what was going on. It turned out to be frogs, hundreds of them, all scrambling together at the surface of the water, climbing on top of each other, sliding off, struggling up again. I asked Matt what they were doing and he said, 'They're mating, Kate. They're making frog spawn.' Though he too looked amazed by the frantic urgency of it.

He told me then that for all creatures, from the single-celled to the most complex, the main purpose in life was to reproduce. I remember being puzzled. It seemed strange that something should exist only in order to cause something else to exist. It was unsatisfactory, somehow. Rather pointless, like travelling for the sake of it.

It didn't occur to me to ask him if it included us – if reproduction was all we existed for too. I wonder what he would have said, that spring, if I'd asked him that.

SPRINGTIME had another significance, of course. Then as now, exams were in June. Matt would have been one of very few at the school sitting the senior matriculation and the only one applying to university. Most of the kids from Crow Lake would have been lucky to get their Grade Twelve. In farming families, if anyone was allowed to complete Grade Thirteen it was likely to be a girl, girls having less muscle and therefore being less useful.

Generally speaking, the farmers' wives I knew had more education than their husbands. It was considered a good arrangement; the wives did the farm accounts and wrote such letters as were called for. I don't think much store was put in education per se. Great Grandmother Morrison was unusual in that.

I remember those months, during which Matt did battle with the Grade Thirteen syllabus (and won hands down), as being the most peaceful since our parents' death. We'd settled down at last. Our financial worries had eased and Matt had come to terms with Luke's sacrifice, if only because he'd worked out how to pay him back. Though he didn't mention that at the time.

For me there was reassurance and even a certain glory in having Luke associated with the school, however humble his position. Sometimes on Mrs Stanovich's days, if farm work permitted, he would come in to school during the afternoon recess to see if anything needed doing. I remember watching him and Miss Carrington down on their hands and knees, peering at the damage done by a porcupine to the wooden foundations of the school. I remember Luke getting to his feet and wiping his hands on his jeans and saying cheerfully that it wasn't too bad and he'd repair it over the summer and treat the whole lot with creosote, and Miss Carrington nodding and looking reassured. I remember being proud of him, and wondering if everyone else had noticed that my brother had reassured the teacher.

Rosie Pye was back at school by then. After Laurie's disappearance she hadn't turned up at all for several weeks – in fact the whole Pye family had disappeared from public view. But gradually things had returned to something like normal. Rosie had been so silent and strange before that she didn't seem much different. Marie was out on the tractor all day, doing her brother's job, and if she seemed more withdrawn than she used to be, well, it wasn't to be wondered at.

Calvin was just as always. Matt still worked for him on Saturdays. He was the only person in the community to have regular contact with the Pyes at that time. He said that in fact Calvin was easier to get on with than he had been, because with Laurie gone he wasn't in a constant rage.

Mrs Pye was the only one who was noticeably changed. The church women shook their heads about her and said she was taking Laurie's disappearance very hard. She never left the house any more and when people called she didn't answer the door. Rev. Mitchell tried talking to Calvin about her and was told to mind his own business.

As for Laurie himself, no sign had been seen of him since the day he'd run away, though Mr Janie's youngest son had been to New Liskeard and thought he'd seen him working in the market there.

It seemed curious, looking back on it, that there wasn't more of a fuss about his disappearance. He had no money, no food, no clothes, no experience of the world outside Crow Lake. You'd have thought people would notify the police or the RCMP.

I suppose the thing was, they'd seen it all before. Laurie was just one more dropped stitch in a family tapestry already full of holes.

*

THAT SPRING I was beginning to emerge from the shell I had been in for the better part of a year. Until then I hadn't been taking much part in things. Like someone with tunnel vision, I'd been able to focus on only a restricted field; Matt and Luke and Bo were clear to me, but everything else was a blur. But finally, that spring, my field of vision was starting to expand. Janie Mitchell, Rev.

and Mrs Mitchell's middle daughter, had been my best friend in the olden days; one day in May she asked if I would come to play after school and I said yes. She'd asked before and I hadn't wanted to. Now I did.

I went on a Wednesday. We played dressing up, as I recall. The afternoon was a success and Mrs Mitchell suggested that we make it a regular thing. Then she suggested that Bo come as well, initially at the same time as me. That worked well too, so she asked Luke if perhaps Bo would like to come for the whole afternoon. Bo did like. The Mitchells had a baby, whom she was intrigued by, and they also had a dog – not as nice as Molly, but pretty nice.

So Luke had another afternoon free. Progress, you see. I remember the anxious pleasure with which he and Matt quizzed Bo and me about the events of those afternoons. What had we played? Had it been fun? Did Bo join in? Had there been any quarrelling? Like a couple of over-protective mothers, the pair of them.

I TURNED eight at the end of May, an event which triggered the dreadful realization that we had missed Bo's birthday by four months. Bo was unperturbed, of course, but the rest of us were guilt-stricken. Mrs Stanovich was appalled. She had baked me a cake, iced with pink icing; now she stormed into the kitchen and produced another one. Around the top edge of both cakes she stuck sugar cubes, each of which was decorated with a tiny pastel sugar-flower. I was fascinated by them. I'd never seen such delicacy, such artistry, in food before. Heaven knows where she got them – they must have cost a small fortune. I'm sure she wouldn't have dreamed of giving them to her own children.

I remember her conversation with Bo. They did converse by then. They had formed a relationship which I think both of them found quite satisfactory.

Mrs Stanovich set the cake on the side-board, beside mine, and said something like, 'There you are, my lamb. Your very own cake.'

'I not my lamb,' Bo said. She was licking out the icing bowl so the cake was of less interest to her than it might have been.

'Well goodness, you're right,' Mrs Stanovich said. 'Aren't I the silly one? You're Little Bo Peep.'

Bo looked pleased. 'Bo Peep!' she said. She disappeared into the icing bowl and then reappeared briefly, waved her spoon at Mrs Stanovich and said triumphantly, 'As lost-er sheep!'

Mrs Stanovich beamed at her but the poignancy of the moment – sweet, pink-iced, motherless child with her tragically late birthday cake – was too much for her and I saw her mouth start to quiver. I tried to slide from the room but she called me back.

'Katherine, sweetie?'

Reluctantly I slid back. 'Yes?'

'Sweetie, as there are two cakes,' she dug a large hankie out of the vast reservoir of her bosom, blew her nose violently, stuffed the hankie back and drew a quavering breath. She tried heroically, she really did. 'As there are two cakes I wonder if you'd like me to put yours in a tin so you could take it to school and share it with your friends tomorrow.'

It was a good idea. I liked it. I said, 'OK. Thank you.'

Maybe I smiled at her, or maybe it was the 'thank you', or maybe it was the fact that by then Bo had pink icing in her hair, but whatever it was it was too much for her and she lost the battle and dissolved.

IN THE background, always, there was Matt with his books. All through April and May while the rest of the household careered around him in its normal chaotic fashion, there was Matt, sitting at the kitchen table, scribbling away. A lot of the time he was baby-sitting and no doubt felt he had to be where Bo was, but even when Luke was home it didn't seem to occur to him to seek the quiet of his bedroom. Maybe we were background noise. Certainly he had phenomenal powers of concentration.

I loved watching him. I'd sit beside him sometimes, drawing pictures on the back of his study notes and watching the movements of his pencil. He wrote so fast that it seemed to me the words just ran down his arm and out onto the page. When he had math to do there would be a great row of numbers snaking across the paper and the pencil would make marks and squiggles between the numbers which I knew meant something, though I didn't know what. When he got to the end of a question, if he'd got the answer he was expecting he'd underline it hard. If it wasn't what it should have been, if he'd made a mistake somewhere along the line, he'd say, 'What? WHAT?' in an outraged tone, which always made me giggle, and score a line through it, and start again.

I don't remember him showing any sign of exam nerves, either before or during the event, though our visits to the ponds became shorter for a while in the immediate run-up. Once the exams actually started he became positively laid-back. When Luke asked him how one or other of them had gone, he'd say, 'OK' in a noncommittal tone and leave it at that.

And then, with no fuss or celebration to mark their passing, they were over. He cleared his papers off the kitchen table, stacked them neatly on the floor in his bedroom, and went back to work for Calvin Pye for the summer.

Think of all that work. The dedication and determination. The hours and hours of study. Work carried out as a tribute to our parents, to wrest something good from the devastation of that year, to prove himself to himself and to Luke, for my sake, for his own sake, for *its* own sake, for the pure joy of it – perhaps that above all. Work so that he could in his turn support the rest of us, work for the future of the family. Work because he knew he could do it, knew his efforts would be rewarded.

As if life were as simple as that.

People say, 'You can do anything you want if you want to badly enough.' It's a nonsense, of course, but I suppose we all work on the assumption that it is true – that life is simple, that effort will be rewarded. It wouldn't be worth getting out of bed in the morning if you didn't believe that. I'm sure it underpinned Great Grandmother's efforts to educate her children. Jackson Pye must have believed it – think of the incredible commitment of energy and effort he put into wresting that farm from the wilderness. The handsome farmhouse, the well-made barn, the sheds and outbuildings, the fields carved out of the forest, the tons of rock shifted, trees uprooted, fields fenced. Arthur Pye must have believed the same – believed that he could succeed where his father had failed, if only he worked hard enough. And Calvin after him.

And all the Pye women – they all must have been filled with excitement and determination when they first saw that farmhouse, seeing in their minds' eyes a large and happy family slamming in and out of the door onto the wide verandah. They must have willingly shared their husbands' dreams, believing in them and clinging desperately to that belief for years. Because in an ideal world, effort, like virtue, is rewarded, and it simply makes no sense not to act as if it's an ideal world.

*

I FINISHED school a week or two after Matt's exams ended and we settled into the summer routine. Mrs Stanovich still came on Tuesday and Thursday afternoons and Bo and I continued to go to the Mitchells on a Wednesday, so Luke worked on those days. Mr Tadworth, whose field he had cleared earlier in the spring, had asked him to help with the building of a new barn. He'd offered more money than Calvin Pye was prepared to pay and was a good deal pleasanter to work for so Luke took the job, though I imagine he felt guilty at leaving Matt to go to the farm alone. With Laurie gone Calvin was extremely short-staffed and Matt worked twelve-hour days. He said Marie worked closer to twenty-four; she spent her days on the tractor and the evening doing the cooking and the housework. Mrs Pye was not in good shape. She was found in a distressed state one evening, wandering the roads around the farm. Mr McLean came across her when he was driving back from town with the week's provisions for the store. She said she was looking for Laurie. Mr McLean said she looked as if she'd fallen into a ditch. He said her hair was all tangled and her face and hands were scratched and dirty and her skirt was torn. He wanted to take her to see Rev. Mitchell but she refused, so he drove her home.

July came. I remember overhearing Matt and Luke in

the kitchen one evening saying that it seemed incredible that it was a year already. I didn't know what they were referring to. What had been a year? I listened, but they didn't elaborate. After a minute Luke said, 'When do the results come out?'

'Any day,' Matt said. There was a pause and then he said, 'You could still go, you know.'

'Go where?' Luke said.

'Teachers' college. I bet they'd still take you.'

There was a silence. Even from my position behind the door I could tell it was an ominous one.

Matt said, 'All I'm saying is, if you've changed your mind it's probably not too late. I bet they'd still take you. I could stay with the girls.'

The silence stretched out. Then Luke said, 'Listen carefully, OK? I'm staying with the girls. And I don't want to talk about it any more, ever. If we both live to be a million years old, I don't want to mention the subject ever again.'

I waited, my skin tight with apprehension. But Matt didn't reply and after a minute Luke said more calmly, 'What's the matter with your brain anyway? I thought you were supposed to be smart. There wouldn't be enough money for me to go now even if I wanted to. That's why you need a scholarship, remember?'

I remember my relief; there wasn't going to be a quarrel. That was all that concerned me. The content of their talk didn't worry me at all, because somehow, incredibly, in spite of a whole year's worth of argument about whether or not Matt was 'going', it had never once occurred to me that he was actually going to *go* somewhere. I don't know how I could have failed to realize it, but that is the case. I had no idea.

I DON'T think anyone doubted that Matt would win a scholarship but I don't think even his teachers realized quite how well he would do. He wiped the board. He won everything going.

I remember the evening after the results came out. Supper was chaotic because people kept popping in to congratulate him, all of them beaming with pride that Crow Lake had produced such spectacular success.

Miss Carrington was the first. The high school must have notified her as soon as they got confirmation of the results, so she would have known almost as soon as Matt did. It had been several weeks seen I'd seen her and I was a little shy of her and hung back a bit. I remember her laughing – all three of them laughing – and Matt looking pleased and embarrassed, and Luke thumping him, quite hard, on the shoulder. I remember watching them, not knowing quite what all the fuss was about but knowing that it meant that Matt was the cleverest person in the world, which I'd always known anyway, and feeling pleased that everyone else had finally realized it too. And still, incredibly, not having the least idea what the consequences would be.

I remember Matt phoning Aunt Annie. She'd have known that the results were due and would have instructed him to call. I don't know what she said, but I remember Matt, red-faced, grinning into the phone.

I remember Marie Pye coming round. Matt got up abruptly when he saw her coming down the driveway and went out to meet her. I saw her smile that nervous smile of hers and say something to him which made him smile back. I remember other well-wishers, Rev. Mitchell amongst them, all wanting to shake Matt vigorously by the hand. The last to come was Dr Christopherson, who'd somehow heard the news and had driven out all the way from town.

I can still see him standing in the kitchen with Bo and Molly waltzing round his feet, saying, 'A magnificent achievement, Matt. Magnificent.'

And I remember him saying, 'When do you leave? Beginning of September?'

And my bewilderment. I remember my bewilderment.

*

I SAID, 'How long for?'

A hesitation. Then, gently, 'A few years.'

'Don't you like it here any more?'

'I love it here, Kate. This is home. And I'll come back lots and lots. But I've got to go.'

'Will you come back every weekend?'

His face was strained, but I felt no pity for him.

'Not every weekend. It costs a lot of money to travel back and forth.'

A long silence, while I fought with the ache in my throat.

'Is it very far?'

'It's about four hundred miles.'

An unimaginable distance.

He reached out and touched one of my braids. 'Come here. I want to show you something.' Tears were rolling by then, but he didn't comment on them. He took me to our parents' bedroom and positioned me in front of the photograph of Great Grandmother.

'Do you know who this is?'

I nodded. Of course I knew.

'She's Dad's grandmother. His father's mother. She lived on a farm all her life. She never went to school. And she wanted to learn so badly. She wanted to know things, and understand things, *so badly*, Kate. She thought the world was just fascinating, and she wanted to know all about it. She was really clever, but it's awfully hard to learn when you have hardly any time to study and you have no one to teach you. So she was determined that when she had children, every one of them would get a proper chance to learn.

'And they did. They all got through public school. But then they had to stop and go out to work to earn a living because they were really poor.

'Her youngest boy – our grandfather – he was the cleverest – he grew up and had six kids of his own. He was a farmer too, and still poor, but all his kids got through public school too, and then the older boys did the youngest's share of the work so that he could go to high school. And that was Dad.'

He sat down on the end of our parents' bed. For a minute or two he just looked at me, and maybe because I'd been looking at Great Grandmother I noticed how much his eyes were like hers. His eyes and his mouth.

He said, 'I've got a chance to go even further, Kate. I've got a chance to learn things Great Grandmother never even dreamed of. I've got to go. Do you see?'

The thing is – and it shows how well he taught me, during our years together – I did see. I saw that he had to go.

He said, 'Look, I want to tell you something, OK? I've got a plan. I haven't told anyone else and I don't want you to tell anyone. It'll be our secret. OK? Promise?'

I nodded.

'When I finish university, if I've done really well I'll be able to get a good job and earn lots of money. And then

I'll pay for you to go to university too. And when *you've* done, the *two* of us will pay for Bo and Luke to go. That's my plan. What do you think?'

What did I think? I thought I would probably die from losing him, but that if I did not, it would almost be worth having lived, to be part of such a glorious plan.

PART FIVE

Twenty

DANIEL SAID, 'You realize this is my first experience of real uncharted wilderness. I've flown over it before but I've never been *in* it.'

I said, 'It's been charted for at least a hundred years. If you look, you'll notice we're on a road.'

'A track,' Daniel said cheerfully. 'A mere track.'

It isn't a track, it's a paved road. And even before it was paved it was a perfectly decent road, a bit boggy in the spring, a bit dusty in the summer, snowed in from time to time in the winter, but otherwise just fine. Daniel was loving it though. As far as he was concerned, this was the Real Thing, this was Nature in the Raw. Daniel knows as much about the great outdoors as your average Toronto taxi driver.

I had no classes on Friday afternoons and he had only one tutorial which ended at eleven, so we'd set off as soon as he finished. It's a four-hundred-mile trip and while it no longer seems an unimaginable distance it is still a good long drive.

The weather was good, a fine clear April day. The sprawl of Toronto gave way quite quickly to fields, and then the soil got thinner and fields gave way to meadows bounded by trees, with the rounded grey shapes of granite breaking the surface here and there like whales. And then the whales began to take over, and the meadows were merely rough patches of grass between the rocks.

We reached cottage country by two. After Huntsville the traffic thinned out, and from North Bay onwards we had the road to ourselves. It's paved all the way to Struan now. It is only when you turn off to Crow Lake that the tarmac runs out and the forest closes in and you really start to feel you're going back in time.

Up ahead there was a clutch of scrubby white pines growing close to the road. I slowed down and pulled over.

'Again?' Daniel said.

'Afraid so.'

I got out of the car and picked my way through the underbrush to the pines. They were growing in a shallow dip between bare ribs of granite; around them tough wiry blueberry bushes fought with the grasses and the mosses and the lichens, all of them struggling for foot-room. In some places there is so little topsoil you wouldn't think it was worth the effort of trying to grow, but they manage. They thrive, in fact. They find every crack, every crevice, every crumb of soil, and send out their tough little roots and dig in, and cling on, and hoard every dropped leaf, every twig, every grain of sand or dust that's blown their way, and gradually, gradually build up enough soil around themselves to support their offspring. And so it goes on, down the centuries. I forget, when I'm away, how much I love this landscape. I squatted down behind the scant shelter of the pines, flapping my hands behind me to fend off the blackflies, and peed into a brilliant green pillow of moss, and ached with love for it.

'You OK?' Daniel said when I got back to the car. 'Want me to drive for a bit?'

'I'm OK.'

I was tense, that was all.

It was the previous Tuesday that I'd had my little crisis of confidence in the lecture theatre. I'd been in a bit of a state afterwards and for the next couple of nights I hadn't slept well. On the Thursday I'd had another class and though it had gone all right – no flashbacks, no drying up mid-sentence, a reasonable question-and-answer session at the end – I was exhausted afterwards. I'd returned to my lab intending to work but my concentration was gone. Matt kept coming back to me. An image of him, standing by the pond. I went into my office and sat down at my desk and stared out of the window at the Toronto skyline. It was raining. Dull grey Toronto rain. I thought, something's wrong with me. Maybe I'm sick.

But I knew I wasn't sick. The old expression 'sick at heart' came to me, and with it a memory of Mrs Stanovich weeping into the kitchen sink, telling the Lord that she dared say He must have His reasons but that it still made her just sick. 'Just *sick*. Sick at heart,' she'd said fiercely, determined that He should know. I don't think it was about us, that particular time. I think Mrs Tadworth's grandson had died of some childhood ailment that people didn't usually die of.

I watched the rain leaking down the window, small snail-trails of light. It seemed that nowadays all I did was think of home. It was getting me nowhere. I thought, You should pull yourself together. Sort out what the problem is and work it out. Solving problems is supposed to be what you're good at.

237

Though I don't have much experience of solving problems I can't even put a name to.

At that point there was a hesitant tap at the door and I turned and saw one of my second-year students, Fiona deJong, framed in the doorway. Normally a student in the doorway is a sight that fills me with unreasoning impatience, but at the moment any distraction seemed worth having, so I asked what I could do for her. She's a pale girl, not very attractive, with limp, mousy hair. From what I've seen of her in class I'd guess she doesn't socialize much, but she is one of the few students of mine for whom, academically speaking, there is some hope, and her work depresses me less than most.

She said, 'Could I . . . talk with you for a minute, Dr Morrison?'

'Sure,' I said. 'Come in, Fiona. Have a seat.' I nodded at the chair against the wall and, still hesitant, she went and sat down.

Some of my colleagues – mainly female – complain that they are endlessly interrupted by students – again mainly female – coming to ask their advice on subjects totally unrelated to their studies. Personal problems and so on. I don't suffer much from that sort of interruption. Perhaps I don't look the sympathetic type. I guess I'm not the sympathetic type. Sympathy and empathy are linked, after all. So I was expecting Fiona's problem to be related to her work and I was surprised and rather alarmed when I saw that her mouth was trembling.

I cleared my throat. After a minute, when things didn't seem to be improving, I said very calmly, 'What's the problem, Fiona?'

She was staring into her lap, obviously battling to collect herself and I suddenly thought, Oh God. She's pregnant.

I can't deal with that sort of thing. The university has its own counselling service staffed by qualified psychologists who have experience in such matters and who know what to say.

I said quickly, 'If it's a personal thing, Fiona . . . if it isn't connected to your work, then I may not be the best person . . .'

She looked up. 'It is connected to my work. It's . . . well, I just wanted to tell you that I'm leaving. I've decided it's the best thing to do. But I just wanted to tell you. Because I've really enjoyed your course and everything, so I wanted you to know.'

I stared at her. As well as surprise, I was conscious of a small flicker of pleasure. Here was a student telling me that she had actually enjoyed my course.

I said, 'Leaving? You mean leaving university? Or changing to another course?'

'Leaving university. It's, well, it's difficult to explain, but basically, I don't think I want to go on.'

I blinked at her. 'But you're doing very well. What . . . what do you see as being the problem?'

So she told me what she saw as being the problem, and it was nothing to do with being pregnant. She told me that she came from a small farm in Quebec. She described it to me, but she didn't need to; I could see it perfectly well. I could practically see the pattern on the blue and white china on the kitchen table.

She was one of five children, the only one interested in learning. She had won a scholarship to university. Her father had been both astonished and annoyed when she said she was taking it up. He couldn't see what good a degree would do her. A waste of time, he said, and a waste of money. Her mother was proud of her, but mystified.

239

Why would she want to leave home? Her brothers and sisters thought she was weird anyway, so their opinion remained unchanged. Her boyfriend tried to understand. She looked at me entreatingly when she told me that. She wanted me to like him, to admire him for trying.

The problem was that she was growing away from all of them. When she went home now, none of them knew what to say to her. Her father joked acidly about how brainy she was. He called her Miss Fiona deJong, BA, BB, B-whatever. Her mother, whom she had been close to, was shy with her now. Afraid to talk to her because she had nothing intelligent to say.

Her boyfriend was angry a lot of the time. He tried not to be, but he was. He saw condescension where there wasn't any. He saw disdain, when in fact she admired him. He had left school at sixteen. When he was eighteen his father had had a stroke and since then he'd been running the farm more or less single-handed. He was kind, she said, and as intelligent in his own way as any of the boys on the course, and about a hundred times more mature, but he did not believe she thought that. He didn't say so, but she was sure that secretly he thought that if she really loved him, she would give up the course and come home and marry him.

Fiona stopped talking and sat looking at me, her face full of mute appeal. I tried to think what to say.

Finally I said, 'Fiona, how old are you?'

'Twenty-one.'

Twenty-one. 'Don't you think you're . . . a little young to be making decisions like this?'

'But . . . I have to make it. I mean, either way it's a decision, isn't it?'

'But you've completed two years of your degree.

You're halfway there. If you give up now, those years are wasted . . . Surely at this stage the sensible thing would be to finish your course, and then . . . then you'd be in a better position to make the . . . other decisions.'

She looked at her lap. She said, 'I just don't think it's worth it.'

'You said you were enjoying the course . . .'

'Yes, but . . .'

'You also said your mother is proud of you. I'm sure your father is too. He may not understand what you're doing, but I'm sure that deep down he will be proud that you've done so well. And your brothers and sisters too, though probably they wouldn't want to show it. And as for your boyfriend . . . don't you think that if he really cared for you he wouldn't want you to give up something so important? Something that can make such a difference to your life?'

She was silent, staring at her lap.

I said, 'I understand what you're feeling, I come from a background that is not all that dissimilar to yours, but I assure you, it has been worth it. The pleasure, the satisfaction . . .'

Something dropped into her lap. A tear. Tears were rolling slowly down her cheeks. I looked away, out of the door, into the ordered chaos of my lab. I thought, that was a pack of lies. You do not understand what she's feeling. You do not come from a similar background. The fact that there were fields and trees around does not make it similar. And anyway what are you doing, trying to convince her to make the decision you would have made? She came to tell you that she was leaving, not to ask your advice. She came out of politeness.

She'd found a tissue in her jacket pocket and was mopping herself up.

I said, 'I'm sorry. Just . . . forget what I said.'

She said, her voice muffled by the tissue, 'That's OK. I know you're probably right.'

'I'm probably wrong.'

She needed another tissue. I got up and searched through the pockets of my coat and found one for her.

'Thanks,' she said, and blew her nose. 'I've been thinking about it and thinking about it and now I just get such a headache that I can't think at all.'

I nodded. That at least was a feeling we shared. After a minute I said, 'Would you do something for me?'

She looked uncertain.

'Would you go and talk to someone at the counselling service? I don't think they'll try to persuade you one way or the other, I think they'll just help you to think it through, so that you're sure in your own mind.'

She agreed to do that, and a couple of minutes later, more or less composed, she left.

When she had gone I turned my chair back to the window and resumed my study of the rain. I thought about her brothers and sisters, who had always thought her 'weird', and I thought about Luke's and Matt's pride in my achievements. No, we did not come from similar backgrounds. No one had ever suggested that I should not go as far as I could. It had been expected of me, and I had been encouraged every step of the way.

And I had never regretted it. Not for one moment. Not even now. Because now, thinking about it again, I saw that whatever my little 'crisis' and my current problems were caused by, they were not caused by my work. That was a red herring. I might not be a very good teacher, but

Daniel was right, I wasn't all that much worse than most. And I was very good at research. We were making a contribution, my little invertebrates and I.

I thought about Fiona. Her fear of growing away from her family. Was that the problem? My conscious mind said that I was prepared to pay that price, but perhaps my unconscious mind did not agree.

But I hadn't grown away from them. Not from Luke and Bo, anyway. There was a temporary split, during my undergraduate years, but now I was as close to them, emotionally, as I would have been if I'd stayed in Crow Lake. We didn't have a great deal in common, but we were close for all that.

Matt, then.

I thought of Matt and there was . . . a moment of truth, I suppose. Fiona was afraid of leaving her family and her boyfriend behind and the truth was, she probably would. Her boyfriend might well be intelligent 'in his own way', but his way was not hers.

Matt's way was mine. It should have been impossible to leave Matt behind.

This crisis I was going through, not to mention the ache which I seemed to have carried around with me for most of my life – of course they were to do with him. How could it be otherwise? Everything I now was, I owed to him. All the years of watching him, learning from him, coming to share his passion – how could I not be affected by the way things had turned out? He had wanted his chance so badly and deserved it so much, and through his own fault – that was the worst of it – through his own fault he had thrown it away.

I sat at my desk, listening to the hum of the university behind me, aching with the pity of it all. I had imagined, once upon a time, that we would always be together. The two of us, forever side by side, staring into the pond. His plan — that absurd, naive, glorious plan. Childishness. Things change. Everyone has to grow up.

But not grow apart, as we had done, surely?

That was the real heart of it. I had never loved anyone as I loved Matt, but now, when we saw each other, there was something unbridgeable between us, and we had nothing to say.

Twenty-One

'IT SEEMS crazy to farm up here,' Daniel said, scratching his ankle. We'd picked up a cargo of blackflies when I'd stopped for a pee.

I'd been so far away that he startled me, and it took me a minute to work out what he was talking about. The landscape, of course. There was a fair amount of rock about.

I said, 'The soil isn't too bad. The land around Crow Lake's pretty good. Though it's a short growing season, of course.'

'But think of the effort – they must have been desperate to come this far north.'

'They didn't have much choice. They had no money, most of them, and the land up here was free. Crown Land. Back then, provided you cleared it you could have it for nothing.'

'I can see why, if you don't mind my saying so.' He scratched savagely. It looked as if his love affair with Uncharted Wilderness was going to be a short one. Daniel knows about blackflies in theory, of course, but there's no substitute for first-hand experience when it comes to bugs.

245

'It's not so bad near the lake,' I said. 'And the farm's fine – except where the fields border the woods.'

'You grew up right on the lake?' he said.

'That's right.'

'You never lived on the farm?'

'No.'

I'd started telling him the story – the whole of it – just before we got to New Liskeard. I hadn't intended to; in the main it is Matt's story and I have protected it from public gaze all these years. But as the miles ticked past I realized that Daniel would have to know; two minutes of conversation with Matt would tell him that Matt should not be where he was. Still, I put off the telling of it until shortly after we passed Cobalt, when Daniel remarked – referring to me – that it seemed an unlikely environment to have produced an academic. That irritated me. Surely the most unlikely place to produce an academic is a city, with its noise and confusion and lack of time for thought or contemplation?

I started arguing the case, trying to explain why Crow Lake was actually the perfect breeding ground for academics, given certain other conditions such as encouragement and time to study. And inevitably I used Matt and his passion for the ponds as an example, and of course that led to questions and the whole thing came out. To my extreme annoyance I had difficulty keeping my voice steady when I told him how it all ended; Daniel noticed, of course, though he didn't let on. If he was baffled by the fact that I was still so upset about it after all these years, well, he was no more baffled than I was.

Now he said tentatively, 'Luke and your sister – Bo. Do they still live there? In the house you grew up in?'

'Yes.'

246

'What do they do? Bo must be . . . twenty?'

'Twenty-one. She works in Struan. She's a cook in a restaurant.'

Still happily slinging saucepans about. She did a cookery course down in Sudbury. She could have done a degree in household economics or whatever it's called – I offered to help with the cost – but she said she wasn't interested in the academic side.

'Does she have a boyfriend?'

'From time to time. Nothing permanent so far. Though she will in due course.'

In a world of few certainties, that is one of them. Matt says some poor guy is wandering around out there still blissfully unaware of what fate has in store for him.

'And is Luke still the janitor at the school?'

'Only on the side. He makes furniture.'

'Furniture? He's started a business?'

'Sort of. He turned our garage into a workshop. He employs a couple of boys off the farms. He does all right.'

He does quite well, in fact. Rustic furniture is all the rage.

'Is he married?'

'No.'

'That girl . . . the one you said kept hanging round him . . .'

'Sally McLean.'

'Yeah. He didn't ever get it together with her, then?'

'Heaven forbid. No, she managed to get herself pregnant by someone else about a year after Luke . . . turned her down.'

'Someone else in Crow Lake?'

'Yes. Tomek Lucas. I don't think he was convinced he was the father, but she swore he was so they got married.

247

But then she saw someone better-looking at the cattle market in New Liskeard and she went off with him. Left the baby with Tomek. His mum brought it up. Sally probably has ten more by now. She probably has ten *grandchildren* by now.'

I thought suddenly of Mr and Mrs McLean. How they would adore ten grandchildren.

'You make it sound like centuries ago,' Daniel said. 'If your parents died when you were seven, it's barely twenty years.'

'It feels like centuries,' I said.

SALLY McLEAN, of the long red hair. When I was thirteen, just starting high school, a new classmate said, 'You're the one with no parents, aren't you? And you've got a brother who's queer.'

I didn't know what queer meant. I can't describe the shock when I found out. I remembered, then, that little scene I'd stumbled on: Sally leaning against a tree, taking Luke's hand and guiding it so smoothly, so competently, to her breast. Luke standing, motionless, head bowed. And then the effort, as if against some huge invisible force, as he pushed himself away.

For a long time I was convinced that it must have been Sally who started that rumour. Now I'm not so sure. I suspect that many people found it hard to accept Luke's sacrifice for what it was. He was only nineteen, remember, and such generosity at such an early age put other people to shame. So they had to belittle it. There's nothing noble in giving up something you didn't want anyway. Nothing noble in resisting sexual relationships with women if you're gay. Nothing noble in turning down a place at teachers' college if you didn't want to go. That was another theory I overheard.

Though maybe there was some truth in that one. I suspect Luke wasn't all that interested in becoming a teacher. It was what our parents wanted and he didn't have any alternative suggestions at the time, or didn't dare to voice them. And it's probably also true that he didn't realize, on that day when he announced to Aunt Annie that he was going to look after us, how much he was going to have to give up for our sakes.

As far as I'm concerned, that doesn't lessen his sacrifice. When he found out what he was going to have to give up – he gave it up. As Sally McLean found out.

I wonder if he knew about those rumours. I wonder if that was another thing he had to contend with.

'So there's still no woman in his life?' Daniel asked. He sounded dissatisfied. I looked at him with amusement. Daniel would be astonished if you told him he was a romantic. 'How old is he now?'

'Thirty-eight. As far as I know there isn't anyone.'

Though strangely enough, I started to wonder about that the last time I visited. Miss Carrington dropped in, as she always does when I come home, and it seemed to me that there was – how can I describe it? – an *easiness* between her and Luke. I could have imagined it, I guess. She's at least ten years older than he is. Though she doesn't seem that much older now.

'Maybe it's become a habit,' Daniel said.

'What has?'

'Self-denial. Resisting temptation.'

'Maybe,' I said. Thinking of Matt.

I switched on the headlights. It had reached that stage of twilight where the sky is still clear and light but the road and the trees and rocks are merging into a smoky blur. Far ahead, you could make out the winking of a light each time we crested a hill. Struan. Half an hour after Struan, we'd be home.

*

THERE'S A lot I have to guess at. I'm guessing, for instance, that Mrs Pye was in a really serious state that summer, and that worry about her, coming on top of everything else, was more than Marie could bear alone. So she turned for comfort to Matt. If she'd had more friends, or if her mother had had family living near, or if Calvin hadn't alienated the whole community to such an extent that no one knocked on the door any more — if any of those things, then maybe Marie would not have needed to turn so hard, so urgently, so appealingly, to Matt.

Matt was available, you see. He was there, though mainly out in the fields, every day, six days a week, all that summer. He was scraping together every penny he could, not for himself — he had so many scholarships even the cost of his books was covered — but to salve his conscience for leaving the rest of us.

So he was available. And they'd been friends, of a sort, for a long time. And I think his grief over the loss of our parents had broken down some of the reserve between them the previous summer. He'd let her see that he was grieving. I think that may have formed a bond.

She didn't tell him everything, even then, but I'd be prepared to bet she wept on his shoulder. I'm guessing that's how it started.

He'd have put his arms around her. Of course he would; it's a natural reaction when someone weeps on your shoulder, even for Presbyterians. He would have held

250

her. Probably he would have patted her back, awkwardly, as if she were Bo. They'd have been round the back of the barn or behind the tractor shed – somewhere out of sight of Calvin.

Definitely out of sight of Calvin. I'm sure they never even spoke to each other when Calvin was around.

He'd have put his arms around her, out of pity and compassion, knowing from his own experience what it is to be wretched and unable to speak. I do not believe for a moment that he was in love with her. But he was eighteen and when he put his arms around her he would have felt how soft she was. She was not pretty, in my opinion. Not at all. Too much flesh on her and not enough definition to her features. But she was undeniably feminine, and when he held her, her breasts would have pressed against him; his chin would have brushed her hair; he would have smelled the warm scent of her. He was eighteen, as I say. She was probably the first person he'd embraced, outside our family.

It would have happened by accident, the first time. They'd have bumped into each other when she was in tears about something. He would have stood awkwardly for a moment and then put down whatever he was carrying, and they would have moved closer, probably not even aware that they were doing so. She would have leaned against him, because finally there was someone to lean against, and he would have put his arms around her. After a few minutes she would have stepped back, and wiped her face, and said, 'I'm sorry,' in that pale, timid little voice of hers.

And he would have said, 'It's all right, Marie. It's all right.'

Twenty-Two

MATT AND I didn't have much time together that summer. He left for the farm before I got up in the morning and by the time he got home in the evening he was too tired to do anything but flop on his bed and read. I spent the days reluctantly doing chores for Luke or Mrs Stanovich, or playing half-heartedly with the children of kindly neighbours who invited Bo and me over to help Luke out. I lived for Sundays, when Matt would be free. And at first he was, and took me back to the ponds as before, and told me how he was going to study about the creatures in them at university and how there would be powerful microscopes so you could see just how things worked. He said that he would write to me, at least two letters a week, and tell me about what he was learning so that when it was my turn I would have a head start. He made me see that although we would be apart we would be carrying on pond-watching, both of us, and telling each other about it. And there would be the summers. He promised that. No matter what the money situation was, he would come home for the summers.

That was how it was the first few weeks after his exams

were over – our usual routine, but full of plans and promises as well. But then things changed. Matt took to disappearing straight after lunch on Sundays. Sometimes he didn't get back until almost supper time and the whole afternoon had been lost.

I was deeply resentful, needless to say. I interrogated him about where he went, and he said for walks. I said couldn't I come with him and he said, vaguely but kindly, that sometimes he needed to be alone. I said why, and he said that he had things on his mind.

I complained about him to Luke.

'Matt's never here any more.'

'Yeah. He's working.'

'No, I mean when he *isn't* working. On Sundays.'

'Yeah?' said Luke. 'Pass me that hammer, will you?' He was repairing the steps to the beach, which got mangled by the ice every winter. Bo was marching up and down at the water's edge, bellowing hymns. 'Jesus loves me *dis* I know, For la la la *dells* me so.' We didn't know whether to blame Mrs Stanovich or whether she'd picked them up at Sunday School.

'But where's he *go*?'

'I dunno, Kate. I need that plank. No, the shorter one. Pass it here, OK?'

'But he must go *somewhere*. And I want to go to the ponds!'

Luke looked at me, the hammer balanced in his hand. 'He's taken you to those damned ponds ten million times. Leave him alone, OK? No kidding, you'd think you owned him.'

He started hammering, loudly. If he minded Matt's absence himself, wishing that he would stick around and help out on the one day of the week when both of them were free, he didn't say so. He couldn't, I suppose, granted how he'd gone on about being able to manage on his own. But also, he may have thought that Matt was worrying about leaving us all and was trying to sort things out in his mind, and needed time alone. Which was true, of course, but beside the point.

I made no such allowances. All that was in my mind was the thought of how few hours I had left with Matt. And when I look back on it now I could weep, because in my resentment, I managed to spoil those few. He did take me back to the ponds now and then and I was incapable of enjoying it. It seemed to me that he was distracted, not concentrating as he should. I accused him. I said, 'Don't you like the ponds any more?'

And he said tiredly, 'What are you talking about, Kate? Look, if *you* aren't enjoying it, let's go home.'

I WAS forbidden to go back to the ponds alone. They were deep and a child had been drowned there once. Perhaps that was why I went – as an act of rebellion.

It was an extremely hot day, heavy and still. I walked tight-rope along the rails, the heat of the steel burning through the soles of my shoes, and then slid down the path to 'our' pond. It felt very strange to be there on my own. For a while I lay on my stomach and stared into the water, but everything that could move was in hiding from the sun. Even if you poked about, you only got a brief flurry of activity and then stillness again. I stood up, dizzy from the heat. If Matt had been there he would have sought the shade on the other side of the bank between our pond and the next. At the foot of the bank I hesitated, thinking I heard voices, though I knew I couldn't have. No one ever came here but us. I scrambled up the side of the bank, using the tufts of grass as hand-holds, and hauled myself onto the flat grassy top. There were voices. Definitely there were. I stood up and peered over the side.

THEY WERE lying in the shade of the overhanging bank, about twenty feet below and to the left of where I stood. Matt had taken off his shirt and spread it on the ground and they were both on that. Marie was lying down and Matt was kneeling beside her.

Marie was curled on her side, her knees drawn up. She was crying. From where I stood I could not see her face, but I could hear her. Matt was saying something to her, the same thing over and over again. I remember how urgent his voice was, almost frightened, utterly unlike him. He kept saying, 'Oh God, I'm sorry. Oh God, Marie, I'm sorry. I'm sorry.'

I couldn't figure out what he'd done. Maybe he'd hit her – hit her ferociously and knocked her down. Though I could hardly believe it; it took such a lot to make Matt angry enough to hit anyone that Luke was the only one who ever managed it. Then I noticed his shirt again and realized that he would not have spread it out in order to knock her down on it, so it couldn't be that.

After a bit he helped her up and tried to put his arms around her. She turned away. She was wearing a thin cotton-print dress. It was creased and rumpled and had come completely undone down the front. She began doing it up, sniffling and fumbling. Matt watched her, his hands clenched at his sides.

'I'm sorry,' he said again. 'I didn't mean it to happen, Marie. I just couldn't . . . But it'll be OK. Don't worry. It'll be OK.'

She shook her head, not looking at him. I remember that in spite of my confusion, I hated her for that. You could see how upset he was but she wouldn't accept it. She finished doing herself up, then straightened and smoothed back her hair.

It was then that she saw me. She gave a cry of absolute terror and Matt jerked back and then saw me himself. For a minute all three of us were frozen. Then Marie started crying hysterically. Her fear was so great that it communicated itself to me and I turned and ran, slithered down the other side of the bank, around the edge of our pond, running as I had never run in all my life, my heart pounding with fear. I was halfway up the path to the railroad tracks when Matt caught me.

'Kate! Kate, stop!' He caught me around the waist and held me. I was kicking and struggling, trying to kick his legs. 'Kate, *stop*! What are you afraid of? There's nothing to be afraid of! Kate, *stop*!'

'I want to go home!'

'We will. In just a minute. We'll go home together. But we have to go back to Marie first.'

'I'm not going back to her! She's horrible! Screaming like that — she's *disgusting*!'

'She's just upset. You startled her. Come on now.'

She was standing where he had left her, arms wrapped around herself, shivering in the blazing heat. Matt brought me up to her, but he didn't know what to say. It was Marie who spoke.

'She'll tell.' She was white as chalk. White as a fish's belly, trembling, weeping, snivelling.

'No she won't. You won't tell, will you, Kate?'

I had recovered from my fright and was starting to feel outraged. Was this where he had been? Could this possibly be where he had been? On our precious Sundays?

I said, 'Tell what?'

256

'Oh Matt! She will! She'll tell!' More weeping.

Matt turned first to her, then to me. 'Kate, you have to promise. Promise me that you won't tell that you saw us here.'

I wouldn't look at him. I watched Marie. Marie Pye, whom Matt preferred to me, though she had no interest in the ponds whatever – you knew that just by looking at her.

'Kate? Promise me.'

'I promise I won't tell on you,' I said at last, turning to him. But he was too smart for that.

'Or on Marie. You must promise not to tell that you saw her with anyone. Word of honour.'

The silence grew.

Matt said quietly, 'Word of honour, Kate. Promise me on all the times I've brought you to these ponds. Promise on the life of every creature in these ponds.'

I had no choice then. Sullenly, mumbling, I gave my word. Marie looked a little less fearful. Matt put an arm around her and led her a few yards away. I watched them, jealousy making my lower lip quiver. He talked to her very quietly, for a long time. Finally she nodded, and walked off across the sand towards the path that led up to her father's farm.

Matt and I walked home together. I remember I kept looking up at him, hoping that he would smile and everything would be as it had always been, but he seemed unaware of my presence. In the coolness of the woods I drew up the courage to ask if he was mad at me.

'No. No, I'm not mad at you,' he said. He gave me a smile of such misery that I was shamed out of my own self-pity.

'Are you all right?' I said, loving him, almost forgiving him. 'Is everything going to be all right?'

He was different after that. He continued working on the farm but in the evenings and on Sundays he shut himself in his room. I did not know what was wrong with him. In fact I hardly thought in those terms. I was too bewildered by that closed door to think of anyone but myself. But I can imagine now what he must have gone through, as one week followed another, waiting and hoping, and no doubt praying too, for we had been brought up to believe in a merciful God.

I can imagine how in his mind he kept trying to turn the clock back to that one final moment when he could have stopped, but did not. In later years, when I thought about the similarity between what happened to him and what might have happened to Luke and Sally McLean, it seemed to me that you could define my brothers' lives by one moment, and it was the same moment for both of them. With Luke, it was the moment he pushed himself away. With Matt, it was the moment he did not.

God was not merciful. One night in September, a few weeks before he was due to leave for Toronto, Marie Pye came to the door, hair wild, eyes wild, asking for him.

He was in his bedroom but he must have heard her, or sensed her presence, because he was at the door before Luke or I had time to fetch him, and he pushed past us and took her outside, and we heard him say, 'Wait, wait. Let's go down to the beach.' But she couldn't wait, her terror was too great to hold, she was doubled over with it, almost crouching on the ground. She said – and we heard her plainly because fear forced the words out far too loudly and we hadn't even had time to close the door – 'Matt, he'll kill me! He'll kill me! Matt, he'll kill me! You don't believe me but he will! He killed Laurie, and he'll kill me too!'

PART SIX

Twenty-Three

THAT LAST stretch of the journey from Toronto to Crow Lake always takes me by the throat. Partly it's the familiarity; I know every tree, every rock, every boggy bit of marshland so well, that even though I almost always arrive after dark I can feel them around me, lying there in the darkness as if they were my own bones. Partly too, it is the sensation of going back in time, moving from 'now' to 'then', and the recognition that wherever you are now and wherever you may be in the future, nothing alters the point you started from.

Normally, the feeling is as much pleasure as pain. It fills me with a sort of all-pervading regret, but it also anchors me and helps me to know who I am. That Friday night, though, with Daniel in the passenger seat, still peering out of the window as if by penetrating the darkness he might learn whatever there was to know about me, the memories were too close. They weighed too much. I could not see how I was going to get through the coming celebrations – the joking, the merry-making, the being-sociable, not to mention bringing Daniel into it all. It seemed to me that they must think that I was flaunting

261

him. Bringing him home deliberately in order to show off my success. Here am I, with my wonderful career and here is my boyfriend with his wonderful career, and look at all of you. I felt I would die rather than have them think that of me.

'How far?' Daniel asked suddenly, out of the darkness.

'Five minutes.'

'Oh! Great! Didn't know we were so close.' He shifted his position, trying to ease the stiffness. He'd said almost nothing for the past half hour, for which I was grateful.

I had to remind myself to turn right at the Northern Side Road rather than continue on to the lake. Normally when I come I stay with Luke and Bo, but the farm is about half a mile along the side road, on the left. You could see it as soon as we turned off the lake road. All the lights were on in the farmhouse and they'd switched on the lights over the barn and the silo as well, by way of welcome. The silo is new since Calvin Pye's day. And the barn is not the original one. Matt burned down Calvin's barn.

Matt and Marie were down by the driveway when we pulled in – they would have seen our lights as soon as we saw theirs, and guessed it was us. Marie hung back a bit while Matt and I hugged each other, holding each other hard. As children we never embraced – it's something we've started to do quite recently. Like coming home itself, it is both pleasure and pain. The feel of him is wonderful, but hugging seems such a symbolic gesture, in our case – a physical attempt to close an emotional distance, to bridge a gap which should not be there.

'Good trip?' he said, wrapping his arms right round me.

'Fine.'

We released each other, and he smiled at Daniel. 'You made it then.'

'Wouldn't have missed it,' Daniel said.

'He's not impressed by the bugs, though,' I said, trying for a lightness of tone and achieving it, more or less. 'Hi, Marie.'

Marie and I do not embrace. We smile the polite smile of acquaintances.

'Hi,' she said, still hanging back a bit. 'You made good time.'

'Bugs?' Matt said. 'Do we have bugs?'

'I should introduce you,' I said. 'Daniel, meet Matt and Marie.'

It was said. *Daniel, meet Matt* . . . After all these weeks of dreading it, visualizing it, living it in advance a thousand times, it was said. And my voice was fine. You wouldn't have known, if you were listening in, the huge and nameless weight behind those words. They were said, and I had survived it. The world was still turning on its axis. I should have felt relief.

'You must be hungry,' Marie said. 'We've held supper for you.'

Simon materialized out of the dark, tall and lanky, like his father. Terribly like his father.

'Hi, Auntie,' he said. 'Do I get a kiss?'

He calls me Auntie to tease. There is less than nine years between us. I kissed him, and he kissed me back, and shook hands with Daniel and said that it was nice of him to come.

Daniel said, 'You're the one it's all in honour of?' and Simon said, 'Yup.' Then he added, 'Well actually, it's just an excuse to get Aunt Kate to come home because we hardly ever see her. But you won't be sorry you came.

Huge amounts of food, Mum and Bo and everybody's been cooking like maniacs.'

'Speaking of which,' Matt said, 'Let's eat. Marie's made all of us wait for you.' He started ushering us towards the house.

Daniel was swatting blackflies again. Matt grinned, walking beside him. 'You'll have to come back in a month or so. Then we can introduce you to the mosquitoes as well.'

'Why is it just me?' Daniel said, smashing himself on the neck. 'What's the matter with you guys?'

'They're tired of us. We've got something in the house you can dose yourself with.'

Matt seemed much older than Daniel when I looked at them together. Of course he is older – he's thirty-seven and Daniel's thirty-four – but the difference seemed much greater than that. It's not physical, exactly – in fact he looks a good deal fitter than Daniel, and he has significantly more hair. But his face seems to have many more years of experience in it somehow. Also, there is a quietness about Matt. There was even when he was a boy, and it made him seem older than he was even then.

'Did you have a good trip?' Marie said, though the question had already been asked.

'Great, thanks.'

'Everybody's dying to see you.' She gave me her shy smile. She has changed very little over the years. If anything, her looks have improved. She still comes across as anxious but her eyes are less fearful now. The five of us began walking towards the house, Simon in the lead. 'Bo and Luke are coming over later,' Marie said. 'We said come for supper, but they said no, they'd just come for a chat.'

'They'll make it in time for dessert,' Simon said. 'At least, Luke will.'

'Well there's plenty,' Marie said mildly.

'Luke's in a bad way at the moment,' Simon said, turning round and grinning at us. 'He's started teaching Bo to drive again.'

'Really?' I said. 'She's worn him down at last then.'

'This is the third attempt,' Matt explained to Daniel. 'He started to teach her about five years ago, when Bo was sixteen, and it wasn't what you'd call a success. So they had a break and then tried again about two years later. I think that attempt only lasted about ten minutes. Bo's attitude to driving is . . .' he made circular motions with his hands, searching for the right word, 'casual. A combination of casual and overconfident. Luke found it a bit stressful.'

'That's an understatement,' Simon said. 'He was a broken man.'

Simon, I recalled, had passed his test the day he turned sixteen. It was virtually the only thing he could lord it over Bo about – she is three years his senior and has done everything first – and he made the most of it.

'Well I don't think you should tease her,' Marie said. 'I'm sure she'll do really well this time.' She turned to me. 'Mrs Stanovich is dying to see you. She's coming tomorrow, of course, to the party. And Miss Carrington. She's coming too.'

'All the old crowd,' I said. Simon dropped back to be with the men. Matt was pointing something out to Daniel. I heard him say, 'Over the top of the house.' I looked and there were half a dozen little brown bats darting silently back and forth, as if they were knitting together pieces of blue-black sky. All three men stopped to watch them, heads back.

'And the Tadworths, of course,' Marie was saying. 'And Simon's friends from school.'

I turned my attention back to her. Marie has no interest in bats, just as she has no interest in ponds.

'What time is everyone arriving?' I said.

'About noon.'

'Sounds good. We'll have the morning to prepare. Is there much to do?'

'Not much. A few desserts, that's all.'

'I bet you've been cooking for weeks.'

'Oh well, you know. I have the freezer, and it's good to have some things prepared ahead.'

That is what we do, Marie and I. We stick to practicalities. What time are we doing this? Where would you like me to put that? What a nice vase – where did you get it? Should I peel the potatoes?

LUKE AND Bo arrived as Marie was cutting the first slice of cheesecake.

'You're here!' Simon said. 'What timing!'

'Just thought we'd wander over,' Luke said, putting his hands on my shoulders and squeezing gently. 'Say hello to the stranger. Strangers,' he amended, seeing Daniel and stretching out his hand. Daniel stood up and they shook hands over the table. 'Glad you could come,' Luke said. 'I'm Luke. This is Bo.'

'Daniel,' said Daniel.

'Hi,' said Bo. 'I've brought a Bavarian Torte.' She dumped it down on the table.

Marie said, 'Oh how lovely. Is it for tomorrow?'

'There's another for tomorrow. This is for tonight. By

266

the way, did you know Mrs Stanovich has made a birthday cake? Giant thing. Three tiers and a little sugared Simon on the top.'

'Yes,' Marie said anxiously. 'I know you've made one, but she wanted to, and I thought, well, I'm sure we'll eat both.'

'Oh sure,' Bo said cheerfully. 'No problem. I just didn't know if you knew. Simon will eat both all by his little self. How are you, Little One? How does it feel to be nearly grown up?' She patted Simon on the head. He grabbed at her wrist but she eluded him serenely. 'Hi, Kate.' She bent and kissed my cheek. 'You look elegant. Thin though.'

She herself looked wonderful. She is an Amazon, my sister, tall and blond and beautiful as a warrior. Simon wouldn't stand a chance against her in a fair fight. In fact I suspect she could give even Luke a run for his money, though he was looking pretty fit himself. Nowadays every time I see Luke I am amazed all over again at how handsome he is. I never realized it as a child. He's nearly thirty-nine and he just keeps getting better. Eat your heart out, Sally McLean.

Matt said, 'Sit down, you lot. Have some cheesecake and some of Bo's mud pie. Go ahead, Marie, dole it out.'

Luke collapsed into a chair. I saw Simon grinning at him and forming a question about driving lessons, but Marie saw it too and inclined her head at him warningly, and he subsided.

'Did you have a good trip?' Luke asked. 'Before I forget, Laura Carrington sends her regards – she'll be here tomorrow. How's the big city? You're having another mail strike, I hear.'

'Aren't we always?' I said. 'Thanks, Marie, could I have a bit of each?'

Bo sat down beside me. 'I need to fill you in on all the gossip,' she said. 'What don't you know?'

'I'm not sure.'

'Did you know Janie Mitchell – well, Janie Laplant as she is now – is getting divorced? So actually she won't be Janie Laplant any more, she'll be Janie Mitchell.'

'I don't think I knew she'd become Janie Laplant.'

'You did. I told you. Did you know Mrs Stanovich is a great-grandmother again?'

'I think I did know that.'

'You're thinking of the last one. This one only arrived last Sunday. Did you know Mr Janie's dairy herd had won a prize? Or at least Ophelia won a prize. She produces more milk than any other cow in North America. Or maybe it's just in Struan County.'

Marie said, 'Daniel? Cheesecake or Bavarian Torte?'

Daniel was looking a bit dazed, due either to Bo or to the noise. He said, 'Um, both please.'

Luke was saying, '. . . so he bought the whole island. He's building this massive hunting lodge. Reckons rich Americans are going to come in their millions.'

'He think they're going to drive all the way up here?' Simon said.

'He'll fly them in. Sea planes.'

Matt said solemnly, 'Experience the Breathtaking Beauty of the Canadian Wilderness. Witness the . . .' he groped for words.

'Wild Savagery?' Simon suggested, equally solemn. 'Untamed Splendour?'

'Both of those. Witness the Wild Savagery of the Raging Rivers. Contemplate the Untamed Splendour of the Forests. See the Awesome Spectacle of . . .'

'How about "Thrill to"?'

'Thrill to the Awesome Spectacle of the Massive Moose . . .'

'Or Mammoth Moose . . .'

'Mighty Moose . . .'

'Jim Sumack reckons he's going to grow his hair and stick feathers in it and hire himself out as a guide,' Luke said. 'Make his fortune. I'm hoping they're going to need a very large amount of rustic furniture. Oh, thanks, Marie. A bit of both.'

'Do you think they will?'

'Well they're going to need furniture from somewhere. Save them money if they don't have to ship it in.'

'Endure the Rugged Grandeur of Luke's Rustic Furniture . . .'

Marie said, 'Bo? Cheesecake or Bavarian torte?'

Her cheeks were flushed, but now that the pressures of company-for-dinner were nearly over she looked less tense than she had earlier. In fact, as she hovered hopefully over the desserts with her cake-knife, it seemed to me that she looked almost content.

I thought, Do you forget it all, then? Living here, in this house which saw such terrible things, do you somehow manage simply not to think about it? Is that how you go on?

*

THAT NIGHT – that memorable September night – it was Luke, stunned and disbelieving though he was, who took charge. Matt wasn't in a state to do anything. I remember him standing with Marie. They were outside still, and she was still sobbing with terror. He was holding her, helplessly, helplessness in every line of his body. I remember Luke going out to them and bringing them

269

both in. He tried to calm Marie down, but she was beside herself with fear. I don't think she even knew Luke and I were there. She kept saying to Matt, 'Matt, I'm two months late. I'm sick every morning and I'm two months late. Matt, he'll kill me. Oh God, he'll kill me.'

Luke said, 'OK, Marie, calm down,' but she couldn't. He himself had the look of someone who had just woken up and didn't know where he was. He said, 'Kate, go put the kettle on. Make her some tea or something.' So I went and put the kettle on, but then I went right back.

Marie was still clinging on to Matt and Luke was trying to talk to her. He said, 'Marie? I've got to ask you something. You said he killed Laurie. What did you mean? Marie, listen to me. Who killed Laurie?'

Matt said, 'Leave her, Luke.' It was the first time he'd spoken since she'd started her outburst. His voice was hoarse and unsteady.

Luke said, 'No, we've got to know. Marie? Who killed Laurie? Was it your dad?'

Matt said, 'I said leave her! Jesus Christ! Can't you see the state she's in?'

Luke didn't look at him. He couldn't look at him. He kept his eyes on Marie. He said quietly, 'I see the state she's in all right. Are you saying we should calm her down and send her home to her father?'

Matt stared at him, but Luke wouldn't meet his eyes. He said, 'Marie, you've got to tell us. Did your father kill Laurie?'

She looked at him. You could see her focus on him, and figure out who he was. She whispered, 'Yes.'

'Are you sure? Did you see it happen?'

'Yes.'

'But Laurie ran away, Marie. Matt saw him go.'

Her eyes were huge in the whiteness of her face. She said, 'He came back. It was cold. He came back for his coat, and my dad caught him, and he took him into the barn. We tried to stop him but we couldn't, and he hit him, and Laurie hit him back, so then he hit him and hit him, and Laurie fell, and he hit his head and there was blood, and there was blood . . .'

Luke said, 'OK. OK, Marie.'

'. . . and there was blood, and . . .'

Luke said to Matt, without looking at him, 'Take her into the other room.'

'What are you going to do?'

'I'm going to call Dr Christopherson and then I'm going to call the police.'

Marie gave another cry. She said, 'He didn't mean to kill him! He was hitting him, and we were trying to stop him, and he was hitting him and Laurie fell! He hit his head on the blade of the plough! Oh God, oh God, don't call the police! He'll kill me!'

Luke said, 'Take her into the other room.'

Marie said, 'No! No! Oh please! Oh please don't, he'll kill us all! He'll kill my mother! He'll kill us all!'

Matt couldn't move, so Luke brushed him aside and picked her up and though she was screaming and fighting him he carried her into the other room, with Matt trailing helplessly behind. He said to Matt, 'Keep her here.' And then he came back and called Dr Christopherson and the police.

CALVIN PYE killed himself three hours later.

The police had driven out from Struan and had come first to our house to talk to Marie, in the presence of Dr Christopherson. From there they went to the farm. Calvin himself opened the door to them. When they said that they had come to ask him a few questions about Laurie's disappearance, he said, fine, but could he just go and tell his wife because she'd be wondering who was at the door. They said yes, and waited uneasily on the doorstep. Almost at once there was a shot. Calvin kept a loaded shotgun above the fireplace in the living room and he shot himself right there, in front of Mrs Pye, before she had time to get out of her chair. Rosie, fortunately, was asleep upstairs.

Calvin died without saying where Laurie's body was, and neither Marie nor her mother knew. It took the police two weeks to find it and they discovered it then only because of a combination of a dry summer and a peculiar chance. Calvin had put Laurie's body in an old feed sack weighted with rocks, and dropped the sack into one of the ponds. The pond he chose – not the one closest to the farm, and not 'our' pond, but one of the deeper ones in between – was steep-sided, and the sack would have sunk a good twenty feet except that it snagged on a jutting piece of rock. By October, when the water level was at its lowest, the top of the sack was just visible below the surface.

Dr Christopherson took Mrs Pye to the mental hospital in St Thomas two days after Laurie's body was found. She died within a year of no disease anyone could put a name to. Rosie was sent to her mother's relatives in New Liskeard. I know Marie tried to keep in touch with her, but Rosie never really mastered the art of writing, so it was difficult. She married very young and moved out of the area. Whether Marie knows where she is now, I've never liked to ask.

Matt and Marie married in October and Matt took over

the farm. I'm sure it was the last thing in the world either of them wanted to do.

The week before the wedding, when the police had finished all their investigations and no longer needed access to the barn where Laurie had died, Matt burned it down. That act was his wedding present to Marie. Luke helped him build a new one. That was his wedding present to the two of them.

Simon was born the following April. It was a difficult birth, and as a consequence Marie has been unable to have more children.

Twenty-Four

I WAS AWAKENED about five in the morning by the tractor starting up. Daniel snorted and opened his eyes and said, 'What the *hell* was that?' and I said, 'The tractor,' but he was already asleep again.

I lay for a while, missing the sound of the lake. Normally, as I said, I stay with Luke and Bo when I come home, and the quiet slow hush, hush of the waves is the last and first thing I hear every day. Here it was farmyard noises instead. And the sound of Daniel breathing beside me.

There had been, as I had known there would be, a moment's embarrassment the night before about the sleeping arrangements. After the clearing up was done, when Luke and Bo had gone and Simon had said goodnight and gone off upstairs, I'd overheard Marie, who was still in the kitchen with Matt, say, 'Well *you* ask her. *I* can't ask her.' And a moment later Matt came into the living room looking uncomfortable.

But I'd anticipated it and worked out what to say. I could have suggested separate rooms just to save embarrassment. Daniel would have gone along with it, though he wouldn't have understood why. But although I had not wanted him to come, granted that he was here I found that I wanted him beside me. I wanted him to be a buffer between me and the rest of them. He was my present. If he was there, then perhaps the past would not spread out in the night and overwhelm me. Besides, I thought, a shade defiantly, what right had Matt, of all people, to pass judgement? Silly, I know. It would never occur to him to judge me.

So when he came into the living room examining a small scratch on his hand with unusual interest I said casually, 'I think it's about time we went up too, Matt. Where do you want us? The front bedroom?' I knew the layout of the upstairs and knew that apart from Matt and Marie's room, the front room was the only one with a double bed. And Matt looked relieved and said, Yes, sure. That would be fine.

We took our bags up, undressed and climbed into the big loose-sprung double bed. I was expecting Daniel to keep me awake half the night dissecting my family, but he must have been worn out by the Untamed Splendour of the Wilderness because after telling me that I hadn't described them properly *at all*, he almost instantly fell asleep. I lay awake for half an hour or so, listening to the movements of the house and thinking about things long gone, and finally fell into sleep like falling into a pit, and didn't wake until the tractor roared.

For a while after that I lay awake, trying not to think too much about the room we were in. It was the largest bedroom in the house and in the best position, overlooking the farmyard. It must have been Mr and Mrs Pye's room — otherwise Matt and Marie would have used it. It was what Miss Vernon would have called handsome; well-proportioned, with screened windows on two sides. Matt and Marie used a room at the side of the house and Simon had a smaller one beside the bathroom. There were three other bedrooms, one of them furnished with bunks, one with a desk for the farm accounts, and the other used as a store room. Apart from the bunks, which were built-in, I was pretty sure that most of the furniture in the house post-dated the Pyes. I imagine Matt and Marie got rid of everything they could, and replaced things slowly, when they could afford to. They'd want as little to remind them of the past as possible.

I lay halfway between sleep and wakefulness, thinking dimly that even so, you would expect there to be a lingering atmosphere of despair in the house and yet, somehow, there didn't seem to be. And then I must have fallen asleep again because the next thing I heard was the tractor coming back and Matt and Simon talking in low voices out in the yard. It was seven o'clock, so I prodded Daniel and got up.

Marie was in the middle of making French toast and bacon and sausages and corn bread and muffins and scrambled eggs. I asked if I could help and she looked slightly panicky at the thought and said, 'Oh, thanks, but . . . I don't think so. Maybe you could find the men and tell them breakfast is in ten minutes? I think they're in the yard.'

So I went out. The sun was strong already, and the sky a pale clear blue. Daniel had joined Matt and Simon and the three of them were admiring the tractor.

'How much did it set you back?' Daniel was saying. 'If it's not a rude question.'

Simon and Matt looked blankly at each other.

276

'How much was it, in the end?' Matt said. 'We beat him down quite a bit.'

'Like hell we did,' Simon said. 'You chickened out. It was tragic. Here's Auntie Kate. How do you like our baby?' He patted the tractor's muddy flank. Where you could see through the mud it was gleaming red; it looked powerful and business-like, with its vast wheels and deep-cut treads, and oddly graceful, in the way anything well-designed is graceful.

I said, 'Happy birthday, Simon. Your baby's lovely. Is she new?'

'Two weeks old today.'

'She's got a terrible cough first thing in the morning,' I said. 'Are you sure she's all right?'

'Spoken like a true city slicker,' Matt said. 'We're just going to take Dan out for a run. If you're lucky you can have a turn later.'

I said, 'Actually, I came to tell you breakfast is almost ready. Marie says ten minutes.'

'Oh,' said Matt. He looked at Daniel. 'Later? After the celebrations? I'd say after breakfast, but I suspect Marie has other plans for us.'

'Later's fine,' Daniel said.

We started towards the house, Simon and Daniel still talking tractors, Matt and I a few steps behind.

'So how's it going?' I asked. 'The farm, I mean. It's looking prosperous.'

He smiled. 'We're surviving. We're never going to be rich, but it's not bad.'

I nodded. At least he had never cared about being rich.

There was a pause. It is the pauses that I dread in my conversations with Matt. The conversations themselves, polite and careful, as if between strangers, are bad enough, but it is the pauses I take home with me afterwards.

'How about you?' he said. 'How's your research?'

'It's going well.'

'What . . . what are you actually researching, Kate? I don't think you've ever said.'

I watched our feet, our shoes stirring the fine dust of the farmyard. No, I had never said. Why rub his nose in the fact that I was doing the sort of thing he would have so loved to do? But now it seemed I had no option.

I said, 'Well, roughly speaking, I'm looking into the effects of surfactants on the inhabitants of the surface film.'

'Things like detergents?'

'Yes. And wetting agents from pesticides and herbicides. That sort of thing.'

He nodded. 'Interesting stuff.'

'Yes. Yes, it is.'

Interesting stuff.

What anyone would say. As if he were just anyone. As if he had not taught me most of what I know. That is literally true, I believe. It is the approach that is important, the openness, the ability to really *see*, without being blinded by preconceptions, and Matt taught me that. The things I have learned since have been mere details.

He was waiting for me to go on, to describe my work to him, but I could not bring myself to do that. It wasn't that I didn't think he would understand — if I could explain my work to an undergraduate I could certainly explain it to Matt. It was the fact that I would *have to explain it*. I cannot describe how wrong that seemed, and how cruel.

He had slowed down and I had to do likewise. The others went on ahead. I glanced at him and he gave me a

278

swift smile. When he is under stress his smile is stretched in a way it isn't normally. I imagine most people wouldn't notice, but I watched him so much when I was young, you see. I know his face so well.

'Daniel seems a great guy,' he said at last.

'Yes,' I said, relieved beyond measure that he was dropping it. 'Yes, he is.'

'Is it . . . serious? Between the two of you?'

'It might be. I think it probably is.'

'Good. Good. That's great.'

He bent down and picked up a flat stone. If we'd been on the beach he would have skipped it, but we weren't, so after turning it over a few times he dropped it again. Then he looked at me, that clear, grey-eyed, steady look of his.

'You should take him back to the ponds afterwards, Kate. They're in great shape.'

I looked away quickly. In my mind's eye, I saw him, stealing a few moments from the incessant demands of the farm, walking back to the ponds, standing, alone, looking into their depths.

I waited a moment, to be sure that my throat would be clear. Simon and Daniel had reached the house. Marie was standing in the doorway.

'Yes,' I said finally. 'Yes, I should do that.'

Marie seemed to be watching us. I couldn't make out her expression.

I said, 'I think breakfast is ready.'

Matt nodded, and prodded at the stone with his shoe. 'Right,' he said. 'Let's go in.'

*

MATT AND Simon and Daniel started moving furniture about right after breakfast. They'd decided that the day was going to be warm enough to hold the party outside so they were taking out tables and chairs and setting them up around the side of the house, where there was grass and a struggling fringe of garden.

Marie and I stayed in the kitchen, doing women's work. Or at least, Marie did women's work, and I stood and watched. She seemed distracted. Normally Marie is fairly confident in her own kitchen, but she was moving ineffectually about, taking things out of the refrigerator and putting them back in, opening drawers and closing them again. She had about two dozen desserts spread about on the counter in varying stages of un-readiness and couldn't seem to decide which to start on first. I wondered if it was the party that was unnerving her or if it was me. I know she does not find me easy to have around. I would have gone out and left her to it, except that it seemed so impolite.

I said for the third time, 'There must be something I can do, Marie. Let me whip the cream.'

'Oh,' she said. 'Well . . . all right. If you like. Thank you.' She opened the refrigerator and took out a jug of cream. 'I'll get you the beater,' she said.

'It's here.'

'Oh. Yes. All right, I'll get a bowl.'

She put down the cream, opened the cupboard and got out a large bowl. Instead of giving it to me though, she stood holding it in both hands, her back to me. Suddenly, without turning round, she said, 'What did you think of the tractor?'

'The tractor?' I said, startled.

'Yes.'

'I thought it was great. I don't know a lot about tractors, but it looked really good.'

She nodded, her back still to me. She said, 'Matt and Simon chose it together. They spent weeks working out just what they wanted. The two of them. They had brochures and magazines all over the kitchen table for weeks. They're very proud of it.'

I laughed. I said, 'I know.'

She turned around, holding the bowl in front of her. She was smiling rather oddly. She said, 'What do you think of Simon?'

I stared at her. I said, 'I like him very much. Very much. He's a lovely boy. An extremely nice boy.'

I felt myself flushing – her question was so strange and my reply sounded so old-fashioned and patronizing. Then it struck me that Simon was now eighteen, the same age as Matt had been that disastrous summer. I wondered if she was worrying about him. I was sure he was far too street-wise to make his father's mistakes, but still, she might be worrying.

I said, 'I also think he has a lot of common sense, Marie. He's a lot more mature than most of the students I see. I think he'll do very well next year.'

She nodded. She put down the bowl and wrapped her arms around herself – the same old defensive gesture, but different somehow. Her face was flushed, but she seemed grim rather than embarrassed. Fierce, almost. It was so unlike her that I was quite unnerved.

She said, 'How does Matt strike you? Does he seem well to you?'

'I think he's looking very well. Very well.'

'Do you think he looks happy?'

I was alarmed now. We do not ask such questions in our family.

'He looks happy to me, Marie. Why? What's wrong?'

'Nothing.' She gave a little shrug. 'I just wondered if you could see it, that's all. Could see that he is well and happy and has a wonderful son who he loves and has a good time with. I just wanted you to see it, for once, after all this time.'

In the silence we could hear furniture being heaved about. Something had become stuck in a doorway. Matt was cursing, Simon was hooting with laughter. I heard Daniel say, 'Maybe if we tried going back . . .'

Marie said, 'If you only knew how much your opinion matters to him, Kate. If you could see him when he knows you're coming home . . . at first he's so happy . . . but then as it gets closer, he doesn't sleep. Luke forgave him years ago and Bo never knew that there was anything to forgive. But your disappointment – you thinking his whole life is a failure, feeling so sorry for him for the way he let himself down – that's been so hard for him to bear. That's been the hardest thing. Everything else that's happened to him has been easy compared to that.'

I was so astonished that I found it hard to take in what she was saying. She was so upset, so emotional, and it seemed to me that her accusations made no sense. What was my disappointment compared to the loss of Matt's dreams?

I said, 'I don't think his whole life is a failure, Marie. I think you've both done very well, I think Simon is a credit . . .'

'You do think his life is a failure.' Her arms were wrapped tight, hands gripping her elbows. I was shocked, not only by what she was saying but by the timing of it, a birthday party, guests about to arrive. 'You think what happened is the great tragedy of his life. You can hardly look at him, you feel so sorry for him and so angry with

282

him still. After all these years you can still hardly look at him, Kate.'

I don't know what I would have said then, but I was spared because Simon came in. He surveyed the desserts and then stuck his finger in one and said, 'What's this one then?'

Marie said sharply, 'Leave it!' and he jumped and said 'OK! OK!' and backed out, looking at her strangely. We heard him say, 'Don't go in there. Mum's getting ratty.'

Marie handed me the bowl. I took it, wordlessly, put it on the counter, poured the cream into it and whipped the cream. I whipped it too much and it curdled and went lumpy.

'I've overdone it,' I said. 'I'm sorry.' My voice sounded odd. I handed the bowl to Marie. She said, 'It doesn't matter. Could you put some on the pies?' and went on decorating the cheesecakes. Her voice was mild now, as if she had said all she had to say and the rest was up to me. But I could think of no reply. If after all these years she still didn't understand what Matt had lost, what was there to say?

When I'd finished the pies I said, 'Anything else?' and she said, 'Not just yet. You might take a cup of coffee to the men.'

I poured three mugs of coffee from the pot Marie always has brewing and put them on a tray. I found a small jug in the cupboard, poured cream into it, found the sugar bowl, got three spoons from the drawer. All in silence. I took the tray outside to the men. They'd set up the tables by then, under the trees, according to Marie's instructions. Matt and Simon were discussing chairs – how many and where.

'What do you think?' Matt asked as I came up. 'How

many will want to sit down? And in the sun or in the shade?'

'Only the women,' I said, holding the tray while they both stirred three sugars into their coffee. 'They'll want to sit in the shade.'

'Right,' Matt said. He looked at Simon. 'How many women are there?'

'Mrs Stanovich,' Simon said, 'Mrs Lucas, Mrs Tadworth, Mrs Mitchell, Miss Carrington . . .'

I looked around for Daniel. He was by the corner of the house, looking with interest at a clutter of machinery in the barnyard. I went over to him. I felt dazed, as if I were coming down with sunstroke. Daniel took his coffee and said, 'Do you ever feel you might like to live on a farm? For real, I mean. Take up farming. Do some real work, where you see progress at the end of the day.'

'No,' I said.

He looked at me and grinned, and then he looked harder. He said, 'What's wrong?'

'Nothing.'

'Yes there is. What's wrong?'

I shrugged, 'Just something Marie said.' Her words were still echoing inside my head. Her accusations bothered me very much. I kept going over them, casting round for explanations, trying to understand how she had come to think as she did. Perhaps it was natural, if you considered her background. She would have no conception of what Matt's life could have been like, had things turned out differently. And even if she had, she wouldn't want to acknowledge it. She'd been the cause of his downfall, after all.

'About what?' Daniel said.

'Pardon?'

284

'You said Marie said something. About what?'

'About . . . me. Me and Matt.'

'What did she say?'

I had told him everything else, I might as well tell him this. 'Oh just . . . she thinks I think what happened to Matt is a tragedy.'

He stirred his coffee, watching me.

I said, 'Which is true. She said I think Matt's whole life is a failure, which is not true, but it is true that what happened to him is a tragedy.'

Daniel put his spoon back on the tray. He didn't say anything. I said, 'The thing is, she doesn't even see it. It's not her fault, she doesn't understand. But that's a tragedy too, you see – that Matt is married to someone who has no idea, really no idea, what he's all about.'

Daniel sipped his coffee, still watching me. Out beyond the fields, along the side road, you could see a cloud of dust boiling up. A car – Luke and Bo, coming to lend a hand. The car was going very fast and seemed to be all over the road; part of my brain puzzled over it, until I remembered; a driving lesson. Daniel said, 'Well I agree with you about one thing, Kate. I do think there's a tragedy here. But I don't think it's what you think it is.'

A mosquito – an early forerunner of the hordes to come – landed on his wrist. He narrowed his eyes, handed me his coffee, and smacked it. He wiped his hand on his shirt and retrieved his coffee and said, 'You'll say I don't understand, just like you think Marie doesn't understand, but I think I do. Some of it anyway. Your family's had a real struggle, all those generations and everything, all of you striving towards this great goal. And Matt's obviously brilliant, anyone can see that. So I can see it was a disappointment. He had his chance and he blew it, which is a real shame.'

He gave me a brief, almost apologetic smile. 'But it's just a shame. It's not a tragedy. It makes no difference to who Matt is. Can't you see that? No difference at all. The tragedy is that you think it's so important. So important you're letting it destroy the relationship the two of you had . . .'

He must have seen my incredulity, because he hesitated, eyeing me uneasily. He said, 'I'm not trying to say it doesn't matter to him, Kate – that he's miraculously discovered that he loves farming, so it's all turned out for the best, or some crap like that. I'm not saying that. I'm just saying that from what you've told me about him and what I've seen of him, my guess is that he came to terms with it a long time ago. The problem is, you didn't. And as a consequence, he's lost what he had with you. That's the real tragedy.'

STRANGE HOW parts of your brain can continue to function normally when other parts have come to a dead stop. I could hear Matt's and Simon's voices; I saw the car getting nearer; in the distance a couple of crows were quarrelling; my brain recorded it all faithfully. But within me, for a long moment, there was total silence. A paralysis of the mind. And then gradually things started up again, and with the return of conscious thought came an absolute flood-tide of disbelief, confusion and furious resentment. Daniel, of all people, an outsider, a *guest*, who had dragged the story out of me, who had known Matt scarcely twelve hours. That he could look at our lives and casually, carelessly, knowing *nothing about it*, come to such a conclusion. I could hardly believe that I had heard him right – hardly believe that he had said it.

I watched Luke's car; kept my eyes fixed on its progress. It disappeared briefly behind the house, then reappeared as Bo hurtled into the farmyard and came to a halt in a cloud of dust ten feet from where we were standing. She was talking as she got out. 'See!?' she said, defiantly. She waved at Daniel and me but she was speaking to Luke, who was in the passenger seat – she bent down and peered in so that he'd be sure to hear. 'See?!'

I watched her, my brain recording the scene. Matt and Simon were coming over to greet them. They grinned at us as they came up; I knew the grins referred to Bo and Luke, but I was incapable of responding. I watched Matt, my mind churning with Daniel's words, with Marie's words. *'If you could see him when he knows you're coming home, Kate . . . at first he's so happy . . . but then as it gets closer, he doesn't sleep . . .'*

Bo slammed the car door, went round to Luke's side and opened his door for him. He was balancing a birthday cake on his lap and had a monstrous bowl of green jello wedged between his feet. I heard Simon say to Matt, 'He looks sort of . . . resigned,' and Matt nodded. 'I guess that's what happens when you face death on a daily basis. After a while it loses its sting.'

Bo had her head inside the car and didn't hear. She took the cake, and Luke bent down and lifted the Jell-O up onto his lap and levered it and himself out of the car.

'How's it going, then, Luke?' Matt said innocently.

Luke shot him a look and gave him the jello. 'Stick that where the sun don't shine,' he said.

'All of it?' said Matt.

'Happy birthday, Little One,' Bo said, ignoring them

and handing Simon his cake, a vast, gothic structure coated in chocolate. 'You don't look a day over twelve. Have you opened your presents? Morning, you two' – this to Daniel and me. I felt Daniel's hand in the small of my back, easing me forward.

'Morning,' Daniel said. 'That's quite a cake.'

'Oh well, it's a celebration,' Bo said. 'We thought he'd never grow up.'

We made our way towards the house. Daniel's hand still rested on my back. His touch made my skin prickle with resentment. I wished he would leave me. I wished they would all leave me. Go away, and let me think. Marie appeared, a dishcloth in her hands.

'Give us a job, Marie,' Luke said. 'We came to help.'

'Oh,' Marie said, 'Oh, well . . . all right. I think you can start taking things outside now. Plates and things.'

The world kept on turning. Marie organized us, after a fashion. I was given the job of washing glasses. As far as I could see they were already perfectly clean, but I was glad to do it; it meant I could stand at the kitchen sink with my back to the room. I washed them meticulously, one at a time, and dried them carefully, and placed them on trays for the men to take out to the tables. Daniel appeared beside me and said, 'Like a drier?' but I shook my head, and after hovering uncertainly for a moment or two he moved away. When I finished the glasses I washed the bowls Marie had been using, and the cutlery, and the cake tins, and the baking trays. Behind me Bo and Marie were putting the finishing touches to the food and the men were standing about, talking and laughing and getting in the way. Daniel was there somewhere. I could feel his eyes on me. Marie's also. Several times she thanked me, and said, tentatively, that I'd done more than my share and wouldn't I like a coffee, but I smiled quickly in her general direction and said that I was fine. I was relieved to find that I was capable of speech and that my voice sounded normal.

I wondered if I could stay there all day, washing dishes until the party was over, and then say that I had a headache and go up to bed. But I knew that wasn't possible. There are certain occasions that nothing short of death excuses you from and this was one of them. I didn't know how I was going to get through it though. There was such turmoil inside my head. Still simmering under everything was my anger with Daniel, but on top of that my brain kept delivering snapshots from the past: Matt, sitting beside me on the sofa in the living room after Aunt Annie had broken the news that the family would be split up, trying to point out New Richmond on the map, trying to convince me that we would still be able to see each other. I could see my child-self, sitting beside him, my mind possessed by a whirlwind of despair.

Another snapshot: Matt in the aftermath of his exam results, taking me into our parents' bedroom, sitting me down in front of the photograph of Great Grandmother Morrison and explaining why he had to go away. Telling me about our family history, showing me that we played a part in it. I saw how important it was, knew it must be terribly important, or he would not leave me. And then he told me of his plan for us. Our glorious plan.

Yet another image, this time twelve years later, the night before I myself set off for university. Matt had come over from the farm to say goodbye. For years I had managed to block that evening from my mind, but now it came back to me, as fresh, as bright, as clear in all its details as if it had taken place yesterday. The two of us had gone down to the beach. We sat on the sand, watching the night creep in over the lake, and talked stiltedly about things that did not matter – tomorrow's train journey, the hall of residence, whether there would be phones on every floor. We talked like strangers. We were almost strangers, by then. The weight of twelve years' worth of things unsaid, unresolved, had made strangers of us.

When it was time for him to go – back to the farm and Marie and his son – we walked back up to the house in silence. It was dark by then. The trees around the house had drawn closer in the darkness, as they always do. At the door I turned to say goodbye to him. He was standing back a bit, his hands in his pockets. He smiled at me, and said, 'You have to write me every detail, OK? I want to know every single thing you do.'

He was standing in the rectangle of light from the doorway and I could hardly bear to look at him because of the strain in his face. I tried to imagine writing to him, telling him about all that I was doing – all that he should have been doing. I imagined him reading my letters and then going out to milk the cows. It was unthinkable. It would be nothing but rubbing salt in the wound, reminding him, constantly, of what he had lost. I didn't believe he could possibly want such a thing, and I knew I couldn't bear to do it.

So I had written very seldom, and said next to nothing about my work. I had wanted to spare him – to spare both of us. And now Daniel was trying to tell me that Matt had not wanted to be spared. That the strain I had seen, and continued to see, was because, try as he might, he could not re-establish the link between us. That he had just wanted me to write to him, regardless of the subject matter, and knew as well as I did that I would not.

I could not – *could not* – believe that interpretation. Daniel thinks he is right about everything, but he is not always right. He is not. I have known him to be wrong before.

But now, when I tried to close my mind to what he had said, when I looked around urgently for more dishes to wash – anything, an egg-beater, a knife, a spoon – his words kept seeping back into my mind, sliding in, like water under a door.

THE GUESTS began arriving just after noon, and by that time I had gone beyond feeling much of anything. I felt light-headed. Unreal. It was almost pleasant. Mrs Stanovich was the first to arrive, and when Marie saw her truck rolling along the side road and urged me to go out and meet her, I did so quite calmly. The men had been sent off on some errand, Daniel amongst them. I was relieved not to have to introduce him. I didn't know how I was going to deal with him. I'd been aware over the course of the morning of his growing concern, and to be honest it gave me some satisfaction. I had in no way forgiven him. It wasn't until later, when I was in a more rational frame of mind, that it occurred to me that it must have been difficult for him to say what he had said. The weekend meant a lot to him, and he would know he was putting it in jeopardy, and possibly risking more than that. At the moment of speaking I'm sure he thought he was doing the right thing, but I suspect he regretted it straight away.

He was right to be worried. My feelings towards him . . . well, I think if you had asked me, at that stage in the afternoon, if our relationship was going to continue, I would have said no. I suppose it was a variation on the

291

theme of shooting the messenger – the bearer of bad tidings. I know it was unfair.

I went out alone to greet Mrs Stanovich. She was heaving herself out from behind the wheel of her truck as I came up, and she gave a little cry of joy when she saw me. She is unchanged, I am glad to say, except possibly for the addition of a chin or two.

'Katherine, sweetie! Sweetie, you look so beautiful, you look so like your mother, you look more like her every day.' And she hauled me to her bosom, just as she used to do, just as she always will. It shows the state I was in that for the first time in my life I almost wanted to accept that bosom for what it really is – a pillow to cry into. A great, soft, warm pillow, into which to unload all your grief and pain and regret, in the sure knowledge that Mrs Stanovich will pass it all directly on to Jesus. But I am me, and I cannot do such things, though I did return her embrace for longer than she is accustomed to.

'Sweetie,' she said, delving around for her eternal handkerchief (Matt once said he bet there were hundreds of them down there somewhere), 'just look at the day the Lord has given us! Not a cloud! And here you are, you came all this way to help in the rejoicing. Isn't Simon the most wonderful boy you ever saw? Somewhere there's a cake.' She puffed her way round to the back of her truck, mopping herself as she went, and let down the tailgate with a crash. 'I couldn't put it in the front because Gabby's put a gear box on the seat. I hope it's survived – now look at that, it's just fine. All you need is to trust in the Lord, sweetie. He takes care of everything. Who is the young man with Matt?'

It was Daniel. Matt was bringing him over to be introduced. They were walking slowly, heads down. Matt was gesturing with his hands, explaining something, and Daniel was nodding. As they got closer I heard Matt say, '. . . only about six months of the year when it's above forty-two degrees, which is the absolute minimum. So you need to get it in as soon as possible after the snow melts – as soon as the soil dries out enough to drill.' And Daniel said, 'Do you use particular strains? You know, more frost-resistant?'

I don't know why I suddenly saw it then. Maybe because they were both so intent on the subject, so absorbed. Two remarkable men, deep in conversation, walking slowly across the dust of the farmyard. It was not a tragic picture. Definitely not.

I suppose the real question is not why I saw it then, but why I didn't see it years ago. Great Grandmother Morrison, I accept that the fault is largely mine, but I do hold you partly to blame. It is you, with your love of learning, who set the standard against which I have judged everyone around me, all of my life. I have pursued your dream single-mindedly; I have become familiar with books and ideas you never even imagined, and somehow, in the process of acquiring all that knowledge, I have managed to learn nothing at all.

*

MISS CARRINGTON arrived while Daniel was being introduced to Mrs Stanovich, and right behind her were the Tadworths; and then several cars and battered farm trucks all rolled in together and the party got under way. It was a good party. As Mrs Stanovich said, we had the weather on our side, and the event quickly took on the air of a large and rather chaotic picnic, with people sitting on the grass in little clusters or milling about near the food tables, talking and laughing and trying to solve the problem of how to eat when you have a plate of food in one hand and a glass of fruit punch in the other.

I would like to be able to say that I threw myself into the spirit of it all, but the truth is, I still felt a bit dazed. A bit abstracted. It's going to take time, I guess. If you've thought in a certain way for many years, if you've had a picture in your mind of how things are and that picture is suddenly shown to be faulty, well, it stands to reason that it will take a while to adjust. And during that time, you're bound to feel . . . disconnected. Anyway, that was how I felt – and still feel, to some degree. What I would really have liked to do was sit quietly somewhere, preferably under a tree, and watch the goings-on from a distance. In particular, watch Matt. Let my eyes absorb this new view of him, this new perspective on our lives.

That's what I would have chosen to do that afternoon, rather than help to host a birthday party. But still, it was good to see everyone – very good, in fact. They were all there, apart from Miss Vernon, who sent a message that she was a bit old for parties but wished Simon well. I introduced Daniel to most of them, I think. He was rather subdued himself, no doubt still unsure of my state of mind. But he rose to the occasion – all the Professors Crane are good at occasions. We talked quite a bit with Miss Carrington. She is the principal of the school now – it has expanded to three rooms and she has two teachers working for her. She was looking very well. There is a serenity about her. Possibly there always was and I just hadn't noticed it before. Anyway, it makes her very restful to be with.

Simon had a good time, I think, which was the object of the exercise, after all.

THE EVENING was the best though. The evening will stay with me. After supper, when the clearing up was done and Simon had gone off with his friends, Matt and I sprayed Daniel from head to toe with insect repellent and took him back to the ponds. Matt has filled in the one where Laurie's body was found and planted a small group of silver birches on it. They were just coming into leaf and looked very peaceful.

The other ponds, our pond included, are just as they have always been.